A Course to a Holy Relationship

Transforming your partnerships

from Fear to Love

To Alan

Belive in yourself
& love

Read it slowly

Bob

ISBN: 978-1-4951-4605-3

Theta Publishing,LLC
1297 South 104th
Broomfield, CO 80020

Dedication

This book is dedicated to all the woman and men who I have been involved with in my spiritual journey for the past 33 years and who have forgiven my lower mind (Ego) and helped me become a higher-minded spiritual being.

This book is dedicated to all my Holy Relationships and how they serve to restore God's plan of love and peace. This book is dedicated to all those who believe in miracles.

A special thanks to all those who worked on this book in helping me edit it and bringing the detail to these messages. You know who you are. So do I. Thanks.

Dedicate your life to making your relationship Holy and you will know devotion truly.

A special thanks to A Course in Miracles, which inspired these teachings.

Most importantly, I want to thank my true self for not giving up on me, and finishing this book

There is a saying I like very much, "If I can do it, so can you!"

Go for your dream…

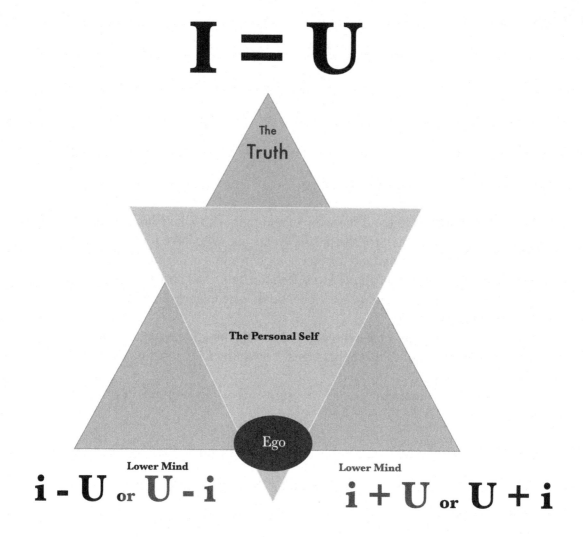

U and I make a choice between

Truth or Ego
Light or Dark

LOVE OR FEAR

Invitation to the Reader

In pure consciousness, you are still as God created you, and this is the foundation for being Holy.

Before we get into the heart of this material, let me say that as you start to examine new ideas and paradigms of thinking, be gentle on yourself and on your partners. Reading this book is a transformative process, and there is no expectation that anyone will perfectly apply all of the concepts outlined here simply by reading this book through once, or even trying to live it for weeks or years. Apply these ideas to your life, for the rest of your life. Expect mistakes, as error happens, and is a part of the No Loss process — it is how we integrate learning! You can make as many mistakes as necessary, because your mind starts out understanding a certain way of being in a relationship.

You are not aware of another way of being in relationships because your parents did not know one, and they didn't know because their parents did not know. No one taught you in school how to make a relationship holy, nor have you likely taken an advanced class in interpersonal communication. You have probably just been following the instincts and reactions that have been handed down for generations. You just thought you knew — luckily, life presents a curriculum to learn new ways of being.

Our relationships are measuring tools to determine if we are learning this curriculum. Remember: you never fail. Failure implies that you cannot receive another chance, and that is not true. In life's curriculum you simply get the lesson over and over again until it becomes clear. You may already be aware that you have been experiencing such patterns in your life. Creating No Loss Relationships mean you are willing to consciously take a step in the direction of knowing who you are as God created you.

Some of the ideas presented in this book use words and concepts that you may or may not agree with. Please suspend any judgments that might arise in your being until you have finished the material and done all the exercises. If you do notice that you are judging, stop being critical of yourself. Let yourself off the torture rack of self-abuse. Any resistance you experience to some of the ideas implies that you are expanding beyond what you were taught. Confusion is not a "bad" state of consciousness; it is a transcendent state.

As you read, you will begin to notice yourself applying the ideas in your relationships with others, and in this process you will discover which ideas best suit you and the people you are involved with. Completely finishing the book and doing the exercises will give you an experience that is beyond the mind that learns. This material is meant to lead you into an experience—not a philosophical or intellectual debate.

This book is not about having all the answers for how to make your relationship what you want it to be in form. About showing you how to receive all the answers. My goal is not to tell you what you should or should not do in a relationship, what to say, or how to say it. I am not here to control your life, say what is moral or proper, or how you should behave. If you want a monogamous marriage or an open marriage, that is your choice. If you want lots of material things or to live in a van, great! I am more concerned about the content of your involvement than the form of it. I am here to give suggestions and guidelines for finding out what works best for your involvement.

My intention is to teach the process of healing relationships, whatever comes from that is holy. So relax—and quit being so hard on yourself about your past! It is all an experiment. Yes, you have been burned. Yes, you have gotten war wounds and felt unloved. Yes, you have experienced many thrills as well. Is it worth it? Well, it's the only game still left to master if you are truly transcending from animal consciousness.

This material is not aimed at finding fault with the past or pointing out what past generations didn't do right. Divorce is the statement of not having the experience of love. We will teach throughout this book that it is not bad to change a relationship that is not growing or willing to change the behavior and/or beliefs that keep us separate. We are not focused on the negative—only observing the process that has occurred and is occurring to warrant conscious relationship transformation.

The goal is to teach a new level of understanding in relationships and help bring in a deeper purpose. Our parents and all relationships were and are doing their best. The past is gone, and we cannot make progress by pointing fingers at what others did not know. Blame heals nothing. Pointing out what is wrong with men or women—as many books on codependency do—or emphasizing the differences between men and women, does not teach how to become whole and complete within one's self. To discern, not judge, and to learn through wisdom without blame or shame, is a focus of this book. Making corrections without punishment is the No Loss approach.

Table of Contents

CHAPTER 1

The New Paradigm

The New Paradigm Shift: from Separation to Oneness

Have you noticed the epidemic of difficulties in yourself and others in intimate relationships? As one reflects on his or her relationship histories (and those of others) it becomes clear that the dynamics of our intimate relationships have become severely strained. "Intimate" means those most close to our heart, our center, and not necessarily sexual in nature. So, relationships are evolving because people are searching for a way out of their feelings of separation and seeking a greater understanding of union. Take heart; now is the time and this is the place for our relationships to evolve. Evolving intimate relationships are the vehicle to facilitate a shift from being separate to being whole. In the new millennium, we are setting new precedents for making our relationships Holy and Whole.

As more individuals turn their attention to Wholeness, society will begin to evolve as One World humanity. Do you see how it is happening now? Relationships are the vehicles that evolve both individual and group consciousness into Oneness. We as a society are climbing the ladder of spiritual development at an ever-increasing rate—and our climb begins with intimate relationships. Relationships based solely on private interests will fail to interest those seeking a greater involvement with society.

We are spiritual beings: units of pure consciousness learning to reunite with each other and the greater Oneness of Life called Wholeness or Holiness. It's an exciting time to be alive, with major changes awaiting us. We're ready to graduate out of the survival mode of existence. We are leaving behind old animal instincts of self-preservation, habitual reactions of "I want it my way" or "I'll attack you if you're not like me" by shifting into a new paradigm for relationships. We don't have time to waste! Wasting time promotes fear, and fear promotes war. Are we going to destroy ourselves or join as one world united?

What's happening to the evolution of humanity is mirrored in our intimate involvements. Couples must move at an accelerated pace because humanity's evolution is quickening. No longer do men and women have to fight to survive, although it may seem that many still choose to do so. We are seeking to learn faster, because spending several years in relationship misery is not a necessary option anymore, nor is living a lifetime with someone and not feeling completely united. Evolution is leading us into loving the WHOLE more than the separate parts. Love is teaching us to join with the "All" and not to remain alone.

If you are finding yourself no longer existing at the survival level of consciousness, spending less time needing to work for material survival (money) and less interest in mindless entertainment, now is the time to focus on your next step in evolution—a spiritual relationship!

What Happened on the Way to the "American Dream?"

When we take the time to look up from our busy lives, what can we see about how people relate to one another on our planet? World peace seems questionable, insecurities of financial gloom and doom continue, wars between governments keep happening, global warming and climate changes frighten us, and disease and advanced warfare cause us to question our survival. Are we using up our resources with no thought for others? Crime and domestic violence are evidence that we are not getting along; our outer world is shrinking while our inner mind has expanded. Outer and inner self-exploration must find its proper balance. Still, few comprehend the greatest advancement in human consciousness—to be WHOLE. With advances in technology, education, self-help, and entertainment, the reasons for being together are no longer together the same. The family structure has already changed greatly. We may be communicating globally through advanced technology, but we lack the understanding of how to live in harmony with a mate or neighbor or intimate friend. However, families are seeking better parenting skills; spiritual communities may be a return to the tribal living concept. Overpopulation and space travel may force the collective consciousness to create a healthier way of being together.

Of all the changes that we have undergone as a society, the most significant change occurred in the latter part of the 20th century when the power between men and women shifted. Women have made a stand for equality and have taken their rightful place in the world. Women have declared their independence from being trapped in stereotypical roles of housewife and mother. A woman has not given up womanhood, but is relishing the idea of being a first-class person. She is no longer dependent upon a man for her livelihood-- any woman can get a job, buy anything she likes, run a household, fix a car, and even do all these things while raising a child alone. Men are as confused as ever, and women are walking on new ground. All the divorces that have happened in the last 40 years are because men and woman are searching to reach a new level of being together.

Of course men are experiencing their own issues as this transformation in roles progresses. Men fear losing their masculine natures—many feel threatened by women entering into endeavors that once were reserved only for men. Now, women are succeeding in every area that men once dominated.

With the arrival of reliable birth control, women have choice. They don't need men in the ways they did before. This transformation has transpired in the last 45 years, happening so quickly and recently, that we are still in a transcendent stage of development. Old mental programming about who is in charge must shift to new thoughts of equality and wholeness.

Women are looking for spiritual men who are truly working on their personal growth. Many women have become so independent that they are living more from their masculine (yang) side than living from the feminine (yin) side. Men are attempting to understand their feelings more, but who is the man and who is the woman when all the roles have changed so much? What is the purpose of all this change in power? Is it a new ball game? The dawn of the goddess is upon us, and it is sweeping the globe.

Women now have power, and make the choice to be in relationship—or not. They are refusing to put up with men interested in controlling, possessing, or dominating them. Many women are insisting that their relationships become healthier.

Many women will not live with a man who is not spiritually, mentally, and emotionally growing. Women will not pretend they are joined when they know within themselves that they are not.

During the first half of the 20th century, most men and women lived together in a "survival consciousness" based on the American Dream of having a family, buying a home, and living happily ever after. Divorce rarely occurred. Women believed a special man would take care of her and provide her with the home and children she had always dreamed of. Men believed they had to be strong, responsible, and a good provider, and from that, should receive total devotion from their wife. Did these couples after years and years of living together grow into divine love, or were they sentenced to exist in the institution of marriage, alone and afraid? The true answer is that only they knew, for if we are honest, we know by our feelings if we are experiencing love or separation.

Men and women existed together each having their respective roles and places. Material goals took priority with the husband in charge, and the wife the faithful servant. Rules of who was in charge were implied and seldom spoken of. Often, when a woman questioned authority, she was verbally abused and sometimes physically abused. Women held silent grievance against their partners, and men ruled with false pride. Domestic violence is still rampant today because of patterns not being transformed. The process of becoming One was making little progress during the early 20th century because relationships were based on inequality and false illusions of security.

The 1960's changed the family stereotype forever. It wasn't "free love" or drugs or even the music—it was the underlying falsehood rising to the surface. Married couples stayed together but didn't really understand love. Couples acted out scripts of what love were supposed to look like, yet they didn't really feel joined, nor did they experience true communication. A marriage can last for years while not progressing to heal beliefs in inequality. The underlying feelings were disillusionment, anger, and repression of expression. They contended with difficulties, tolerated each other, and coexisted, never reaching the real purpose for being in a relationship.

The children of the 60's and 70's watched and realized something was not working—even though parents lived together, made babies, and looked like a family (much like Ward and June in "Leave it to Beaver"). These children started the rebellion: the divorce rebellion. I call it the "relationship revolution."

At first it was called "women's liberation", and men reacted with their own movement—they started getting in touch with their feelings. Males gathered and bonded, attempting to figure out this drastic change. We developed the term "dysfunctional family." We worked on our addictions and we went looking for our inner child. We blamed it on drugs and material freedoms, but in truth, the old ways of being in relationships lacked understanding of how to achieve real love.

What Doesn't Work: The "Dream Lover" Idea

It goes like this: boy meets girl, girl becomes attracted to boy, boy pursues girl, girl pretends she is not interested, boy pursues girl, girl gives in, boy marries girl, and they live happily ever after. This fairy tale "love scenario" has been played out for hundreds of years with leading characters such as Snow White, Cinderella, and Sir Lancelot.

So often today, the knight and his princess are full of resentment and disillusionment, and the happily ever-after couple often ends up in divorce court. What happened to the loving couple with all their dreams and hopes for finding love? More than 65% of adults over the age of 40 are highly disappointed and unhappy about how their relationships have turned out. Just ask them!

Has our society taught us that the fantasy is more attractive than the reality? Have we bought the package due to its fancy ribbons and failed to look at what is really inside? Are men and woman really so different that we can't get along without one dominating the other? Are we so independent that we really don't need each other? These are important and relevant questions with 72% of first-time marriages ending in divorce, and over 55% of singles still looking, most of them quite unhappy with the possibilities out there. What has happened to love?

Today, it often requires two or three marriages before couples find the solutions to correcting dysfunctional relationship issues. An interesting truth is that even false reasons for being together can be learning opportunities that lead to real purpose. You cannot fail in a relationship that has false values because they always through pain teach you what you do not want. Letting go of what doesn't work leads to what does!

An unholy relationship is based on not truly joining in love and instead making separation real. You will then be living in a constant state of emotional fear. Whether you call it fear or not, you will notice unrest or lack of peace. A major reason most relationships don't work is that we are reacting only to the behavior and how we feel about that behavior.

Only the pure mind, one free of judgment, can join and experience Oneness. Relationships that never reach joining are in pain and discomfort, which leads to disease or divorce. The prefix "dis" means, "Two kept apart." Remember that the emotion of fear keeps you apart and different. Fear is a separating emotion that comes from the decision to move away from love. Emotions move in one of two directions: toward love or toward fear. The main purpose of a Holy Relationship is to shift the focus away from the physical and toward the spiritual. It requires that we learn to relate correctly to the emotional, intellectual, and spiritual bodies. We must learn to join and relate in these bodies, which can be the hardest and most confusing part of becoming one.

When we can admit what doesn't work, we get closer to understanding and embracing what does. Let us remind ourselves that on a spiritual journey to love, we can't lose; we may get lost or meander off the right path, but life will correct us if we allow it and ask for help from our higher selves. If you think you have failed to produce a desired result in a relationship, you can invite yourself to examine the deeper causes and correct them. To find what blocked your past relationship from working is a blessing! You are changing yourself, reaching toward complete forgiveness and healing fearful programming that may have been in your family for generations.

Remember: you are only working on yourself—no one else. It is time to embrace a no-blame consciousness, especially toward oneself. If you bring in a new self to a new partnership, along with a new way of dealing with past mistakes, you are evolving and transforming towards the positive goal of wholeness.

I have identified the following seven issues that often prevent relationships from reaching the positive results of love. See if you can identify any that may have harmed your past or present relationships:

1. Pursuing Superficial Attractions

We live in a materialistic society, and the majority of our interests revolve around the body and body appearance. A materialistic society values money and physical possession more than inner realities. Printed ads, television, radio, the Internet, and fellow Americans are trying to sell us a certain type of lifestyle to maintain these illusions of love. Our society brainwashes us by promoting physical attractions, sex, and materialism. We are like a donkey chasing a carrot on a string—and several new carrots are invented each day. We are so caught up in all the latest gadgets of success and inventions and ways to spend our time, we find we have little-to-no time for a spiritual relationship. When do couples find that quality time they need to bond and experience a unique state of consciousness called "Oneness?" The attractiveness of the illusions of love are greater than ever, with society promoting the form of a relationship as more important than personal integrity, one's true inner character, and the Spirit.

2. Resisting Bonding/Commitment

Bonding is essential to a healthy relationship. If love is the highest reason for being involved in a relationship, then bonding must occur, because it is love that binds us together. If we are not bonding to our partner, we are not pursuing love. What are we pursuing? We are looking for a fix, a thrill, or a high. We are looking for specialness. (I will explain specialness in great detail later in the next chapter.)

Bonding, or joining, is a primary need we all have, and that is why we seek a meaningful relationship. Joining causes a higher purpose and understanding of life. Bonding proves the Oneness of life.

The fear of being committed or truly joining comes from the internal messages that bonding means bondage, imprisonment or entrapment. Those who have commitment issues have misinterpreted the bonding process as a loss of freedom. No one wants to lose freedom.

When we were growing up, we may have received messages that seemed controlling, confining, or limiting to our abilities. When those messages are associated with a loved one, they teach that love = prison. When we attempt to force someone into a commitment or to change, it promotes fear. Look at the ways to make someone feel guilty and how they resist; realize that each attempt to force bonding is weakening love.

The fear of bonding comes from experiencing pain, such as children of "coping" families as they watch and feel their parents fail to properly join. If you have an "authority problem," or resentment toward a controlling figure, you may have developed a defense against bonding. If you were given messages that made you feel there wasn't room for your difficult feelings, like anger or sadness, bonding can become very difficult.

Any codependent behavior you witnessed growing up made you think bonding was happening, when in fact, it wasn't. When bonding doesn't happen, we feel unworthy of love. Cycles of rejection and not finding a suitable partner come from false reasons for being in a relationship and an unclear spiritual purpose.

If real bonding is occurring, it becomes increasingly difficult to give up on each other. If healing is happening, each experience brings you closer. Joining always occurs in the mind and has little or nothing to do with what happens in form. We have a very mistaken belief that if we are bonded, our partner should act according to our expectations and wishes. Joining means that thoughts are in harmony with each other.

The woman must teach bonding. Men must be willing to listen. The women yearn to teach with an inner instinct to breed and to protect the young. This doesn't mean that men don't bond—they do more than we think they do. A myth women carry is that men don't hurt when they break away from a relationship. This is not true. Men deal with the hurt differently, but they do bond and do experience the pain of the change.

A Holy Relationship causes joining, which is the bonding of real love. Ask for help in understanding what it means and how to achieve it, and your relationship will never fail.

3. Failing to Communicate

Couples who fail to commit to real communication cannot remain together in today's society. Communication is the most misunderstood form of connecting known to couples. The greatest barrier to joining is the false ways we think we are communicating with each other. Many couples model the communication styles they learned with family members—and often those methods did not work then and are not working now. When a couple gets together, each partner assumes that the other came from the same family style of communication as he or she did. Many times during communication we think we are communicating and in fact, no valuable communication is happening at all.

The purpose of communication is to bring two separate parts back into union. If communication is giving us the opposite results, we must realize we are not communicating, even if words are coming from our mouths. When couples continue to not communicate and are convinced they are communicating, the relationship becomes blocked and dysfunctional. Hundreds of books are written about communication and many methods are provided in self-help book sections, so you can learn much about this subject.

Failing to communicate means two people cannot cause healing in the emotional level of life. This is another teaching job for the woman. Men know very little about this. I am not saying men are to put it upon the woman to do the healing for them; I am saying that a man doesn't understand emotions as well as a woman does, because men were forced to be in their heads to figure out how to survive. Let the woman be in charge of the healing process of the couple, listen to her advice, and if she is truly bonding with a man she will study and find ways to heal his emotions with him. Isn't it the women who are constantly taking the men to counseling or to workshops (or perhaps, isn't it your wife who is getting you to read this book?)? She has a genuine interest in emotions, and if her emotions are clear, she will enjoy a sexual connection. She knows that without a balanced emotional experience she will feel unhappy, and that blocks her sex drive. She knows more about feeling and can read a man's feelings much better than even he can, even though his pride has a hard time admitting it. Men still think that being in charge is to their advantage and to be a man means that he has control over the household. In this area, he needs to be willing to be a student.

The illusion of communication—not really communicating—governs our minds and our involvements more than we are willing to admit. Ask anyone why the relationship doesn't work, and it is often said, "We failed to communicate."

4. The Dark Issue: The Darkest of the Dark

Most people believe couples break up because of issues like fighting, not enough sex, money matters, going bankrupt, children, overworking and addictive patterns, wanting different goals, and running away from a business deal. Granted, all couples face specific problems and challenges, but usually one major thing presents itself as the motivating force to abandon the relationship. I call this, The Dark Issue.

The Dark Issue is your core negative belief system that convinces you that you are unworthy or incapable of being loved. It is the darkest part of your soul. The darkest part of your Ego is your fear of being loved—and it takes on many forms and acts out in many ways to sabotage your relationships.

When the Dark Issue surfaces, and it always will, it attempts to break up the heart connection. It is the darkest cornerstone of every Ego's foundation. Examples of the Dark Issue being acted out are: sexual affairs, authority issues, harming another physically or verbally, noncommittal involvements, stealing, habitual lying, murder, rape, drug addiction, con-artistry, money schemes, long term unemployment, religious differences, abandoning children, on and on. If you say, "I haven't seen anything this major in my relationships," but you have experienced several relationship changes, ask why the Dark Issue is kept hidden. It can also seem to play itself out in many minor ways like repeatedly being late, getting fired often, being very opinionated, stubborn, and other character defects in which you refuse to change. It often is seen as the faultfinding self.

Little disagreements or fights, minor likes and dislikes, or conflicts present problems in the relationship, but they often don't cause the couple to break up unless the relationship is weak in purpose from the start or meant to be a casual involvement. These little problems will never get resolved when the combined force of them make up the Dark Issue. When the Dark Issue happens, the Ego is at its best (and worst), doing everything possible to extinguish the love spark. When we choose to engage in enough surface healing from minor disturbances, be prepared, healing the Dark Issue is not far behind and must be dealt with.

Dealing with it, is dealing with the Ego and much more will be addressed in this material on this topic. Often the more you face your Ego; the more it tries to destroy love. The "I" doesn't want to lose its grip on the you that is Spirit.

5. Respecting and Trusting

Respect, like trust, is earned and strengthened by finding appreciation and loving thoughts to exchange with our partners. Respect is a way of viewing one another, and trust is required to accomplish union. If we lose respect and trust in our partners, whom so many of us do, the relationship becomes irreconcilable. Without respect, we become critical. Without trust, we make our partner feel guilty and then we doubt them. When thoughts of judgment, doubt, and guilt control our vision of our partner, our involvement is in serious trouble.

Monitoring our thoughts is a primary way of understanding the health of our relationship. Healthy thoughts about our partner promote healthy feelings about our partner, which promote healthy communication—and behavior always follows those thoughts. Disrespectful thoughts with "good intentions" cancel each other out.

Selfishness is the core reason we remain separated and indifferent and in judgment of those around us. Selfishness is just another way of saying "self-absorbed" and "Ego-focused." One of the main reasons we get involved in relationships is to learn to get out of our Ego, referred to in this material, as the lower mind. Your Ego wants to dominate you and your partner, and its advice leads to the death of your relationship. It always advises you to leave or to fight against your partner. It never appreciates the higher qualities or the divine attributes of one another. The Ego wants to substitute your partner for a different one and does all the dirty tricks to sabotage the trust you and your partner are attempting to build.

The journey from selfishness to wholeness is accomplished when you learn the skills to relinquish the Ego and choose a higher Mind. The selfish (lower) mind is filled with past considerations, expectations, and demands that weigh heavily upon the relationship. Like a donkey carrying a heavy bundle up a steep hill, piling on more weight causes the donkey to move slower. The more conditions and demands we bring into the relationship, the harder it will be to join successfully. Generally, the older we get, the harder it becomes to find a suitable partner—not because we are less lovable, but because we bring so much baggage, narrow viewpoints of what we want, and expectations into the relationship.

6. Being Attached to Independence

Sometimes, we have an unhealthy commitment to independence that refuses to CO-create or change. The phrase, "Can't live with them, can't live without them" certainly applies to today's couples. The balance in CO-creating is not easy to maintain. We swing between co-dependence and independence claiming that we are safer in a certain posture. The Ego always maintains that an independent stance protects you, and the more you withdraw from others, the less likely they can harm you. An unwillingness to change is a front for the need to be right and to be validated. The stance of "knowing at the expense of the ones we love," which says, "I win, you lose," promotes independence, but independence is not holiness, nor is co-dependence. It requires much introspection and self-evaluation to understand these differences and to learn to choose the path of co-creating. Few follow it, and many find themselves living with a partner while not being joined with their partner.

When we become attached to a form and adept to the belief that something can harm it, we become protective of our creations and defend them even at the expense of the ones we love. This is just a mistake and can simply be corrected when we turn our minds over to the Holy Spirit. So let's stop bargaining, pleading, begging, or manipulating plans with the hopes that we can get our way. Every time we do get our way, it becomes a witness to our independence, and what seems like a win, is a loss to our partnership.

7. Longing for Agape Love (Unselfish Love)

Finally, we come to a very profound reason why couples don't stay together—and it is an issue our guilt would rather not deal with. Inside all of us there is a thorough desire or driving force as powerful as, or even more powerful than, our sexual desires, and that is to reach for a divine union with God. Our desire for knowing God can be classified much like salsa: mild, medium or hot.

Our desire for God can become stronger with age or seemingly be put out entirely by our critical opinions about life. The passion for God cannot be explained, as its source comes from the depth of our soul. When it changes in intensity, it can affect our relationships dramatically. Many couples have fought over religious differences and spiritual experiences. To "out grow" a partner, or to assert oneself on a personal spiritual path can affect our involvement—but it doesn't have to change the love. To love is the purpose of any religion.

In the No Loss Relationship, setting another person free to pursue spiritual adventure only brings you closer together in a higher Agape love. We release any co-physical needs. Quite frequently when someone has outgrown a partner, they look for a soul mate, a spiritual companion that causes them to pull apart. Be careful that this does not become a "spiritual special relationship," as our guru will fall off their pedestal, for sure. We can be legitimately meeting our next stage, which may be necessary, but be sure to keep it clean. Do not substitute one partner for another. Include both in our lives and let all parties know about each other. Openly and honestly discuss all that is in our awareness, no matter how painful it may appear to be.

If it is right to change involvement for a greater spiritual advancement, no one will lose, and the primary partner will find his or her rightful next partner as well. The outcome of this honest shift is that we remain friends forever. Letting partners go is not loss if we release them to their highest path, knowing that what we envision for them is what we create for ourselves. We all want to participate in certain activities more or less than our partners, and when we really love someone we allow them to do as they wish.

Always be supportive of someone's genuine interest in pursuing a spiritual path, go with him or her if you can—but if you cannot, don't hold him or her back.

It is our guilty self that wants to keep someone from growing. We are mostly mad at ourselves because we are not interested in growing at this time.

Every relationship must find: a way to heal, a method of forgiveness, and a correction process for dealing with the dark part of our egos. A common mistake with modern couples is that they often have little to no foundation for deeper inner work. They bought the attraction to love: the thrill and the high of being in love—without looking to see what was inside.

The Three Stages of Relationship

Stage 1: The Act of Attraction

Every person seeks or wants to be in a special love stage of relationship: the stage of specialness that makes everything looks and feels perfect, like a rose. You cherish your new partner; the whole day seems brighter because of him or her. The more focused your mind is on your new partner the stronger the passion, and the stronger the passion the greater the intensity of emotions. You cannot stop thinking about him or her. You feel so happy and the excitement is consuming your full attention. The dream of someone loving you with all of his or her heart is irresistible. This stage of the involvement generally lasts for months, weeks, or can only be felt in a one-night stand.

In the erotic stage, the word for specialness is often called "chemistry," and the relationship is based in illusion and fueled with good intentions and expectations. The illusion of the relationship is that the root of the exciting feeling is coming from the other person.

They are making you feel what you feel.

The pleasure we get from loving someone can be based on false ideas of the lower mind. The greater the pleasure your lover seems to produce, the more likely that special love will swing quickly into Stage 2.

Romantic love originates from the thought of being alone, and we believe someone passionately loving us can solve it. I will write much more about specialness and its pitfalls in the next chapter.

Stage 2: The Act of Hate or Healing Hate

From love to hate, from pleasure to pain, from acceptance to rejection—here comes our dark side. The unthinkable happens when that extended moment of "falling in love" turns into an even stronger feeling of being unloved. It can't be explained, it just happens; we see another side of that 'love partner.' You hear it every day on the radio in blues songs and on television. When you are fully in the special love stage, you think it can't possibly happen to you—but eventually it does.

Most of us think Stage 2—or special hate—is bad. It certainly is painful and can lead to the most destructive behavior known to man, but it is as necessary to Special Love as winter is to spring or as fire is in the cycles of growth in a forest. Special Love is a mistake in perception, and Special Hate is the flip side of that misperception. You can't have one without the other. When a Special Love relationship advances—yes, advances—it flips to Special Hate.

By the time you reached puberty, you were already conditioned by fear to hundreds of misconceptions about life, as well as many false self-images of who you thought you were. The good, the bad, and the ugly all existed in your childhood program. Dad called you a good child if you cleaned up your room. Mom said you are fat and ugly and needed to lose weight. How many times were you criticized or told some belief that essentially meant, "You're not good enough," translating to "you're not loved?"

Special Hate is the stage in which our misconceptions of self are acted out. In other words, we begin to show our love partner a part of us we keep hidden from the world and very often even from ourselves. The unconscious conditioning is brought to the surface by the feeling of the Special Love.

Hate is defined as any act or experience of separating away from or angry with another person, place, or thing. Any attack, no matter what the degree of emotions it displays, generated by a lower mind is Hate. Hate can be mildly explained away using other words such as: irritated, concerned, and numbed out, passive aggressive, aloof. It can also be exaggerated as rage, violence, physical, and emotional abuse. The temperance matters, but the effects are the same. Hating causes us to validate the experience of not being loved.

To think that someone doesn't have an unloved self (dark side) is the mistake in perception made in Special Love. Because in Special Love, these things are ignored or agreed upon (verbally or non-verbally) to be kept secret. It is not a matter of if the dark side is going to reveal itself; it's when. The big question that we deal with in this book is how to use our Special Relationship to recognize and heal our self-misconceptions and false self-images. All the relationships that have failed were based on not being equipped with the understanding or the methods of how to heal each other's dark sides.

To get through the hate stage of a relationship is very difficult without spiritual help.

It's impossible if you don't have proper understanding of true forgiveness. Your critical thoughts come from your unwillingness to look at your dark side and your judgment of that part of yourself. No partnership can escape from illusion without the willingness to look at it fully and let it go. The Special Hate stage of an involvement can last for years, is rarely completed in months, and is finished when you learn to move correctly into Stage 3. When love contains drama, it is not really love. When love contains hate, it is not really love. Both of these conditions are indicative of the Special Love-Hate relationship.

Stage 3: The Act of CO-creating

Once the participants in such a relationship are willing to look at their dark sides, an experience of real love can occur. The CO-creating stage of relationships turns happy dreams into reality. This is where you choose peace and put the lower mind's misconceptions and false self-images to rest in favor of an agreement with your partner and with Spirit.

CO-creating is the loftiest side of the Special Love-Hate relationship and is how the relationship transforms into holiness. Through clear purpose followed by well-defined spiritual goals, each participant in the relationship can move forward into realizing Oneness. When we put aside our separate interests and selfish "wants" based in self misconceptions and false self-images, to strive for a mutually agreed-upon creative expression, we join with the natural flow of what life is about: creating. Avoiding this stage is choosing to remain in the illusions you carry about yourself, thinking you have achieved a stalemate with your partner or won a battle over them. To CO-create is to realize that no one loses by creating, and only the Creator is truly important. Your inner work leads to inspiration that serves everyone and everything.

Just look around you at the world's natural order. Get out of the city and spend a weekend in the wilderness; you will feel an inner peace, and it will become clear to you that creation is happening all around you. If you understand its process, you can create the same natural flow in your own relationships.

True Oneness with All Life

Think of these stages—Special Love to Special Hate and on to CO-creating—as the transformation process that will take you out of your separate identity into a real union and then beyond into a sense of true Oneness with all life. If a relationship is stuck, ends, or a change of partners occurs, the spiritual process of moving through the stages to CO-creation can still continue. What many people fail to realize is that this process, its content, and mental patterns continues, even if the participants in the relationship change. Becoming aware of this is how to make all of your relationships into No Loss Relationships.

If a relationship should end, it should not be seen as a failure. You never totally fail in the universe because this is a no-fail zone; through relationship, all paths lead to healing or to nothing. Nothing means that your mind doesn't change. Let's say you exist in the perception of separation and enter into a relationship with a set of beliefs; if you change nothing in the way you think, you simply remain the same. Nothing happened—the separation is still there.

Through conscious cooperation with life's curriculum, you advance out of separation and closer to a sense of Oneness that is the goal of a holy involvement. Each step leads to a healing and each healing removes an illusionary thought of being separate. Each illusion that was subsequently brought to light is a victory for your spiritual transformation. Every relationship is another opportunity to look at your beliefs so they can be healed. Love gets suppressed, covered up, and distorted, and our illusory views of each other cause us to forget about love. It waits for you quietly, to remove what isn't love so that you can remember what truly is love.

"You can never fail" is the no-loss teaching if you work on yourself from within. It doesn't matter to the universal mind how many partners it takes. It only matters that you are willing to learn and arrive.

A No Loss Relationship understands how to go from Stage 1-Attraction into Healing, and then on to CO-creating. First we must understand more about a special relationship.

A No Loss Relationship is willing to see specialness for what it offers a relationship.

A No Loss Relationship means you examine the past ways you did seek partnership. It is by admitting our strengths and weakness in "past" relationships and owning how our "lower self" has affected those involvements that we can start 'seeing' what works and doesn't work in relationships.

A No Loss Relationship is not 'blaming or fault finding.'

A No Loss Relationship is not judging or condemning.
We are discovering what doesn't work so we can change our minds, not changing the other person or ending a relationship.

A No Loss Relationship is 'looking' for causes of 'lack of love' to transcend them, not attack or defend them.

Complete the exercises for this chapter in Chapter 10.

CHAPTER 2

Special Relationships

Attraction to Specialness

We have to take a closer look at Attraction, and how it manipulates our minds. The majority of people go through life being attracted to this or to that and never understanding how their minds work. They never understand how they give their power away to these attractions, and the effects it has upon their lives until suddenly they are thrown into hate, pain, and disillusionment. The consequences are sickness, guilt, and death. All beliefs in lack and loss come from the illusions of our attractions. What is attracting your attention? Let us find out by fully studying this phenomenon.

 Most relationships start off special. The purpose of this book is to teach about Holy Relationships through transformation. Denial of specialness prevents the process. You would not be looking for, or be in a specific involvement, unless that relationship had some aspect of specialness in it. If you had already transcended specialness, you would not be reading this book, nor have a need to heal your relationships.

Special relationships, our starting point, show us what is valued from our past involvements. Looking carefully at specialness is not to label it bad but rather to help us change course and take the relationship in the direction of Wholeness. Specialness is our defense against loneliness. Even if it does not work, no one wants to be lonely.
Give yourself much self-appreciation because you are at least looking for answers and not settling for less. Relationships that are painful and seem like failures are simply saying, "There is a different way of looking at relationships."
Going from Specialness to Holiness is a soul journey, an adventure, and a required study.

 Although the definition of 'attraction' is 'being pulled by inherent physical force or to have emotional or aesthetic appeal for'; attraction is also responsible for the illusion of joining to things, people, personalities, or concepts. I call it "specialness" throughout this material, and you must fully understand this for what it offers you and your involvements. When we feel drawn to someone, we have made an association of him or her with an inner image. An inner image draws an outer representation of its likeness. We call it desire, but the effects are the same.

What is "Specialness?"

Specialness is a thought form the illusion of love takes by wanting specific objects, concepts, or people, more than Reality in its pure nature. Attraction, often a primary component of specialness, is frequently referred to as romantic involvement, desire, passion, or "that certain magical something" we are all looking for. The mind's field is narrowed, allowing the desired object in focus to become the center of attention, with all else being in the background, causing us to crave that one thing. Another way of saying this is we have "selective perception."

Being attracted to someone, some quality they possess, or to their spiritual conscious-ness is rarely recognized for what it is. The allure of someone can be quite deceiving. Attraction is an illusion where the belief that something external to you is holding your attention, rather than that your conscious perception is maintaining a fixed limited view. "You are my dream woman." "I couldn't keep my eyes off him." "From the moment we met I knew you were the one." "You make me feel so magical." "You're so special." We believe the object of our attention, the person, is causing the emotional passion and energy high. However, all real attraction comes from deeper thoughts, because real thoughts have magnetic energies.

When under the influence of 'specialness', our "selective perception" is a limitation, a loss of the awareness of Wholeness, so it becomes a block to the awareness of real love. The intensity of the attraction is expressed through our emotions and physical expressions of passion, which ultimately governs our behavior. If we are not aware of the reasoning behind our behavior, the illusions of specialness take our relationship for a big ride. Who is driving these forces of energies?

We are sold specialness in many forms such as romance, fantasy, eroticism, and glam-our. We are constantly bombarded through media as to what is special and what is beauti-ful. To be a model, a figure of attractiveness is the Ego's false notion for getting attention. If you fear being alone, you may seek a special, single perception to fall in love with as protection against your loneliness. The search for this special "something" is often equated with the search for something "better than." It is extremely difficult to avoid the lures of specialness in today's society because the "sold" specialness is quite alluring.

Specialness usually turns our focus away from who we really are, and directs it onto an external subject that serves as diversion from our personal truths. What we find special is generated by the Ego's need for acknowledgment and validation. The more "special" atten-tion we think we are receiving, the more worthwhile our egos will feel.

The law of mind attraction is "like attracts like." In addition, if we dislike something, we will attract someone who dislikes what we dislike; or, we will attract someone who thinks differently so that we can see what attracts us. We then create memories with that person. Memories are crystallized thought images with a layer of judgment. The magnetic forces occur because of the judgments. Everyone draws nigh unto what they love, and what they love draws nigh unto them.

Within our minds are many images of physical specialness. Being physically attractive is of enormous importance to the lower mind, which values specialness. We are attracted to the body and then to specific parts. We are attracted to emotional expressions, behaviors, and fixed personality types. There always exists an attraction to Spirit; we can be attracted to someone for the spiritual qualities they seem to manifest. We can even be attracted to pain and rejection.

The problem of attraction is not the object of interest but the way the inner image and the judgmental energies force the focus. The problem is what we do with the intensity of the energy charge that is directed toward the person or thing. The error the mind can make is that it doesn't recognize that the inner image and the judgment are causing the magnetic pull towards the desired object. The mind believes that the object is causing the pull.

The Ego believes it lives on getting attention, and it tries to convince you that you must be attractive to get attention. The more special attention we think we receive, the more worthwhile we seem to be. However, there is no "special" attraction to a certain person from the higher perception of a Holy Relationship, for it holds no concepts of being "better than."

Your judgmental images are your blocks to the awareness of love. This is not what the Ego part of your mind wants to learn. Without judgment, you realize the deceptions of the Ego. The thoughts you have drawn across the awareness of love will disappear the moment you recognize them.

However, if a judgmental image is not corrected, the power remains to force you back into specialness. This is why we so often repeat patterns of attraction. We keep looking for the same type of personality, look, or lifestyle, but we blame a relationship not working out on the specific person for not turning out according to our expectations.

Judgmental images are also an expression of self-hate, which occurs through judgment by picking a certain limited perception to dislike, such as your hair, your nose, or maybe a part of your behavior, such as shyness. To compensate for our inner self-hate, we often become attracted to an outer object/person. My special attraction to a woman's body or a certain physical appearance is my projection of wanting to look beautiful myself. My negative perception of my own physical looks seeks an outer correction. We want what we believe we cannot have. If I believe she is so attractive that she probably would not be interested in me, what happens to my self-hate? It is justified and now more intense.

All attraction to specialness is an illusion. We are attracted to dreams of "becoming better." We hope to get, or become, what attracts us. We also think the object of our attraction must pay us attention by our choice to be attracted to it. If it doesn't, we become rejected. But who is rejecting whom? Is what we are attracted to rejecting us, or did we just demand a condition so that life proves again, that we are really unlovable? This illusion of attraction will not bring about a holy joining.

Learning that we set up our own illusions of attraction by taking responsibility for our inner images can save ourselves a lot of pain and rejection.

I knew a woman who was attracted to my friend, who was a musician. He had long hair, was tall, and quite good-looking. She fell in love with him on sight and was always talking about how attractive he was. I asked what she would do if he cut his hair and was paralyzed by a car accident. Interestingly, she answered that her real attraction was to his music because she always dreamed that one day she would play the piano like him. This is an example of how we can project ourselves into multiple levels of attraction—it may seemingly start off one way and manifest into others.

What you think you are attracted to only veils what is really there. We must admit that by becoming attracted to someone and falling in love, we are not seeking to know the true individual. We do not love all of them but just selectively a part of them—and even that part is not truly seen because it is seen through the projection of our inner image. It is influenced by our judgments. We desire to be with them, and we see them at first through the eyes of our secret wish to have what we are so attracted to.

All thoughts have a magnetic nature, including thoughts based in fear and thoughts of love. Often I am asked, "What causes bad things to happen to good people?" Fearful thoughts cause us to draw fearful experiences to ourselves. Good people can carry fearful images within their minds. When we find this out about ourselves, we can become even more disturbed or learn to watch our thoughts. We are not a victim nor does what happen to us come by chance. Fearful thoughts manifest what we call negative experiences, by way of attraction.

When we fear losing a partner or being abandoned—we are asking for and attracting exactly that. What we fear comes upon us. What we resist persists. The average person takes little responsibility for negative attraction and magically wants to take credit for the good things they attract. However, thoughts are things, and the emotional vibrations they emanate set the laws of attraction into movement. Our private world is filled with figures of fear that we have invited into it, and the love that is offered to us, we do not see.

The undoing of specialness is the way to return to love. The balancing of emotional energies leads to peace. Those whose lives are not controlled by their desire for specialness are freed from the prison of lower thinking and false attractions.

In the beginning stages of remembering Wholeness, it may seem like a loss to give up attractive energies. Don't worry—we do not want to give them up entirely. As you and your partner start working on letting go of selfish "getting" patterns, you will both experience expanded awareness and an inner peace, and these wonderful and healthy experiences will replace your limited perceptions.

Are there healthy types of attractions? Yes! Healthy types of attraction cause the mind to go inward versus focusing predominantly on the outward. Everything is seen for the beauty and glory of its uniqueness as a creation. No-loss consciousness holds the awareness and acceptance of the rightful place of everything, and how everything serves a holy purpose.

Attachments to Specialness

Now that we understand the entrapments of attraction to specialness, let us look at how our attractions can become attachments, obsessions, and addictions. The illusion of specialness causes an attachment, which becomes a false type of bonding. The belief: "I have to be with this person" is painful and controlling. Real attachment is love, while false attachment is co-dependence based in lower mind gratification.

Holding hands, kissing, or a lustful sexual encounter is physical attachment, which is sometimes a fear-based emotional bonding. Being bonded physically together gives a false impression of joining in the mind, which seems absolutely true to the people it's happening to. But, the glue is not truly sticking.

The mind has a driving force to heal, and a driving force to be apart. The connecting force of life—the cosmic glue—is love. Physical attachment is a way of pretending, an incorrect method of trying to realize love. The yearning to be together is deep; the only problem is we do it in an incorrect way.

Our Ego attachments to the physical give us the message that physical attachment is love. That lie is the source of most pain and suffering in relationships. No physical attachment occurs in the mind of God. The part of your mind that believes in physical attachment is very powerful. Although it does not have the full power of God, it has the power of your belief, your faith, and conviction that bonding is happening.

Don't try to tell someone they are not in love, when they believe they are. Learning the difference between true love and the illusions of love can only happen from the inside. Change your own beliefs in the illusions of love, but don't try to change those of others. The Holy Spirit is the true teacher.

Correction of your own mind means we relinquish all thoughts that promote specialness and illusions of attraction to a limited form. Correction involves stopping the projection and looking to the causes. We don't move away from a person but release the inner image that makes us dependent upon them in a fixed way. This frees us and them to love truly.

Let me put it this way: if real physical attachment could happen, I would always have to take you with me wherever I go, even to the toilet. It is only made up as happening in the mind of the Ego. Living with someone for 30 years doesn't mean that you will experience a true attachment, and that is why so many go through a divorce. Real attachment occurs only on the level of the mind.

Living in codependency is a dysfunctional involvement with life. It may be all that we have been trained to understand, but it is still a block to understanding real love. Special moments become crystallized memories. Repressed crystallized memories make up our private mind of illusory attachment. Escaping from fear is our goal. When we achieve it, Heaven is seen.

We want to attach to someone else to avoid looking into our own inner issues. We are all learning to return to love through our relationships, and we must learn that Holy Relationship is the correct way to return.

Who hasn't felt the pain of a false attachment to someone we call special? If we are in a relationship that is based in physical attachment, the first signs of realizing it are to observe how each partner is trying to control the other. Controlling a person or situation indicates our own need to be attached to the illusion of love. False attachment is also demonstrated by unaccepting opinions about an event. We will then notice passive aggressiveness, anger, and fear of failure or loss. Thoughts of specialness and physical attachment will start to ruin your relationship. Your partner may start begging to have space.

When one partner is trying to control another by force, the false attachment is convincing them that they can gain greater attachment through controlling. Wrong. Forcing attachment only causes emotional fear, not love. Submission is the opposite of freedom.

Remember, physical attachment is an investment in our own inner images—not reality. Detachment is not loss, but a connection to what is real. Releasing inner fantasies is not sacrifice. It achieves attainment of enlightenment.

False physical attachment can also be recognized as anger. If we are angry in any way, we have falsely attached to a mental image and may be attempting to keep that image by demanding something from an object or person. Each demand requests that the person remains the same as our inner image—or else we cry, "I can't have what I want!" Attempting to possess a person or thing is only a reflection of not letting go of inner images, crystallized thoughts within the mind. We cannot possess anything because everything in the material realm is temporary. False attachment to a form only causes greater discontentment, because we are not keeping up with change. Reality is always trying to advise us that attachment to form won't work. If we keep attempting to hold on, we will need to keep adding energy to our presumed possession. When we fail, which we will, pain and suffering will occur.

Try holding a 30-pound weight at a 90-degree angle to your body. The longer we hold on, the more our muscles hurt, and relief occurs the moment we let go. Similarly, we hold onto mental beliefs and allow them to possess our thinking. LET GO. The answer to all demands of attachment is to release an inner image and work with our thoughts and not the outer person, or object. Letting go ensures a true relationship of joining, which is what we really desired before we bought into this false way of bonding.

All pain and suffering associated with past partners can be traced to a special, crystallized moment in our mind. We shouldn't be self-critical about it because we did not know how to release it. This material will show how to release any crystallized special moments that may still remain in you. Do not underestimate the importance of this work, because only when it is complete can we have a healthy relationship.

The illusion of physical attachment increases our need for affection, and how we receive affection determines our self-perception of Wholeness or lack.

Real attachment always has been, always will be, and always is—and no thought of "not attached" can enter into the Holy mind. It has nothing to do with the physical and everything to do with Wholeness. It proves the Oneness of life. False attachment never happens, cannot happen, and the illusion of it comes out of attraction to specialness keeping us in "lack." It's a joining that did not occur. It's a physical connection that's not permanent, despite our attempts to make it so.

Attachment to Affection

Showing affection through physical attention causes the mind to believe that it is achieving love. Touching, kissing, flirting, hugging, pleasing and speaking flattering words, or building emotional tension toward physical sexual passions are all examples. It is not love; it is sensory gratification. Sensory gratifications can deceive us into believing that we are loved, and once again, we must see the difference between what is illusion, and what is real. Physical affection without emotional awareness causes unhealthy attachments. Sensory gratification is a drug of sorts. It has a limited effect. It has a high and a low energy release. It becomes addictive and cause s us to be constantly looking for the next fix. The Ego convinces us of the need, and turns it into a craving. Lovesick people are always on the prowl for physical affection. Affection is not a bad or wrong experience. It simply must be understood for its effects. We must get honest with what is driving its needs and wants because without this awareness we cannot achieve a No Loss Relationship.

Many people starve themselves of affection, calling it bad, or blaming themselves for the pain they have experienced, until they reach a state of depravation—and then reach out and grab a bite of unhealthy attention. Who do they reach to but an addictive sensory grabber, one who lavishes them with affection to make sure he or she gets theirs. The effects of these attractions are not binding, and these relationships never last. The pain of getting and losing causes inner dissatisfaction, and often the person gives up on love. Mostly the person loses trust in their choice of partners and blames it on their need for affection.

I have met many women who go for years shutting off their sensual drives. Men think about sex several times a day, but if a man is wounded inside, sex becomes merely exercises of sensory gratification.

Showing affection is very personal and intimate. We all have defined comfort zones of acceptable boundaries for allowing someone into our being. When we find someone who seems to understand or resonate with our comfort to being touched, we call it "being loved."

Why are some people starved for physical affection while others can't stand to be hugged? Some want to have sex daily while others prefer very limited amounts. Physical affection is a conditioned behavior. While growing up, I lived in a home where little to no touching occurred between my parents, and my sisters and I fought a lot. As I grew older, I sought affection in sexual ways. No one worked with me or showed me the difference between physical affection and energy exchanging. If this information is new to you, look out--you are in for the greatest discovery of your life.

Physical affection is different from energetic affection. It is a perceivable difference. The focus of the mind on the physical without the awareness of the energy involved is unholy, and often called "lust." We become ignorant of the important aspects of someone's soul and Spirit. This is not a judgment, but a fact of observation. Energy affection is an awareness of energy moving. It is the awareness of exchanging, of giving and receiving. Energy affection looks beyond the behavior, the form, and reaches into the essence of an individual. It deals with feeling and knowing, and doesn't concentrate upon the physical sensations as much as the energy that dwells around and through the body. Our physical bodies thrive on energy. Touching, kissing, and sexual activity is very stimulating, causing us to crave sensory gratifications. What happens on the energetic levels? We will explore more about energy exchanging in Chapter 5. For now let us look at energy affection.

In our desire to have a Holy Relationship, we must look beyond the body to something deeper—this is a commitment to looking at energy and to understanding it. Physical affection is limited to two people being in the same physical space, within touching distance from each other. Energy affection is unlimited and goes beyond form.

In a Holy Relationship, each person learns to receive first from his or her inner source and then to extend. Their extensions are the way they keep the energy moving, like ripples in a pond, they keep reaching out in an ever-expanding circular motion. By moving energy correctly, a Holy couple feels the affection and exchange on many levels and remains constantly content. Why would we not want to give and receive it all the time?

I am not saying to stop touching, kissing or hugging each other. I am only suggesting that we explore a deeper level of affection. The deeper we go into energy, the closer we get to pure gratitude. Gratitude is a divine awareness of God's affection for us, as praise is our appreciation for what already has been given. Praise is acknowledgment of what God gives: love. It certainly is OK to see love in the physical affections we exchange; the trick is we must see it along with the non-physical presence of our partner. If we fail to see the energy affection, we will believe in loss. A No Loss involvement expands the awareness of affection to the connection in the mind.

Outside Approval

When we seek approval from others it often signals that we haven't given it to ourselves. The search for approval becomes a mystery—once found it quickly leaves. The need comes from the nature of doubt—and those who doubt can never know. When we are looking for approval from our mate, remember that no matter what they say, it will only cloak our dark inner feelings of doubt and fear of being unloved.

Of course it is appropriate to reassure a partner that they are on the right path and to encourage him or her, but to say that we approve of who he or she is only promotes insecurity. It is a childish need. Those who have low self-esteem issues are looking for approval because their parents did not nourish that part of them.

The key to a whole relationship is not to give false praise or buy into mental reassurance that can appear flattering. This is manipulative and co-dependent by nature. The Ego can talk a good talk, but it cannot walk the walk. Real approval is silent, its source knows. Don't let the voice of "getting" replace the voice of "knowing." Help each other know; do not encourage co-dependence. It is better to teach a child to do their own homework than to do it for them.

Admiration

Again we come to the awareness that the Ego has one way of doing something and Spirit has another way of expressing the same idea. Of course, we all want to feel admired, appreciated, and adored. We are seeking a feeling of being loved. We also can be seeking a feeling of being "better than" and that comes from how we are admired and valued. We simply have to learn to be aware and observe the direction of the energy. We must look for the expectation and the source of the need. Look at how this need is being met and by whom. If we think that it is our partner's duty to keep us feeling high, then we have given him or her an unhealthy job. If we feel any form of being unloved and believe that our partner can fix that, we have created an illusion of specialness. That mistake must be corrected or we will constantly misunderstand real love.

Love doesn't need to be reassured or admired or coerced into knowing itself. It is only because we are looking for it in the wrong way that we feel a need to be admired. Remember, the higher the pedestal, the longer the fall. The more someone makes us special the more they may grow to hate us as well.

What About Romance?

Loss in relationships is perceived when happiness is not recognized for what it is. We feel rejected and abandoned because we sought happiness in the wrong way. A false concept of "getting" (also known as "I want") leads to the obsession with romance. I am not saying not to buy flowers for a sweetheart. I am saying not to buy flowers with the intention of "getting" the sweetheart to give you happiness (pleasure) or thanks for it. Give flowers with the pure joy of sharing, with no expectations or fantasy that something more will come from the moment of just giving.

The difference is subtle. It is a quiet joy, a selfless extending, based in certainty of purpose and not wishful yearning to be complete. It requires examination of motive and inner awareness that we are not giving for a specific result. This is the problem with romantic love; we expect a hidden result. If we achieve the hidden agenda, we think we are happy. If it doesn't turn out as we dreamed, we become unhappy. We also compound the problem by believing that our partner caused us to feel what we felt. To tell the difference between romance and true love is a process of self-growth.

Sexual Bonding Without Purpose

Another problem with erotic love, romantic sexuality, or lust is false bonding. False bonding occurs without a foundation for healing the emotions. Healing emotions plays a major part in any healthy relationship. In lust, we never really see beyond the body or pleasure seeking.

Sexual energies cause bonding, and by being sexual we are opening ourselves to the other's emotional state of mind. If a couple has not established a solid way of healing their emotions through communication and the relationship does indeed become toxic, they exchange their emotional baggage and dump it on each other. Sexual pleasures focused on the body, line the path to emotional drama. No relationship can join or find purpose if the drama of emotional love and hate become predominant. Like a small boat in a heavy storm, the rise and fall of the waves will sink the ship. Happiness is never found until each partner balances his or her own emotions.

Few know how to do this, and it is a catch 22 because we rush into a romantic sexual relationship hoping the other can fix what feels wrong. Because we have lived with our Ego mind for many years, we carry with us a deep sense of unhappiness. Those who are chasing a mate are simply saying, "Who can take away this unhappiness? Can you?"

It takes a lot of learning to discover the illusions of love. The sooner we learn what is false, the sooner we can seek what is true. No relationship is a failure because we can always learn what is false—and to find this out is a success.

Dreaming The Dream

The dreamer's of the dreamare dreaming of remembering that they are the dreamer.

The dreamer of the dream is asleep, unaware that they are dreaming. The dreamer cannot awaken from his dream while dreaming because he is so invested in the dream. He believes in the dream as his reality and is unaware of himself without the dream. All spiritual leaders teach us that we need to teach ourselves what is the nature of the dream, and what is the dreamer. The need to teach ourselves is of utmost importance because it is an experience, a revelation, quite often referred to as spiritual awakening.

The dreamer is you, the real you, devoid of any false notion that you are the dream.

A spiritual relationship must set a primary purpose of waking up and helping each partner wake up. Relationship problems stem from not being awake or being able to tell the dream nature of the mind. Problems seem true or real because the dreamer cannot comprehend that it is just a dream. We forget that we are the director and creator of the dream. We believe the images are real and solid. We, of course, take the dream seriously. We have forgotten to laugh in life and take our images as real.

The idea of being asleep is the idea of being unconscious, ignorant, and unaware of the real essence or nature of our creative self. When we are asleep, we dream, and it matters not if we believe we are in bed asleep. When we are asleep we think of ourselves as being something different from what we are as God created us.

The unhappy dream is our romantics "special" wish that we would "get" the happiness from a different self. Our Ego waits to repeat the pattern of "special love." We are always in a relationship with some aspect of our self.

You are dreaming when any judgment enters into your awareness.
You are dreaming when you feel any person has hurt you.
You are dreaming when you entertain a concept of loss.
You are dreaming when you believe you can gain at another's expense.
You are dreaming when you think of yourself as a separate self-afraid of other selves.
You are dreaming when you live out of some identify other than what you are as Spirit.
You are dreaming when you think something can replace Real Love, like money, a car, and a beautiful body.
You are dreaming when you think you can die or be sick.
You are dreaming when you think you are stuck or bound by a limitation.
You are dreaming when you become fearful in any way becoming emotionally imbalanced is caused by dreams
You are dreaming when you alone are thinking about your future.
You are dreaming when you think you are in a body and are a fixed personality.
You are dreaming when you put others in a body or a fixed behavior.
You are dreaming when you feel guilty about hurting someone else.
All beliefs that someone else can give you something you do not already have, is a dream.
You are dreaming when you think you are alone or separated from the ones you love.
All enemies are dreams. All beliefs that you are attacked and killed are dreams.

Each dream can be very specific and personal, causing you to forget you are the dreamer. Can you add to this list?

Types Of Dreams

Dreams in Sleep: Unconscious dreams, dreaming in symbols and surreal images.
Dreams in Waking: Conscious thoughts which we often call thinking.

    A. Walking Fantasies: Dreams of wanting or lacking
    b. Time Dreams: Past and future projections dealing with time and space.
    C. Nightmares, Death wish dreams: Dreams of terror, dreams that
      include attack, sickness, and death.
    D. Happy Dreams and Dreams of Joining: Miracles.
    E. Dreams of Forgiveness: Dreams of correcting and healing.

Each type of dream occurs at a different level of mind. The level of sleep is a thought of unconsciousness. The level of thinking is a level of unconscious mind also. Nightmares and death dreams come from thoughts of lack, and the entire premise of this book is that through our Holy Relationship, we can teach each other to awaken from such lower mind dreams.

Dreams turn to nightmares when the dream gains power over the dreamer. All power is given to the dreamer, but even that can be forgotten. Each time we believe the dream is real and reinforce it by developing a defense against the dream, we leave some energy and power with the dream.

If a dream frightens us, we must see it as within and not outside of us, for no correction can occur as long as we place the dream out there.

Dreams have only the power that we give to them. If we dream that we are poor and lack recourse to pay bills, that dream can control our creativity. It can make us less productive. However, if it is offered for healing it can change who we see ourselves to be. Each dream can be transformed because we are the dreamer. Learn to be in charge of our dreams, not let the dreams be in charge of us.

The partnership learns to share thoughts and dreams in the light of forgiveness. The AAA Mind Healing Method (Acknowledgement, Acceptance, Appreciation) works particularly well with dreams, for each dream melts away when we look upon it with acceptance and gratitude. This method will be discussed in more detail in the next chapter.

In forgiveness, the judgment is removed and the power balanced. All figures in the dream are seen as our creations, along with each part we invited them to play, their respective role as we directed. Ask a past lover who made an idol, a special relationship out of the past involvement. Who gave the power to the idea of loss? Who wanted an outcome that was not CO-created?

By returning the mind to a right perception of an event, the dream is accepted. Once a dream can be accepted it becomes a happy dream. All happy dreams honor the creator of the dream. Make your relationship happy, and you are very close to seeing the dreamer. Knowing yourself in this light causes joining, and the experience of love.

The happy dreams occur when we uplift our mind to the conscious level of Spirit, the level of mind that can dream in joy. Happy dreams come when we see life as it truly is with no thoughts of lack. My happy dreams are usually dreams of flying, playing, and being in wide-open spaces. I love freedom and the openness of Life.

When we know the true nature of dreams they become something to advance our spiritual growth. A No Loss Relationship shares dreams and learns to dream together. They set their minds on happy dreams with purpose and intention. A No Loss Relationship uses dreams as a tool for transformation. Even waking, thinking dreams are shared to be changed into awareness of Reality. Happy dreams shared are the way to revelation.

Friends First

Each person of a Holy Relationship makes a commitment to place spiritual values at a priority above the lower mind, physical desires, and pursuits. This commitment is the safeguard that prevents the relationship from moving into a dream involvement or into a sexually dysfunctional attachment.

By making the decision to be friends first while also choosing a spiritual focus, you are actually setting up ways to protect yourself. In today's society, we need more than just safe sex; we need spiritual protection as well. You need protection, not only from a potential partner, but also from your own Ego and its lower habits. The risk of putting yourself in danger will more likely be the result of your own actions rather than the result of actions that others may take against you. By setting certain agreements in the relationship before becoming too entangled, you enhance the chance of effectively healing together.

The partners in a No Loss Relationship are not interested in selfishness, and they are not interested in holding on to behaviors from past relationships that did not provide desired results. They are interested in supporting spiritual principles. If a partner is possessive and wants to control the way that we love him or her, then the relationship is stuck in special-ness. A true friend will support our efforts of being free. A friend may encourage us to seek higher counsel, but he or she will also allow us to make mistakes and learn from them. Each person in a real friendship is interested in supporting the other person. Neither person is interested in controlling the other person, and there is no motive of "getting something" from the other person.

The supportive partner will have a desire to learn. In a spiritually based friendship, each person agrees to practice together and make it fun. A good friend doesn't engender fear; our own Ego mind supplies enough fear already. A good friend doesn't set limits. Although a friend may not always act according to our likings, we are certainly more likely to overlook the behavior of a good friend than the behavior of someone with whom we have given the required task to love us. We lower our expectations with friends and often raise them with a "special" partner. When basic friendship is lost, the Golden Rule becomes highly distorted. A No Loss Relationship is one that promotes true friendship and reflects unconditional love.

Freedom from the body is what each Holy Relationship strives for but not through death or any attempt to make a partner experience lack. If we believe the body is a source of freedom and joy, we will look to what bodies do for our enjoyment. A Holy Relationship chooses to change the focus away from the body. Matter is a by-product of energy, just as energy is a by-product of consciousness. If we value matter more than consciousness we have a backward view of what's important in the universe. Simply put, if anything in this material universe makes you unhappy it is a sign of this up side down perception. If we value Spirit more than the material, then nothing can disturb our peace and joy. A Holy Relationship is the means to teach us how to change our values.

A Holy Relationship can make all corrections and remove all pain regardless of its na-ture, provided that we give everything we think to the Spirit that knows how to change our thoughts. Each time we entrust each other to jointly offer unholy thoughts to Spirit, healing does occur. Do not forget that the purpose of forming a Holy Relationship was to teach us the power of a joined Will. In a Holy Relationship, there is no concept of a separate mind. The separate mind was only a mistake, and in the inner Light of our spiritual vision we see how the error is corrected. How happy we will be when we let this vision be given.

The partners of a Holy Relationship bring only love to each person they meet, and with-in each person they see a reflection of the same mind they found in themselves. They look on each other in perfect love seeing only the pure consciousness of what made them. How blessed they are, and they bless others by desiring to look past the body and judgments of the lower mind and look for the Wholeness.

Teachers of Light bring a joy that others have forgotten but can remember because they see it in a Holy Relationship. The ability to share this joy is the purpose of a No Loss Relationship that is based on putting Spirit first. Within the No Loss Relationship, what one feels the other feels, and what one thinks the other knows as well. What can this mean, but that we share and are joined in the same mind? Do not be afraid of this concept of feeling and thoughts. Do not think that we must protect the mind that has kept us separate and alone. It has only made us miserable.

When the sense of separation is finally overcome, we will learn that we have not lost our individuality or anything else. The body that we thought was so valuable will be seen for what it really is—a place to hide and a place to protect our identity of lack. The Whole cannot lack, thus the No Loss Relationship contains everything.

Complete the exercises for this chapter in Chapter 10.

CHAPTER 3

The Components of a Holy Relationship

Holy Relationships

Taking off for the moon requires a set, calculated course. Entering back into the Earth's atmosphere must be at a precise angle or the craft will disintegrate. Our relationships are similar even though we seldom realize it. If two people meet and the direction of their encounter is set for the right course, then the relationship will be guided toward true love. If the relationship gets off course in the beginning, how much more off course will it be if it travels in time in the wrong direction?

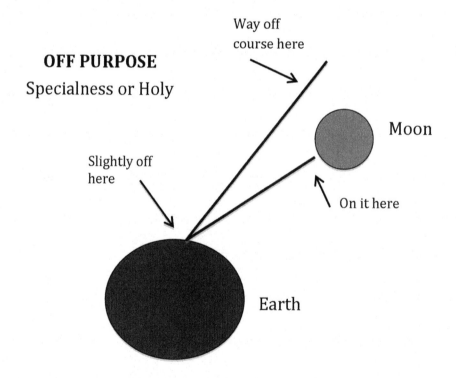

Our minds see in two directions. The mind is directed either toward the body or toward Spirit, much like a telescope, which has a narrow focus or an expanded view. The transformation of a relationship into Holiness begins with setting the purpose. How can we get somewhere if we don't know where we're going?

As we enter into this new era of spiritual involvement, people are committing to spiritual disciplines to replace the need for physical addictions. Many are looking to the idea of lasting friendships with their intimate partner to replace the romanticized notion of a 'one and only special someone' who will complete us. Holy Relationships are the answer to the sense of isolation people feel as a result of generations of dysfunctional relationships.

A Holy Relationship is the means for raising our consciousness, which will help us complete our training to be a teacher of love. Each person in the relationship is given specific instructions on how to help the other person. These instructions come from a space of recognition of wholeness and not from a place of codependency.
Few people understand what it takes to have a healthy relationship because they have rarely, if ever, seen one modeled. If we want to feel a sense of Oneness and we want to know God, then we will need to evolve our personal relationships into relationships that are devoted to spiritual principles.

A Spiritual partnership is different from a non-spiritual partnership. Each partner in a Spiritual partnership learns how to be whole and complete within him or herself. Each partner extends that awareness of wholeness not only to the other partner but also to every person he or she encounters. A Special Relationship is dependent, which means that a partner is not aware of his or her personal sense of wholeness and sees something particular in the other that is better or special. This type of involvement depends on one person supplying that "something better" trait in which the other person feels he or she is lacking. Each person believes that he or she becomes complete by being with the other person. We refer to this as a "Special Relationship." One person is perceived as "having it" and the other person is perceived as "getting it."

A Holy Relationship must reverse this tendency. Through carefully laid out plans made by the Holy Spirit, our relationship heals the mind that believes it lacks something. If we knew what this endeavor entailed, we probably would not be so willing. Be assured that the Holy Spirit has picked a helpful companion for this endeavor. We cannot look at our own fear parts alone. We can't heal alone. The collection of errors that our lower mind has made is so persuading to us that it requires another person and the Holy Spirit to undo the mistakes we have made about ourselves.

The goal of a Holy Relationship is to undo any programming of thought that teaches us that we are lacking in any way. The means for learning this are our relationships in time and space. The means are the lessons we teach each other to prove what is true. The meaning we give to anything leads us closer to, or further from, the truth. The further we are from the truth, the further we are from a healthy relationship. Our Holy Relationship mirrors our inner commitment to find our higher mind.

No one who has a unified shared purpose can fail. A Course in Miracles states, "And through Him have all your Holy Relationships been carefully preserved, to serve God's purpose for you. Your question should not be, '"how can I see my brother without the body?"' Ask only, '"do I really wish to see him without making him special?"' As you ask, forget not that his wholeness is your escape from fear.

The Mind—High and Holy, Low and Slow

Our mind has three parts—the lower part, the sane part, and the higher part—known as the Holy Spirit. The lower part of our mind is the domain of the Ego and identifies with us as a body. The sane part of us is our true self and the part of us that understands reason and truth. It can also be called consciousness, which is not to be confused with conscience. The sane part is the neutral decision maker or Will to choose. It is the switch (so to speak) that chooses between the Ego and Spirit. The conscious mind can see both worlds but must make a choice for one or the other. This mind is either in the OFF position (Ego) or the ON position (Spirit), but it can't be in both positions at the same time. Our sane mind can't be in fear (Ego) and love (Spirit) at the same time. We choose whether to listen to our Ego and follow its advice or to listen and follow the instructions of the Holy Spirit. The higher part of us is the Absolute Real Self, which is the one whose home is with God, and this part never separates from Spirit. The Real Self is called the Child of God. It is the Holiness of this higher part that knows nothing of bodies. It knows nothing of evil, sin, or hell. It lives not inside our body or our brain. The Holy Spirit, an idea in our Higher Mind, appeals to the part of us that can reason, and the Holy Spirit teaches us to direct our faith to our higher thoughts.

Our Holy Relationship supports our being able to listen, to learn, and to teach as our higher mind directs. Think what it can do. Listening to the Holy Spirit as our higher mind helps us to change our judgments about our partner's differences. It will also help us release our hold on conditions we're requiring within the relationship. In the Holy Relationship, we can reach beyond fear and experience enlightened moments of union. The concept of the Holy Relationship will eventually reach all minds because all minds are the same, and all minds want the same experiences. These experiences will never end, and No Loss is possible. A Holy Relationship leads to God directly by teaching that there is only one mind, and it is shared.

You are both joined in that one mind. A Holy Relationship's teaching is practical and reasonable because its goal is to have Earth return to the state of mind that is like heaven. When you learn that you share this mind with your partner, then you realize that you are not separate and your wills are not different. It is within these concepts that you receive a glimpse of heaven.

In heaven, minds are not separate from each other, and the one-shared mind is not separate from its maker. In heaven, the concept of one shared mind is perfectly clear, and there is a complete understanding that only God exists. In a Holy Relationship, partners learn to receive together and to give to others as it was given to them.

When we exist as a separate mind, the experiences of the shared mind seem impossible and difficult to understand. By having a willingness to learn the concepts of the shared mind, we will notice how easy it is to move beyond the concept of separate minds since it is only a trick that our lower mind is playing on our relationship. Our lower mind will no longer be able, neither to trick us, nor to block us from learning how to join within the relationship. In the Holy Relationship, both partners share the Real Mind, and it is available to both of them. A Holy Relationship is formed when two people decide to become spiritual teachers, first to each other and then to the World. To become a teacher only requires a willingness to become one, nothing else. Your qualifications are already established by being a spiritual human. No one is denied admittance into the institution of wholeness. Love waits upon your interest in learning. When you hear an inner calling to know God, and find a fellow companion who also feels the desire, your joint decision to participate creates all the means necessary to fulfill your training. Unlike any earthly college, which requires an entry exam, the Holy Spirit accepts your applications without reservation because you are a part of a plan greater than anything you can possibly imagine.

In the beginning stages a clear purpose must be set. By setting this purpose and placing the relationship in the guidance of a higher mind or Holy Spirit, you both do something you never have done before. You start the process of truly listening and surrendering. You make a conscious decision to be trained for a higher purpose than your selfish interests. You find you're ready to learn something different—something you have never been taught before.

You have a "readiness" to seek a higher method of correcting mistakes. You say to each other, "Let's learn together in a higher way." To evolve means to move on and to grow beyond old patterns and old ways of living. This readiness to grow is why you have sought out a spiritual relationship. It is very important to realize that you don't want to repeat old habits of love and hate. The higher mind, now referred to as the Holy Spirit, can easily place the right people in your life to help you evolve.

Your "readiness" is often increased by meeting a "special significant other." Most relationships start with each person making the other person special, and neither person have a clue about what is required to make the relationship holy. The Holy Spirit accepts where you are in your process of evolving, and if you are willing to allow it to do so, then it takes what you have made and uses it for a higher purpose. A Holy Relationship is seen as a relationship with the Spirit of wholeness as the guide.

The person you met did not come to you by accident or by chance, and the groups of spiritual friends you know were carefully selected to help you in your personal transformation. So we say, "Thank you Spirit for my friends." The Holy Relationship is an incredible way to learn, and in all aspects is the greatest method of accomplishing what you truly want—to be whole.

We need to see our relationships as the method we use to heal our mind, emotions and soul. If both partners agree that the function of the relationship is healing, then the relationship has a good opportunity to be healthy and happy. The relationship will also allow each partner to advance into a realization of Oneness.

A No Loss Relationship is when two people make the agreement to seek holiness. This agreement can be made between any two people—friends, business partners, coworkers, lovers, family members (siblings, spouses, parent/child), etc. The only requirement is that a conscious agreement is made to work toward wholeness together. You can have one or an infinite number of Holy Relationships and each support the desire to know who you really are—a being created as whole and complete.

Focus—Connections to a Higher Path and 4H focus

When we meet someone, we acquire a first impression of who we think they are. That first impression often entails examining their physical appearance. If we like the person's physical appearance, then we seek to know more about his or her personality and intellect. If we still feel an attraction, then we make a subtle evaluation to determine if we feel safe with this person or if we consider the person to be a threat to our sense of well being. We notice any sexual energy present, and we make several judgments to determine if this person can fit into our lives or not. It isn't until much later in the involvement that we get a glimpse of that person's emotional side and spiritual interests, even if we happened to have met the person in a religious or spiritual environment.

Every person inherently possesses four levels of self: the physical, emotional, mental, and spiritual. We all know that we have a human body, which is necessary for the expression of our physical existence and our physical life force. We also know that we have a brain, which contains our beliefs, concepts, and memories. We have a mental body that holds and projects our thoughts and feelings on both a conscious and a subconscious level. We also have an emotional body that evaluates and judges our personal experiences and determines how safe and secure we feel. Lastly, we have an often less-understood spiritual body. The spiritual body consists of pure energy Light and is "self-conscious and whole. (Our spiritual body doesn't necessarily have anything to do with religion.)

Each partner we choose has all four bodies, whether we notice them or not. We see maybe one or two bodies, but often fail to notice all four. We see the physical because we use our body's eyes. We "see" the mental because we use our ears and can feel each other's emotions.

The spiritual body is seen and felt through developed spiritual awareness. If each of these bodies were in perfect alignment and functioning properly, they would produce health, happiness, knowledge, and wholeness. Each person has varying degrees of Health, Healing, Happiness and Holiness. We call these qualities the 4H's.

To achieve the type of relationship that we truly desire, we need to make choices that support physical health, feelings of happiness, emotional healing, and a constant awareness of our true divine self, which we call "wholeness." Who wouldn't want a relationship where both partners have an exuberantly healthy body, a happy attitude, a willingness to be healed emotionally, and a continuous flow of thoughts that reflect spiritual knowledge? Who wouldn't want a partner who is whole and truly giving love all the time? Who wouldn't want a relationship in which each partner views him or herself as complete? Who wouldn't want a relationship where the games of judgment and "better than" have been relinquished? When you view the personal ads of singles looking for mates, these are the qualities that are listed as desirable.

When we live with the 4H Focus as a priority, we are reminded of the direction to take to experience the relationship that we truly desire, and this directional reminder helps us to remain on our higher path. The 4H Focus serves as a guide for measuring how close we are to achieving a Holy Relationship with our partner. The 4H Focus provides the framework for achieving healthy and holistic goals for ourselves, for the people presently in our lives, and for the people who will become a part of our lives in the future. By committing to the process of healing our own minds, we will be led to the knowledge and the understanding that we are already whole.

The Lower Self—Driven by the 4S Focus

The opposite of a Holy Relationship is an unholy relationship. It is based in our physical existence alone and originates from our animalistic consciousness.

Let us look at how the animal inside of us thinks. Our animal is interested in survival and procreating. It knows that in order to survive, its security is paramount. It also wants to be noticed and to stand out above the rest. It seeks to be "special."

Very often, our relationships are based in Sexuality, Survival, Security, and Specialness. We call this list the 4S Focus. Each person has a lower self, which is a dark part of the mind that is directed primarily towards the physical existence. In biblical terms it is called the "carnal mind," or the lower self.

We can also refer to it as the Ego. Our lower minds tend to operate like mazes, and we spend a great deal of time navigating the many ruts we have worn in our brains that lead us around and around only to keep us locked into our conditioned programming. Our lower mind can gravitate towards negative thoughts and ignore our Higher Self. When a relationship is driven by the lower mind, it is generally attracted to the illusions of love, and there is a predominant focus on Sexuality, Survival, Security, and Specialness.

When we operate within the 4 S's, we tend to look for security in misleading ways such as through money, competition, control, and/or domination. The Ego is designed to want to be superior over others. Its goal is to keep us from focusing on our spiritual nature because by avoiding one path, we ultimately must choose another.

This is not to say we deliberately set out to operate from a lower-self state of consciousness. It is simply that many of us are not aware that we have alternative ways of viewing our relationships and that we may be allowing the 4 S's to govern our interactions with others. The 4 S's ultimately move us in the direction of separateness and isolation from our partners if we are not willing to examine our intentions and purpose for the relationship that we have entered into.

By choosing to focus on the 4 H's as described above, we can eliminate the 4 S's, and our relationship can transform from carnal thinking to an evolved spiritual consciousness! Each step we take to let go of one thought of specialness will open the door to welcome a thought of holiness. A lower thought and a higher thought can't occupy the same space. Spiritual evolution through a Holy Relationship is about transcending the maze and transforming the programming. By choosing to explore how to progress toward Holy Relationships, the 4 S's can be viewed in a totally different light and will lead us on the path of the 4 H's: Health, Happiness, Healing, and Holiness (and Wholeness).

Understanding the difference between these levels of consciousness is called an awakening. Undoubtedly, it is the fastest and most effective way to experiencing real love.

The AAA Mind Correcting Process

Acknowledgement of What IS, Acceptance Through Appreciation

Acknowledgment is awareness of self-consciousness. Divine presence exists in everyone and everything; through acknowledgment, we recognize that.

Acceptance is the divine awareness of what IS, without any past or future or judgment of any kind. Acceptance is the consciousness of now—exactly as it is.

Appreciation is a divine awareness of what God is in expression. Appreciation is the ways we know each other without the illusion of specialness.

Acceptance through Appreciation, with Acknowledgment of what is, is the way to make your relationship become holy. It's the means to achieve a 4H Focus. With these attitudes, you evolve out of the lower mind. If these divine attributes are not present, your partner will forget how to love you. No matter how distorted your vision of love is, acceptance through appreciation will correct it. Every mind is searching for acceptance without judgment. Every mind needs to be appreciated: not appreciated for what is "good or special" about them, but appreciated for what is true about them. The difference is the removal of judgment.

Appreciation, like any idea if distorted by the personal mind, can lead to a confusion of its purpose. If your appreciation is based on your need to get something from your partner, that admiration is manipulative. To prevent manipulating appreciation, include the ideas of acceptance and acknowledgment. Teach yourself to accept your partner exactly for whom he or she is. By coercing him or her into being what you want him or her to be—instead of allowing him or her to be what he or she is—you forget what true appreciation is. Only through acceptance of the Is-ness of a situation can you have an understanding that it is not selfish. The Is-ness is another term I use for naming a moment without judgment.

Your partner is your greatest gift, and who wouldn't appreciate such a gift if you truly understood what your partner was doing for you? He or she is the one who is your greatest fan, the doctor who heals your mind and the mirror that reflects your fears or your inner light, the lawyer who pleads for your innocence, your jailer who frees you, your chiropractor who makes a mental adjustment that straightens out your kinky thoughts. He or she is your Spiritual Savior, your best friend, and your greatest lover who leads you to the greatest pleasure of life—to know love. What else can a holy partner do? Just ask him or her. Each time your partner comes to your mind, observe your thoughts about them. What are those thoughts directing you toward? Any thought other than deep appreciation and gratitude must be an error in judgment. Would you really want your partner to think any other way of you?

You need but leave the mirror clean and clear your mind of all the fearful images you have drawn upon it. God will shine upon it by itself, and you shall know Spirit by your awareness of your appreciation for Life and of your partner. The reason you find it hard to appreciate your partners is because you have placed a guilty thought over the Is-ness of a situation. You have darkened the event with your personal dreams. Non-acceptance is condemnation in some form. Those who condemn know not how to reach for appreciation or acknowledgment. It becomes a cancer in the mind. You grow a different outlook than the acceptance of what is.

The healing part of any relationship is to return your mind to the acceptance of the past without any need to change it. Acceptance is the necessary step you must take to reach love.

The AAA mind perception allows you to end the sense of being separate. A thought that is judgmental makes a false perception of what happened, and a "story" is formed from that perception in your mind as a crystallized script. Love doesn't have a story; it only sees the Is-ness of creation. Acceptance becomes the bridge, and appreciation encourages crossing over.

People often ask, "How can I accept what seems like a tragedy or a major loss? How can I accept a 'wrong' my partner has done?" People ask this because the wrong has trespassed your beliefs of what you think should have happened. Forgiveness is the process that makes acceptance possible. Once again you have to remember you are not alone, and that is why God created the Holy Spirit. The Holy Spirit will work with your mind and show you how to make the shift from fear to love. From your expectation to acceptance to pure knowledge is the direction the guidance of the Holy Spirit takes. If you can't find acceptance, ask for help.

Of course, it is not possible for you to be totally accepting all the time, for if you were, you wouldn't be on Earth. It is natural for you to shift back and forth. When you start to learn the value of acceptance and how it helps heal your relationship, you will learn to appreciate even the healing process. At first, it may be a gradual process to accept and appreciate everything your partner does. The test of the method proves its worthiness.

Always remember that it is your choice to hold onto certain types of thoughts. It is your choice to experience certain types of energies. When you learn that a thought image doesn't serve you and that another type of attitude will change the image, the willingness to practice increases. Practice acceptance through being appreciative of the events and the people involved in them as a tool to bring yourself and your partner closer to love.

Acceptance is true perception. Most people's perceptions are based in specialness and guilt. When you make a choice to accept, you are making a change in your perception. True perception leads to truth. An illusory perception is a false view of life. Your partner is the mirror to inform you which view you are taking.

If you find anyone doing something you consider unacceptable, ask your partner's help in shifting the awareness until you do find it acceptable. If you still can't make that shift, ask for help from the Holy Spirit together. If you still don't feel you have been helped, ask what condition exists in your mind that you are not willing to relinquish that makes the unacceptable stance more attractive. That thought-image is a core threat to your Ego, which wants to make you listen to its guidance instead of Spirit's. It illustrates the idea of being victimized by someone.

For example, having an opinion about an event that didn't really physically involve you, like watching a crime on television, and having an unaccepting thought about it, leads to holding a fearful view about life. When we live from a fearful stance about life, acceptance becomes harder and harder to accomplish. The more you hide from life, the less you can understand about it. The more fearful you become of life, the more you live in your unconscious, and your unacceptable thoughts become your dream reality. Dream realities manifest as the world of special hate mixed with special love. These catch-22 cycles become such a vicious merry-go-round that few know how to get off of. The way off is acceptance through appreciation of your partner.

Many a person will find rape or physical aggression toward a child "unacceptable." Please don't be confused in this teaching—I am not saying you should accept violent actions. I am saying that to prevent violence, you must forgive all the images your personal mind holds. All healing of violence comes not from fighting against it, but from searching your mind for your unacceptable attitude toward it, and through acceptance, letting those thoughts go.

People think the fight against something unacceptable is justified, and that's what will prevent it from happening again. What people don't realize is that by resisting it, they cause it to persist in the mind.

Acceptance is the way thoughts are freed and not held in the dream energy that causes it to be acted out into material manifestation. Thoughts repressed into the subconscious cause the dream to happen. Violence is a dream, an act played out, with this world as the stage. Its ending occurs when you accept your personal part in it, and give no power to it. By accepting something you are not advocating it. You are not participating in it. You are not supporting it or encouraging it. You are really neutralizing it. By condemning behavior, you are participating in the dream, thus keeping the action happening.

This can be so hard to understand from a human-animal level of consciousness. It requires a super-human awareness—the awareness that a Holy Relationship provides, awareness that in the past had been reserved for spiritual masters and gurus. You may have to prove this to yourself in little ways before you can move to larger issues. To be impartial and still compassionate to all parties is an inner attitude that only the Holy Spirit can teach. Acceptance lifts you out of the human-animal consciousness of existence and into an awareness of appreciation for what it took to return your mind to God. You will never fully appreciate your journey until you appreciate all those who played their parts in your transformation. It is so difficult to see that the ones you "hate" only played the part you asked them to play.

When you see the collective consciousness as one mind, you see that each part of that mind volunteers to play out certain thoughts; the weaker parts choose to play the victimizer, and you must learn to thank them for doing so. The weaker parts of society are our criminals, and the stronger parts of our society are the saints that love. They forgive through acceptance. They heal by not condemning others. Each condemning thought can be transmitted to a weaker mind until that mind becomes so weak that it can't resist acting out the unacceptable deed. It is like a black hole, which keeps sucking in planets until it explodes and spits them out. Dark minds are the black holes of this society, which collect our fear thoughts. The spitting out is called "action."

The only way to correct this problem is to recognize that minds are joined and that we have to take responsibility for what we think. No longer can we pollute or refuse to recycle. We must realize that we are affecting the entire planet. Similarly, we have to realize that as a whole, each thought has some effect on the collective mind.

Let me warn you that the Ego hates acceptance through appreciation and acknowledgment of what is. It knows that if you get the hang of it that it will cease to exist. Acceptance is the death of the Ego, so remember, it will scream to not practice. The Ego warns: if you accept, you will be allowing the event to happen again. You don't accept something because you fear it repeating. This is the self-deception that the Ego invents to keep the game alive.

Have all the unacceptable thoughts and guilt in our minds prevented "criminals" from acting out? Are we putting an end to war by finding people's actions unacceptable? We keep building more prisons, we have more criminals, and we certainly need larger police forces. Why? Because not one of our unaccepting thoughts has changed the mind of our brother.

Each time you practice turning an unacceptable thought into an acceptable one, you actively participate in healing the mind of the entire planet. Since a Holy Relationship works for the whole, each time you practice forgiveness in your personal involvement, you contribute to God's plan.

The reason we are so attracted to the illusions of specialness is because we don't know how to heal our minds and the minds of our partners. We substitute specialness for acceptance, forgetting how much joy comes from true appreciation of what is. By forgetting the values of acknowledgment and appreciation, we dwell in the pain of "thinking" about how to find pleasure. The Ego then advises us, and we follow its guidance toward its chosen path of attraction to the body. No wonder our fellow humans are unhappy!

Acknowledge what is; appreciate what is, and pay attention to what is. The Is-ness of any moment is the door to knowledge—and knowledge is God. To know God is the greatest pleasure possible. Anything less is a misstep.

Direct your mind to be attracted to Spirit. Become addicted to God. Attach your attention to light; practice acceptance through appreciation, and you have a firm basis for making all of your relationships Happy, Healthy, Healing, and Holy. The AAA mind stance leads to this 4H Focus. When you achieve a Healthy, Happy, Healing, and Holy Relationship you will do much for this planet, and the weaker minds that have become toxic with judgment will look to both of you as examples of love.

A Holy Relationship makes acceptance through appreciation of a goal (although it may be hard to practice at first) by finding its partner's actions totally acceptable. To have a Holy Relationship it is possible with the help of Holy Spirit and achieved through practice, Practice.

The average Ego-driven person thinks five critical, judgmental thoughts to one positive, uplifting one. Most couples put down their partners eight times more than praising them. Couples are starving for appreciation, often misunderstood as affection, or sexual impulse. Couples are not trained in acceptance unless they do many meditations together. Couples in an unholy involvement focus on the body and not the knowledge of what they are as Spirit created them. A Holy Relationship reverses these lower tendencies and replaces them with thoughts of AAA mind training.

A No Loss Relationship is full of divine praise and spiritual aliveness, accomplished simply with right thought. A No Loss Relationship is the truth of what you both are in love, and the consistent remembering is done with correct vision of each other.

Communication

The Holy Relationship focuses on communication as the primary way to cause joining, and joining is the way to remember God's love. Communication that is directed by will means coming together in union. However, when communication is directed by the Ego mind, which is really not communication but an expression of selfishness, focus is placed on personality. Maintaining a self-centered personality is not communication. Expressing a perception that attempts to prove a certain point of view can only reinforce separation and the desire to be right.

Communication is of God, and Spirit creates a channel for its voice to extend to every mind, thus establishing God's will forever. This communication link joins us to all minds and all creations. Its quality is universal and abstract. It has no judgments and no exceptions, and it cannot be changed by anyone or any event. Communication is guidance and when directed by the Holy Spirit it properly aligns the relationship, centering it on sharing Spirit.

The Ego mind can distort or block this function, but this communication link can never be taken away. It is not possible to totally block or lose the ability to communicate, but we can refuse to notice the constant signal that this voice sends to us. The reason that the voice of the Holy Spirit can be unnoticed is because our Ego voice is too familiar and valued by us. A Holy Relationship realizes that Spirit is in constant communication with itself. Spirit is always expressing its certainty, knowledge, and love without question. When we do not hear it we are refusing to listen; we are listening to our own beliefs instead.

Believing that our own perceptions or our own words communicate is as silly as believing that our anger attacks make others love us. Ego minds do appear to join together by sharing concepts, but the appearance of this joining is used to promote attack or to gain something from a particular situation. We often share concepts in hopes that others will not only understand and agree with our point of view, but also serve as an ally with us against those who disagree with us. This act of joining does not lead to communication, and no one receives spiritual help. Overpowering another with judgmental beliefs only reinforces our blocks to sharing. Getting is not giving; attacking is not joining.

Revelation is communication from God, and our gratitude is communication to God. Those who communicate gratitude for being created complete the circuit. Words are the battery of communication and never cause real joining. Words can either establish the conditions that make joining possible, or words can cause future separation and block the channels. It is not the words themselves but our interruption of the message and the secret meaning we give to them.

Words act like a boat that takes us across a river; once across, we no longer need the boat. Words have a certain function, but we may not recognize this function because we have forgotten how to remain joined by the mind, and because our abilities to communicate have been seriously impaired.

If we remembered how to use our higher mind, thoughts could be transferred and received telepathically. A Holy Relationship that has done lots of healing can practice and regain these abilities.

Healing consists of removing the distorted perceptions that block real union. Language is a tool for returning to love but so often it becomes a weapon for remaining stuck in our intellect. "Silence is golden" is an old quote that most couples today have forgotten. We can talk ourselves out of love. We talk to prove a point. Talk can certainly be driven by fear. Words can be used to free or they can be used to control and demand. No matter how spiritual our words seem, they can be misdirected and used by the Ego to command obedience to a fixed concept.

Used by the Ego mind, words are swords and knives that cut us apart. Used by the Holy Spirit, they close the gaps of separation. Observe the effects of your words and you will understand if you are getting closer or creating more distance between you and your partner.

Never blame your partner for distancing; look to your own method of communicating instead. Bodies, like words, never join. Only minds that know how to extend pure thoughts can join.

The biggest problem we face is we believe we are communicating when in fact we are not. We are separating and attempting to prove we are right about our personal perceptions and concepts.

All wars start with words of attack. If we seem to be fighting with a mate consider reviewing the words we used. What type of relationship would we have with a mate if our words were never used to cause division? We mature as spiritual partners when we are discerning with our thoughts before speaking any words. If our thoughts are clearly aligned with our purpose, then our words will follow accordingly. Ask yourself this question: "Which purpose do I want to serve by speaking these words: joining or separation?"

Many relationship theorists have certain communication techniques to improve understanding. Some are easy and very helpful; others can be quite complicated, and we forget them when we become emotional. The one simple thing that always works is to learn to ask Holy Spirit to speak for us. Never practice what we will say. The act of rehearsing our words will limit our ideas to the directions that come from the Ego.

Tones and sounds promote more healing than words. Physical posturing always proves the unconscious thoughts that exist in the lower mind. A major reason we fail to communicate is because our tones and sounds are vibrating at a level that our partner is resisting. When we hear a tone that is outside our programmed comfort level, we block ourselves from hearing what is being said. The block is a response that is based on past experiences. We become threatened by the feeling that comes from our unconscious past, not even connecting to the person in front of us.

We also read a person's body language and intuitively feel what their unconscious beliefs are expressing. Don't underestimate how much we react to the hidden ways our partner distances him or herself from us. The walls we have made are not as invisible as we think. Communication occurs when our words, tones, body language, and hidden past beliefs are in alignment with the principles of joining.

Arguments and Blocks between Partners

When we verbally fight with a partner, we communicate with no one, and we are as Isolated from reality as if there were no one else in the entire universe. We are actually relating to our own inner images. In our madness we overlook reality completely, and see only our own concepts and perceptions. We communicate with the past, and it is the past that answers us. When we are listening to our Ego, we are not talking to each other but instead abandoning each other to focus on our own private opinions. Keep not what breaks communication, for it prevents us from hearing Spirit's voice. Life waits on us to discover what doesn't work in restoring communication and invites us to listen within to what does. Our relationship is the playground in which we learn.

The disruption of communication happens through judgment, for each judgment distorts thoughts and splits them. Judgmental thoughts have no meaning since their purpose is not to communicate. Meaningful thoughts are whole, pure, and complete like their creator. They do not express opposition or any thoughts of evilness.
In the idea of peace, minds do communicate. The Holy Spirit can't teach if we remain fearful.

In addition, guilt, whose only purpose is to disrupt communication, has no place in true communication. Our brother's behavior is as little use to us as it is to him. When our idea of guilt is used only as the Holy Spirit teaches, it serves one function, and that is forgiveness. To focus on what the body did or said is not to understand freedom. Whatever our bodies communicate is but another chance to teach the value of freedom.
No communication can happen when each word has a different meaning to each partner. The words carry different meanings because our minds have different memories associated with each concept.

The Holy Spirit's goal gives one meaningful way to look at all our words. Meaning is a way to Is-ness. This common purpose lets us speak to all our brothers in one meaning, so that we relate to them, and thus, we can communicate again. Understanding produces relating and relating means acceptance. Those who choose to accept the Is-ness of any event will be able to relate and then to join.

Scripts and Stories

Our lower mind writes our stories, our scripts, and our interpretations of events and uses them to keep us from communicating. Our stories are the way we think a past event happened. We write our personal view of what we thought happened and how we felt about it. These stories often refer to people and things from a place of specialness and fear. They speak of dark strangers that were harmful.

We believe in our scripts, as well as the concepts that we learned from others. We have also conveyed him or her to people with no consideration or question regarding the logic or validity of the content. We believe our scripts to be true, but really they are only the programmed opinions that we have repeated and unconsciously recited without considering the illusions that might reside within them. In our Holy Relationship, we question these scripts and learn to undo and change the programming, thus removing the blocks in communication that they cause.

Our interpretation of events color the way we think. Take the Bible for example; how many millions of interpretations have come from reading it? Each person that reads it compares it to his or her own scripts and chooses a meaning that may not match another person's meaning.

Each interruption will lead us in a direction of either feeling safe or feeling threatened. If we feel safe and happy about the people and events of the interpretation, then the meaning of the story and its scripts must be leading us toward Spirit and towards communication. If the story and the events foster feelings of fear or guilt, then we are being directed further away from communication. Our feelings help us determine if the interpretation of the situation is promoting our ability to communicate or block it.

If we believe that we can communicate through acts of attack, harm, or fear, then we are misunderstanding the true nature of communication. We often share thoughts based on attack, harm, and fear in an effort to be liked by our partner. If our partner understands our view, then we hope this will promote allegiance. If these efforts do not lead to communication, no one receives spiritual help, and the blocks to communication become reinforced.

When we think we are communicating and in fact we are not, we are only reinforcing our own viewpoints, proving these images are more valuable than the person with whom we are trying to relate. When this happens we call it arguing. We are relating to those who are not present. The response will always be that they can't answer us with the love we were seeking. If we only want someone to agree with our viewpoint, we are asking for our partner to be a puppet, a slave. We are not connecting with him or her but are connecting only with our Ego mind.

By using language to prove our point, we disrupt communication. When we understand the power of energy and the true nature of love, words lose importance. We have been taught in so many ways about the control that comes from speaking words with our tongue, but this twisted effort to join only distorts our true function. Spoken words invoke feelings and interpretations that are unsolicited by the mind that shared them because each idea that is shared reflects a hidden experience along with a hidden meaning.

At the level of personality, our past dictates the meaning we give to words spoken. Therefore, we cannot rely on words as our means of communication in a Holy Relationship. Words directed by the Holy Spirit can invoke a willingness to communicate but don't cause us to experience communication. Joining is union, two views uniting or becoming similar. Spoken language only starts the process; actual communication really has everything to do with energy and thought. Words must be seen as a lower order and have no value if directed by the Ego mind.

The partners of a Holy Relationship learn to meditate together and to value silence more than talking. Guilt and criticism have no value because real communication has been restored and is understood. Belief systems of the Ego are released rather than reinforced. The body and its senses are seen in their proper relationship when real communication is understood as an interaction that comes from the mind and not from the body. Minds do not need the body to share ideas and express love. Only in a codependent relationship do couples believe that they have to be together in form and time in order to relate to each other. Since we have believed for so long that communication comes from our words and actions, we may find these new ideas difficult to accept. It may take some time before we can believe in these new concepts of communication and learn to rely on them. My advice is to develop a consistent habit of meditation and ask for help in learning this higher way of joining. Only through giving up one method can you learn another.

Communication through Forgiveness

Forgiveness is a major function in a healthy relationship. When understood it becomes the most valued tool in sharing. We are conditioned to misunderstand the real purpose of forgiveness and we fail to put it to the test of effective communication.

As children, we were taught the false reason for forgiveness: we were told to forgive as a method of correcting behavior. We were often shamed with guilt and then told to ask for forgiveness. The "bad feelings" were suppressed and the incorrect behavior was magnified by the need to be forgiven. Most forgiveness has sent the message "you're guilty, don't do it again."

The association of forgiveness with punishment and shame makes forgiveness undesirable. It is often expressed in a phony way to avoid criticism. The Ego mind uses forgiveness as a way to manipulate the situation, but forgiveness is a major step toward returning to communication. Recognize that the Ego mind has been guiding us and leading us to experiences with forgiveness full of disagreement and separation. Forgiveness is the means for healing the mind, not the behavior. Until the mind is healed or put in the proper alignment with Spirit, no correction can occur. By seeking forgiveness we are placing our mind in the care of higher guidance. Only then can we be taught how to communicate.

The AAA mind method is an example of real forgiveness. This method not only promotes concepts such as Acceptance, Agreement, and Appreciation, but it also helps us place the mind in the right attitude before attempting to communicate. If we are not in a state of acceptance, then we are not in our right mind and no communication will occur. The wrong mind is the Ego personality mind. The right mind is the mind of acceptance. In our right mind we can listen to the Holy Spirit. We can also say the right mind is the mind of Light and the wrong mind is the mind of darkness.

Forgiveness is the process of going from one state of mind to the other. It has nothing to do with our behavior. True forgiveness only deals with thought. Only the Holy Spirit's judgment will lead us to our right mind. Learning to forgive each other is fun and rewarding because it results in feelings of joy and eliminates negative feelings associated with past behaviors. Real forgiveness releases the concepts retained from the past. Those who truly forgive have no past.

We wouldn't feel the need to manipulate another person unless we believed that we have something to gain over them. Those who manipulate others only believe they can be deprived of something. Those who are in communication are denied nothing. Who would not want forgiveness if they understood that it would lead to real communication and that real communication is the only way to be truly abundant?

Remember:

A No Loss Relationship wants forgiveness to be a very important part of the relationship. Each partner wants to practice forgiveness, remembering its benefits. Any partner who is afraid to forgive has forgotten that guilt and criticism don't cause communication and is associating forgiveness with punishment.

A No Loss Relationship understands that the Holy Spirit teaches forgiveness because it is the perfect lesson and the simplest way to return the mind into the awareness of peace.

Fighting About Disagreements: Agree to Disagree

Couples shouldn't fight each other to prove they love each other. Be at peace if one person is asserting his or her point of perception. It's not making our partner "right," it's honoring his or her right to have a perception knowing he or she wants to release it. We hold the purpose for our partner if they start to attack. We learn that we don't have to defend or attack back. We become great models or teachers with the help of Spirit.

Out-of-balance emotions combined with an active mind cause the mind to spin. Such a mind can never communicate because a state of peace is needed before true communication can happen. This imbalance is experienced when couples argue in an attempt to solve their problems. Most of us are aware of the damaging effects of arguing and how arguments can get out of control and can seem unstoppable. This perception is correct. Once a spinning mind gets started, it is very hard to stop it, just like a snowball rolling down a hill.

Our challenge is to prevent the snowball from forming, much less rolling, into a big ball by preventing our mind from getting upset and forming grievances. Stop the avalanches. Practice forgiveness and meditation regularly with your partner to address the little issues that will help prevent the bigger issues from occurring. Meditation slows the mind. Chanting or repeating a single affirmation or phrase, such as, "I am Love, I am Love, I am Love," slows the mind as well. A quiet, still mind is ready for real communication.

The Three Paths to Sacred Love

In every soul is a desire, a longing, often felt as a craving or an inner pain to know Spirit. It is a hunger, a thirst, and a crying out from the darkness, which seeks to know that I am not alone. No one really is alone in truth, and in the absolute knowledge of God, we are one with God, always have been and always will be at this very moment, we are held and completely embraced by the Divine. We are still as God created us, and we have never been separated from the presence of God-Spirit or from it's inheritance. Spirit has not changed, and the nature of life is whole and complete.

The complete and total embrace of Spirit is love because all that is Spirit is shared with all of life. We would say that gravity is everywhere, and there is no place on this planet where we could walk and not be influenced by the natural forces of gravity. We would say that air is everywhere and that our atmosphere surrounds the earth completely; we can breathe air anywhere, provided our lungs are functioning normally. We can say that water and earth make up the surface of the planet, and always, we are either on water or on earth. Together, water and earth make up the surface of the entire earth. Fire is energy express ing itself, and energy is everywhere. Physics proves that energy is everywhere and in every atom. No lack of energy exists.

We must receive and exchange energy to live in physical form and in Spirit. Energy is the elemental nature of life, and it is everywhere. No lack of it exists, yet we can block this energy exchange, and we can be prevented from receiving the energy we need in order to live in form or to live by Spirit. This energy exchange is blocked when we block our aware- ness of love. Just as a lack of food, water, or air can starve the body, a lack of love can starve the soul. Love is the giving and receiving of Spirit as one and creating as one. The absolute reality of life is slightly different from the personal perception that is derived from the lower self; one difference is the idea of lack. Lack is the cause of all misperceptions of life.

Now, the question is, "What happened, and why are we experiencing lack?" This "event" from which the idea of lack derived is called the "fall" from Spirit. The "you" that is the child of Spirit caused an idea to occur in the mind of itself—an idea with the belief that it could create outside the wholeness of the God self or that it could create beyond the "void" or from the "void." This is also called the "original sin" or "separation."

This "event" was the start of the making of perceptions regarding the self and the start of the self-concept of the personal self. When this "event" occurred, not only did the mad beliefs of lack, darkness, and loss come into the mind of the soul, but also the concept of death became a perception.

This once-perfect whole and complete soul self split its mind into two parts with one part higher and still true and one part lower and false. The mind is still one, but each part formed a different concept of self. The lower part makes up ideas of an "it" (the Ego), and that self is the cause of all your suffering, all feelings of a lack of love, and all feelings of abandonment.

How deep or identified into that self you have traveled is reflected in your perceptions of life. How much you identify with the lower self is reflected in the self-concepts that you have made and are now holding. When the "soul self" becomes immersed into the darkness, it will seek a way out. This is called the "seeking" or the "call" or the desire to "know."

Spirit provides three paths out of separation. It also created an idea of returning and shared it with all of life. This idea, which we refer to as the Holy Spirit, is the call from within ourselves that beckons for us to return to the Light.

Path 1: Path of Many

The first path is the path of "The Many," and about 12% of people are naturally on it. We see the avatar, the saint, the priest, the politician, the healer-teacher, the entrepreneur, the world adventurer, and others who were born with great purpose. They serve and devote their lives fully to the good of a greater cause. By loving and serving the many and giv- ing to a vast number of people, they become full and abundant. When lived with a strong purpose that includes being truly helpful and not being selfish, the mind is able to expand out of the lower self. Service and giving are often seen as acts of sacrifice, yet within the spiritual path, they become a transformation back to the knowledge of God.

Path 2: Holy Relationship

The second path is the Holy Relationship, or intimate partnership. When two people choose to be fully committed and devoted to each other, they can open the door to holiness, or you could say, they love as one. Complete merging of self into self is love, and love is wholeness. Of course, in this book, we are teaching how to make a relationship holy, and indeed, many know this path is not simple—it can even lead to feelings of being more separate. This is the path that 80% of humanity is naturally meant to take. Eventually, through evolution, the people on the Holy Relationship path will jump onto the path of "The Many." Great indeed is the Holy Relationship that serves the world in a special way.

Path 3: Path of None

The final path, which resides in the darkness, is the path of "None." This is the path of abstention or emptiness. It consists of a complete denial of family, community, and social involvement for the purpose of knowing the "void." It is the hermit. It is the path of solitude, meditation, and complete withdrawal from the world. About 8% are meant to walk this path naturally, and believe it or not, it's a great gateway to the Divine. From complete emptiness comes the realization of the all. Yes, death is a great door because emptiness is everything. Buddha and many spiritual masters have walked this path.

The path of "None" is being experienced by 30% of the population, who are dating or looking for a mate. When you are dating from a place where you are seeking specialness, then the path of "None" is very painful because it produces a sense of wanting and loneliness. The path of "None" is not fully embraced nor valued for what it offers. Not being in a relationship is rewarding only if you are seeking Spirit and accepting that self-love is a path unto itself. Dating to "get" love is often the act of looking outside of the self. It reinforces the sense of lack, making it a lower pattern and causing us to be stuck in fear. Only by teaching ourselves to be fully on the path of "None" can we learn to release the longing for another person.

Granted, this view is very difficult to achieve, and many suffer from this attachment of "wanting a soul mate." Remember, Spirit offers you two other ways out. One way is to fully live in and follow the path of "None," and the other way is to jump onto the path of "The Many." Stop wishing, pleading, begging, or fantasizing about your desire to be on the path that includes an intimate relationship that is based in specialness or on a longing to be loved. Begging Spirit to bring you someone to love is not facing your specialness, and it's only your specialness that is keeping you out of your higher path. When you perform the exercises on healing specialness, you will increase your ability to release the blocks that exist on your path of "None."

You can always form a Holy Relationship if you read and practice this material; it is not a requirement that a Holy Relationship involves sexual relations. If you form a Holy Relationship that does not meet your sexual desires, conflicts can still surface that will provide learning opportunities, and your feelings of pleasure and sensual longing will remain within you until they have been healed correctly by the Holy Spirit. On the true path of "None," the desire for pleasure can be healed. When we embrace the path correctly, our desires for the pleasure of being in a partnership with another person along with our gratification of the senses are replaced with Spirit; we receive a fulfillment from Source that includes pure bliss and unconditional love and joy.

The conflict that we feel is occurring because we have not fully embraced the path of "None." We've become caught between the path of the holy relationship and the path of "None," and being in this space is very uncomfortable because it lacks substance. Frankly, we are not being "fed" from either path, which leaves us feeling stuck and not on any path. Suffering from lack of joy, the Ego is happiest because it maintains our allegiance to "seeking and never finding." The circle of this thought system is like the hamster running on a wheel in a cage. The images on the wheel can be appealing, but the Ego remains in charge and we stay in the same position, lonely and lacking.

A No Loss Relationship can occur when we remain fully in the state of seeking the path of "None." A person who is involved in a No Loss Relationship has no fear of being empty or alone. Once we learn how to receive from emptiness or how to surrender completely to death, then we are able to find great pleasure. The greatest pleasure of all is found in the "void of being." So, it matters not whether we are single, divorced, widowed, or dating someone casually, we need to choose to become fully on the path of "None," and life will offer us its greatest reward, which is love.

When the path of "None" has ended, the soul finds itself to be a leader on the path of "The Many." The deeper we can go into the real "void," the quicker we can merge with the absolute. The difficulty occurs when we do not let go of the lower mind, possibly because we feel that the training we must undertake to let go of the lower mind identity is enormous. Some people have sat for 12 years in the silence trying to reach Samadhi, which is, essentially known as "becoming the void."

Every day, in some way, we are on this path, struggling not to be on it, or attempting to accept it. To embrace death or nothingness, which is often felt as the fear of dying or the fear of anything else, is to seek or to hunger for Spirit. Hopefully, I have successfully demonstrated the idea of seeking as the circle of the snake eating its own tail, or as eternity. The Holy Spirit is the answer. Spirit will show us the way out of the mind that perceives loss and lack. We could say that, in every mind, these paths exist and we simply have to pick one, get on it fully, and follow it to reach our knowledge of Oneness. No path is better or worse than the others because they all lead to the same awareness.

The problem is not that Spirit has provided a way out. The problem is either that we refuse to take or choose a path, or we are in conflict how to follow our naturally chosen path. The lower mind loves to hold us onto parts of the path of "None" because the beginning steps of darkness on this path are the home of the shadow Ego self. Our lower mind lives in the shadow or valley of the "void." Mistakes are made when we develop attachments to the gifts of the Ego, and they hold us in a state of feeling lost and wandering amongst the levels of darkness.

We choose to maintain our qualities of selfishness and our false concepts instead of deepening our experience on our chosen path. If we know which path we've selected, then as we follow it, we will make choices every day to stay on that path, and that path will lead us to the "Light."

The majority of us will try each of these paths, or we will switch from one path to another path at any given time throughout our lives. We can also say that we get off a particular path without immediately jumping to another path. Switching between paths will cause confusion. The difficulties we experience occur when we do not complete a particular path or follow it to its final destiny. The lower mind does not want us on these paths and attempts to keep us in a state of feeling incomplete or stuck, which prevents us from finishing the journey. The Ego says, "Seek and do not find. Stay stuck and lost. Be lonely. You are unworthy."

Forget the body; where are you? Where is your mind? Which path are you following? Choose one. Complete it and follow it home. Home is always wholeness.
Being stuck, trapped, and imprisoned in the lower mind is the only mistake we experience. Being a slave to the lower mind prevents us from leaving "nowhere" and keeps us in a "nothing" experience through some form of lack. From within this experience, we form and make all darkened concepts of self, including a belief in the ideas of being lonely and of being without love. Whenever we believe we are lonely, think of it as a lie, or an alarm clock that is ringing to remind us that we need to get back onto a spiritual path.

With 7 billion people who need us, how is loneliness possible? Loneliness is a choice for no-thing. We say "no" to opportunities from many things and people, and it is our repeated "fault finding" behavior that leads us to the feeling of being alone. This choice we make to find fault originates in the lower mind, more often than most of us are aware. If we are feeling lonely, which by the way, is different from being alone, then it's time to examine our thought processes with honesty and determine how often we find faults in other people. Recognize how much effort we exert in looking for a special someone to "cure" our loneliness. Since this effort originates from our selfish self, it will narrow our perceptions; thus, the effect is "I am feeling lonely."

There are two ways to get stuck. One way is through the glue of fear, and the other is love. If we are stuck on someone and we are experiencing love, then that fusion through the holy relationship will cause us to complete the journey by being the driving force for enlightenment.

Being stuck in fear is the way of getting off the path, and loss is the effect.
Desire is the passion bestowed onto each soul that provides a way for it to break free and move on to a chosen true path.

The sense of "wanting" is the Ego's way of keeping us stuck and not allowing us to move. The Ego's goal is to offer us the carrot and to keep it out of reach. "Wanting" is that false longing; and, its cry or call for love is pain. Pleading is begging, and begging is "wanting" to the degree of desperation. Like bleeding, if it continues, then we die. So, learn to stop all lower method behaviors that come from a sense of wanting or from a sense of "not having."

"Need" is the awareness that fuel is required, and it is a propelling feeling that causes us to be "looking" for the path. Souls with a distortion of "need" are in a state of greed. Greed is the Ego's method of keeping us off the path of "The Many."
Through greed, the Ego can deceive us into believing that we are on the path by convincing us that we are getting "The Many" through various forms, such as money, power, and pleasure. When greed has a role in intimacy, it is played out through excessive selfishness where the choice made by one partner to perform a selfish act takes precedence over the choice to learn how to give and receive as one. A taker reacts based on greed for love or for another object, and in the process, he or she maintains the separate self. Sadly, the person who reacts with greed will never feel like he or she gets enough and ends up feeling

very lonely.

The elements of a No Loss Relationship will teach you and your partner not only how to remain on the path through daily practices and reminders, but also how to return to the path if either of you should stray. A No Loss Relationship is the path for any two people who are seeking Oneness through partnership. Spiritual growth is defined as being on your chosen path and feeling its rewards. The holy relationship is the greatest answer for most people, and it is the reason the mode of partnership (marriage) is the way home.

The path of following a spiritual teacher, or guru, is the path of devotion and is the path of "The Many." It's great to make a partnership with a master soul who is on the path of "The Many." People who devote themselves to the path of intimacy and the path of purpose for "The Many" through the Holy Relationship are on the super highway to enlightenment. Time has nothing to do with us, or our path, and time is not required to complete our journey.

In fact, we could eliminate time completely and still reach our purpose. Be joined with many now. Be totally committed to our partner now. Be 100% empty now. Now is the end of time. Don't let time trick you for it's the realm of the lower mind. Everything you ask for that is "real" is given in the now. A No Loss Relationship has nothing to do with time, for its chosen path is eternity.

Into It or Not Into It

We are all in life, and life in us! LIFE is IT. To life, we are the fish in the sea, and without the life, we don't exist. The question is, "Do we realize that we are all into it together?" Are we into the Oneness? Are we having an experience of being out of it or not into it? The idea that we are able to have feelings is the awareness that we are into it or not. Our feelings teach us about our intuition and our intuition is our way to knowledge.

Our sense of being into it can be detected when our intuition is serving as a compass that tells us where we are in relation to Oneness. We must know where we are before attempting to create a somewhere. If we are not into it, then we will experience all the lower emotions of fear. If we are into it, then we will experience all the higher feelings of the Light. I have been asked so many times, "How do you know? How do I get guidance? How do I know God's voice is speaking to me? How do I trust my intuition?" Well, it all begins in our awareness of being into it or not.

Spirit speaks from within when we are being still and aware that we are into it or, said another way, connected to it.

One of the advantages of a Holy Relationship is that both partners agree to practice listening together, which is often called meditation or being in the silence because this is the place from where all intuition arises. When we know we are both into it, then real love is recognized. When we are in this state of being and our partner is not, we hold the space for his or her return. Through the act of receiving guidance together, partners experience the birth of CO-creation.

We are in it or we are not in it. These are the only two experiences we can have with any person, thing, concept, or truth. We will need to name the IT. There is only the it without name or explication, without perception or cause, void of judgment or conditions, and it is. We have attempted to name it, and we have given it 10,000 names in every language. Everyone is seeking it. Every religion has many different names for it.

Of course, we name it, we talk about it, we make up a story about it, we think about it, and we are in fear of it. We have judged it. We think we can be in control of it. We believe we can influence it or change it. We think we can be without it. We seek it, we look for it, we feel lost without it, and we are never quite sure it is. Yet, it is always. Without it, we don't trust our self and we make many poor choices and decisions. Every real relationship we have ever had is it. What is it? How do you know it?

It is the purpose of the Holy Relationship to provide the opportunity for us to be into it and to be joined for it. Partners of a No Loss Relationship seek to know it as it is. It is found when we are in it, knowing we are never without it. It is completely understood when we have no words or when we are attempting to explain it or concepts about it. We know by being into it. We have knowledge of it by having no perception of it.

We have lost it only when we are not into it. All relationships, which have not stayed connected, have been more not into it, than into it. They have been into the me (Ego) self, or the you self, or another self, but never joined to be into it. The " into" it is a commitment to know our true self as the same one self and to live as One. In other words, two are in it as one. Intimacy without the "not" is what we seek in our Holy Relationship. Everything learned through the Holy Relationship is about the removal of the "not" and the ability to just be into it. The not into it is the cause of all darkness.

Developing the skill for recognizing the not into it moments is intended to be a fun learning experience. Be willing to admit it when these moments occur and return to the only remaining choice, forgiveness, because choosing forgiveness is at the crux of all healing.

Here is a list of some not into it.
You are not into it when:
When you meet someone to whom you feel very attracted.
When you argue with someone with whom you are living.
When you are independent of others.
When you are codependent. (When you are interdependent, you are seeking how to be into it.)
When someone rejects you or you reject someone.
When you feel hatred or you feel hurt by another.
When you attack someone.
When you defend your position.
When you have a position of being against anything.
When you dream about winning or losing.
When any part of your mind believes you are separate from your whole mind.
When your behavior is a reaction to negative thoughts regarding a past event.
When your behavior is a reaction to negative thoughts regarding a possible future event.
When you are fearful or upset emotionally due to judgmental thoughts (in fact, far removed from).
When you are passing judgment.
When you are in a state of mental worry.
Can you add to the list?

The thoughts we think are always not into "it." However, we can choose thoughts that will either move us toward it or away from it.

Life is the University of Living Love

We are all in the schoolhouse of Earth. We are all students learning the same one curriculum. That curriculum is Sacred Love.

As students, we are being tested and learning the same lessons over and over again. The master teacher is the Holy Spirit. Our spiritual partner in our Holy Relationship is our teacher as well. Actually, every person who we meet is teaching us a lesson or we are teaching him or her a lesson regarding our belief in love. Each of us is receiving a grade for each moment of our lives. We may not have liked academics in school, so we may find this concept difficult to accept, or maybe we loved school and found learning to be very enjoyable. Whether we like or don't like academics is irrelevant. In this schoolhouse of Earth, we either receive a passing grade or we continue to return to Earth to repeat the curriculum until we have mastered Sacred Love and can demonstrate it fully.

Learning how to know Sacred Love is the only class we need to pass. Many of us don't like tests, and we can easily choose to judge the idea that we are being tested. Testing is natural, and it is an important activity that promotes learning, not for the sake of pleasing others or for looking good, but for the chance to know that we know.
We are graded on how well we know love within a relationship. We are graded on how well we give love and how well we receive love. We are never graded on how long a relationship lasts. Spirit has nothing to do with time. We are graded on how into it you become or how not into it you behave. A grade is a measurement of Being or a standard of living. Those who get high grades in loving correctly receive many benefits and rewards, while those who get low grades feel separate and alone.

The grading system is defined below.

A+... Complete transcendence and enlightenment. This grade applies to our most famous spiritual leaders, saints, and you who are very, very constant with little regard for physical form.

A... Absolute knowledge of Sacred Love shared with everyone and everything. Experiencing unconditional love toward all, in all. Deep inner peace and joy.
Harmony in CO-creating with all of life. Includes souls who are very devoted to a path.

A-... Complete Realization of Sacred Love in partnership. This grade applies to the majority of souls who may retain a few minor grievances. Aware of Ego thoughts but not acting on them; releasing Ego thoughts correctly. Endures complete forgiveness of the past. Experiences inner peace and joy at least 90% of the time. Able to experience CO-creation with minor challenges. May be living as a monk, minister, teacher of god, or even a homemaker. This grade could also apply to a couple that has mastered the sense of Oneness within their Holy Relationship.

B+... Complete realization of Sacred Love in partnerships, family members, and business associates. Holds out some separation for certain types of people. Strong spiritual beliefs. Manifesting many happy dreams. Experiences inner peace and joy at least 80% of the time. Quick to forgive other people as well as one's self.

B... Complete Realization of Sacred Love, yet love is limited to a family, with many holdouts for special interest groups. Experiences inner peace 70% of the time with lots of joy and true happiness. Gives one's best behavior to each relationship. Has a purpose for living and is determined to achieve goals.

57

B-... Doing your best to practice Sacred Love in your Holy Relationship, practicing most of the time, Ego thoughts challenge your practices. Relationships cause minor upsets. Experiences inner peace 60% of the time. Needs more discipline and focus on goals. Paying bills and making most goals happen. Understands forgiveness, but is staying stuck in Ego for 30 minutes or more, yet, not usually more than a couple of hours before returning to Spirit.

C+... Attempting to practice to the best of your ability in a Holy Relationship. Remaining committed to practicing but missing many sessions. Experiences 50% in and 50% out of inner peace and joy. Processing conflicts with reactions that range from mild irritation to anger. Working strongly on goals, strong in courage and faith. Understands the purpose of not judging. Practice forgiveness regularly at night and remembers to pray.

C... Multiple attempts to practice. In and out of relationships due to old patterns. Experiences 40% of time in joy. Questions a life purpose. Experiences glimpses of Light and anger-to-sadness swings. Seeking help. Studies spiritual growth. Learning to meditate. Still holds resentments and regrets in life. Focused on special group interests, such as politics, religion, or environment concerns.

C-... Experiences depression, disappointment, and addiction patterns in relationships and holds many grievances. Is often making decisions that are hurtful to loved ones. Experiences 30% happiness. Forgets to seek guidance. Very independent and alone. Fearful of others. Feels anger regarding past events. Experiences health challenges, often, with pain.

D+... Damaged relationships are like a plague. Focused on self centered gratification and power. Has many addictions. Lack of sleep. Disliked by many people. Has few friends. Feels anger toward Spirit. Lives in poverty and minor criminal behavior. Reacts with blame and judgment. Is victimized by others. Experiences mental sickness and emotional dysfunction. Experiences 20% happiness, yet it is often for false reasons. Loss of awareness of soul. Directs 80% of focus on self and physical reality. No true friends. Few family members with whom he or she can stay associated.

D... Destroyed and destroying others. Harming, hating, or hurting others. Deep depression and emotional pain. Predominately controlled by Ego thought system. Has no goals or purpose. Has no happiness or peace. Locked in an addiction center or in jail.

D-... Isolation and destruction occurs with most relationships. Engages in killing activities and lives from a place of total mental illness. Locked in fear. This grade represents the bottom of the human experience.

No F... There is no such thing as failure in the view from Spirit. The soul would just repeat the class.

Grade only yourself, never another person. Don't let your ego grade you, nor be critical of where you are. Always see there is room for improvement, and enjoy this life for who you are and how you are advancing. Love this school and all your teachers.

The Atonement

The Advanced Teaching of Being Centered

Stillness is "it." Being in the now is "it." Being centered in it completely is "it." Knowing when we are 100% is "it." Knowing is the atonement. True knowing is being in our center. Core problems in life occur when we live from the place of "not knowing." Everything has a center point. Everything has a tone. Everything has knowledge of itself. There even is a true perception of all things, which we have termed Is-ness.

Partners of every Holy Relationship seek to practice being "into it," for a spiritual relationship means living the truth of the Oneness of life. The big advantage partners have within a Holy Relationship is they assist each other with the objective of staying in the center "0" point, and this objective becomes the purpose of involvement. The "0" is the perfect now. The "0" is the atonement. The "O" is the "O" in One.

Our natural awareness through our feeling nature can tell us where we are and how centered we are. With practice, we learn how to atone and how to continually move toward "0." With the Holy Spirit as our guide, we are able to shift toward the center. When we are at one with the "into it," we are complete and whole. Recognizing how to shift is the key to returning the mind to wholeness.

Our Holy Relationship offers us the greatest method for us to know that we are "into it." Be "into it" fully within your Holy Relationship and all the rewards and benefits of being "into it" will be revealed. Your intuition will grow stronger and stronger, and as your intuition strengthens, Spirit will speak to you and your partner directly, rather than through perception or reflection. Using your intuition is the key to trusting yourself and your partner. Listening together on a regular basis is the key to atonement and the return to center, known as being in your heart. Learning to tune out Ego and to tune into center will cause the Spirit to flourish and the truth to be revealed. "IT" is what you have been seeking your whole life.

This shift toward the center is a major training of the Spirit and could be your one true purpose or function within your Holy Relationship. Like all advanced spiritual disciplines, practice through mastery becomes the greatest joy possible. It is the simplest of alignments, yet the result is total fulfillment. When you are staying centered, you are being present in the now.

Visualize this graph and think of a three dimensional cross in your mind.

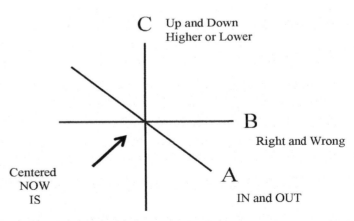

C Up and Down
Higher or Lower

B
Right and Wrong

Centered
NOW
IS

A

IN and OUT

The point where all three lines connect is the center, and this center is where the atonement can be experienced. Visualize the center as 0, the perfect now. Then, number each line from 1 to 6 as you move away from the center. If you remained at 0 within any spiritual chakra center, then you would know it because this is the point that we refer to as "all knowledge." Line A (the IN line) represents a time line that can run from "in to out", "front to back", "future to past" or "past to future." Line B represents the judgment line (horizontal line) and it oscillates from "left to right", "good to bad", or "bad to good." Judgment also occurs when choosing between "this or that." Line 1 also oscillates for feelings of worry, doubt and guilt. Line C (vertical line) represents "up to down" or "high to low." Highs represent false pleasures and addictions. Lows represent disappointments and feelings of depression.

Knowing yourself means you can be aware of how off-centered you are on each line of the axis and what that means to your intuitive feeling self. When you are farther away from "0", then you have a greater need for correction. Also, you are out of knowledge and into false perceptions. The more you are far away from the center, the less you can access true intuition, and the more you will be guided by feelings of fear. If you register yourself at a 7 or 8, then you are really off. If you register yourself as being closer to 3 or 2, then you are mildly to slightly missing the mark.

Use the chart to evaluate your distance from the center. Always ask for help when you are trying to determine where you are and when you are trying to understand the amount of healing and releasing you will need to practice in order to return to center. Returning to center is simple once you understand where center is in relation to your current position on the chart and once you understand your guidance from Spirit on how to return. Recognizing that you are lost from center can be a challenge, so remember that you may need your partner to help you.

Through practice and loving feedback, your process to return to center will become natual, easy, and simple. Staying in center is spiritual growth and consistency is mastery. The act of forgiveness will move or shift you toward the center. Inner listening is intuition and guidance from the Holy Spirit. Sharing spiritual growth with your partner and practicing together joyously will result in you and your partner living as a Holy Couple and serving in a purpose to save the world. Your feeling of knowing "it" and listening to "it" and recognizing "it", which is called the "now", will cause you to live fearlessly in the world while being a spiritual teacher to your holy partner and to all whom you encounter.

The gifts of Spirit come from knowing the center. Intuition is a great gift. "It" all begins when we know our true self as centered or atoned, who occurs when we feel like we never walk alone, through intuition, we are truly helpful to all others. Partners of the Holy Relationship understand the power of atonement, and they see it as the way to knowledge. When two people live centered in the heart, they constantly replace fear with love. They work miracles through the power of their true thoughts, which are the thoughts that Spirit's knowledge would have them think.

Partners of a No Loss Relationship have no fear because they are always guided out of fear and they are always protected through their understanding of the atonement. The atonement is the means for the partners of the Holy Relationship to achieve Oneness love.

Complete the exercises for this chapter in Chapter 10.

CHAPTER 4

Guidelines for Creating and Maintaining a Holy Relationship

The following guidelines are to help us keep our relationship moving in the direction of the 4 H's. (Holy, Happy, Healed, Healthy) They can be considered agreements, not one-sided rules. These guidelines are suggestions for how to stay within certain boundaries to maintain a healthy relationship. Guidelines are not walls but signs, which say, "Do this, go this way." Rules are walls, and because most of us are so rebellious, the more demands made on us, the more we want to do the opposite. Be gentle with the guidelines. See them as a corrective device and not as a way of punishing our partner or ourself. The challenge of relationships is to rise above the battleground of conflict with each other and into the awareness of Oneness where we can then co-create what we want. We can meet the challenge best when we stay within the guidelines and set the purpose that promotes the highest experience possible.

You can change them, add to them, take away parts, or put them in your own words. As your relationship grows, you will learn how easily they can help you work with situations in which you go insane and move out of a loving space. Guidelines point the way for you to return home. When you seem to stray away from joining, it is important to have a clear way home. Guidelines prevent you from wandering too far away. Just as a boxing ring, a football field, or a game board keep the game activity within a set perimeter, guidelines set a circle around your involvement to keep your activities headed toward love.

We all know that communication is an essential ingredient for maintaining healthy relationships. As you discuss and agree to each guideline, view them as principles for creating the relationship you truly desire. Use these agreements when you feel that you and your partner are drifting apart, or when you want to deepen your involvement, or when you want to increase your community of loving friends.

Develop your own guidelines by answering the questions in the workbook. Write them out, sign them, and hang them on the bathroom mirror, on the refrigerator, or any place that will serve as a reminder. Spend several sessions memorizing them and refer to them often until they are built into your inner programming. The largest problem most relationships have is that they have no agreements about the relationship; therefore, each partner tends to resort back to the behavioral programming and mental images that he or she grew up with. We often expect our partner to know if we feel that a particular behavior is unacceptable to us! This assumption is wrong. Assumptions are like ships without rudders or boats without captains. Most couples fail to set agreements before they choose to become sexually and emotionally entangled. As a result, no friendly method to heal can occur when the lower personalities try to destroy the involvement. Be certain they will try!

Guidelines for Creating and Maintaining a Holy Relationship

1.Admit that you do not know how to transform your relationship from specialness to holiness. What is this relationship for? Create a purpose and a vision for the relationship. Pray together in a peaceful state of mind asking that the Holy Spirit to be in charge of making the relationship holy. Be willing to learn.

2. Open your heart. You're with the perfect partner because he or she is able to teach you how to know your higher mind. Don't substitute another person for your partner in Holy Relationship; include everyone. Have no secrets and hide nothing from each other. Strive to put an end to jealousy, envy, and greed, and all the lower emotions of the mind.

3. Act as mirrors (equals) and heal each other. God's children are equal and the same. Neither of you is less or more advanced than the other. Refrain from being "better than" or "less than." Be open to being both a student and a teacher to each other. Nothing happens that is not affecting both of you. You're both equally dealing with the same issues. Make choices that promote joining.

4. Create a safe space for sharing and healing. Start by sharing feelings first and be willing to use your feelings as a vehicle for healing. Communication is for growth and healing. Tell the truth about your experiences. Choose to work past the Ego illusions of communication. Don't hold grievances against your partner. Practice forgiveness by not attacking each other when faults are discussed. Admit your own errors, but don't seek out your partner's errors.

5. See the Is-ness in each other. Admit judgments for the purpose of correcting them. Don't make them real. Ask the Holy Mind to judge for you and show you the true perception, which is called the Is-ness. Agree to disagree by allowing each other to have a different perception of the situation.

6. Love your partner as yourself. Agree not to be verbally or physically abusive. Do nothing to each other physically without his or her full consent. While it is appropriate to release emotions in verbal form, it is not appropriate to focus the anger or sadness toward your partner. Proper expression of feeling is to be targeted into the Holy Spirit, not your partner. You have the right to leave the space if the verbal expressions of your partner would trigger an emotional reaction in you that surpasses your comfort level. Pray while your partner is releasing.
Make peace within yourselves and make your home a priority. Practice the Golden Rule.

7. Have no separate interests or ways to end the relationship. Turn all decisions about the relationship over to the Holy Spirit, and make no major decisions without each other and the guidance of the Holy Spirit. Share the miracles and inspire them to happen. Create fun and happy dreams.

8. Choose to be happy. Admit expectations and addictive needs with the willingness to see them as healed. Make no demands, rules, or conditions of how the relationship should be in form. Understand pure happiness as a way of being.

9. Enjoy spiritual disciplines with each other. Pray and meditate daily, both morning and evening. Commit to spiritual principles that apply in your daily practices. Affirm spiritual truths daily.

10. Not my will but Thy will be done. Find a purpose for the relationship that is greater than your personal interests are. Holiness works for causes greater than sensational pleasures, power, or survival. Let the Holy Spirit show the way of serving God's Plan for humanity. Build trust in God's plan for your mutual freedom.

Each guideline is fully discussed in the following sections. When you learn to apply them, you will see how effective they become in maintaining a healthy, happy, healing, Holy Relationship. The form of the involvement is called your happy dreams; the content of your relationship is called your purpose.

The manifestation of your purpose and goals proves your holiness, showing you that the joining is real. Nothing in this world can threaten what purpose joins.
Your repeated pattern of unsuccessful relationships is over. You will no longer be controlled by thoughts that the 4 S's produce. Fear is no longer in charge nor does it have the power to convince you that you should leave a partnership. Without support, a structure falls. Support the development of a Holy Relationship, and the power of the Holy Spirit will come to the aid of you and your partner.

Entering into the new humanity marks the advancement of spiritual relationships and the end of an era where people live in little caves, separate and different, afraid of each other, and afraid of the world. The end of war begins with you and your partner. The end of the world is not the destruction of humanity by judgment but the spiritual evolution by relationship transformation. We live in Oneness with each other. The world of separation ends when a Holy Relationship is achieved.

1. Admit that you do not know how to transform your relationships from specialness into holiness.

Create a purpose and a vision for the relationship. What is this relationship for?
Pray together in a peaceful state of mind asking that the Holy Spirit be in charge of making the relationship holy. Be willing to learn. Build trust in God's plan for your mutual freedom.

Our mind can see in two directions. The mind is directed toward the body or toward Spirit, much like a telescope that has a narrow focus or an expanded view. The transformation of a relationship into holiness begins with setting the purpose. How can you get somewhere if you don't know where you are going?

By examining your reasons and purpose for being together, you set the direction of your relationship. What is this relationship for? What is to come out of this encounter? Do you have a clear intent for this involvement? Often in relationships, people fail to ask these questions and assume that the outcome will be based on their dreams and fantasies. It matters not if your relationship is several years old or just a few weeks old. A clear, defined purpose is mandatory for a Holy Relationship to develop.

When we become very attracted to someone, we think we know the purpose of the relationship. We react to our physical impulses of desire before examining our direction. Do we stop and examine where this attraction will take us? To bed maybe? To marriage? To better communication? Will it lead to more pain and loss or will it heal the loneliness that we feel inside?

The direction of any relationship leads either toward wholeness or toward separation. These are the only two directions possible. One leads to the experience of love, and the other leads to aloneness. The problem in relationships is that we don't know what it feels like to be whole. We are confused because we do not understand which interactions promote joining and how joining will occur.

From a space of non-judgment, we need to admit that we do not know how to accomplish this task. Are you willing to learn? Everyone is searching for answers that explain why they are not experiencing love. A relationship is a teaching device that serves to bring our mind back into correct alignment with that which is real and true. A Holy Relationship is formed to correct the mind of misperceived ideas regarding reality. The first step is to admit that we have many misconceived ideas about what a relationship is for. Until we admit this, we will be guided by false concepts. Here are two examples of the false ideas that most of us carry within our minds: "I am incomplete and in need of someone or something to complete me," and "I am lacking something that must come from something outside of me."

Codependency, a twisted view of co-creating, teaches that you are only complete when you are with a special someone. Independence teaches you that you don't need anyone, but you also know that you are not complete or content on your own.

Wholeness teaches us that we are the same self. A Holy Relationship teaches, "I am whole and complete and nothing is lacking." It teaches us how to continuously co-create with other individualized parts of creation in harmony and peace, and never is any part better or less than any other part. Each unique contribution joins to the whole contribution, and nothing is taken away. If the purpose of a relationship is not clear, our minds will divert back to old patterns that we learned in childhood. An unclear or false purpose will lead to rejection and disillusionment.

After a clear purpose is set, we need the means to achieve that purpose. The way to fulfill any purpose is called the means. The means and purpose both belong to the Holy Spirit. By setting the purpose we call upon our higher mind to arrange the teaching lessons so our relationship can be transformed. The purpose of the Holy Spirit is to transcend relationships and to help relationships return to Love. A holy purpose such as this, without the means, is inconceivable.

A purpose has no end. A goal does have an end. The means is the way the goal will be achieved so the purpose can be expressed. If we want a relationship that will never end, we must be certain of our purpose, and know that our purpose is the realization of our holiness. Write it in your own words and language. Make a commitment with each other to support the realization of this purpose.

Businesses create a mission statement. Any successful organization has a written plan of what is to come from its endeavors. Why do we make our relationships so unclear? Without the clarity of a purpose, we let assumptions and exceptions guide us, and we give the other person the task of fulfilling our fantasies.

The goal of a Holy Relationship is to undo any programming of thought that teaches us that we are lacking in any way. The means for learning how to undo this programming are our relationships in time and space. The means are the lessons we teach each other to prove what is true. The meaning that we choose to give to anything will lead us either closer to the truth or further from the truth and further from a Holy Relationship.

It is God who has placed the Holy Spirit in our minds to bring us back into proper relationship alignment with God. A true purpose can only be established when we have learned how to put our relationship in the guidance of the Holy Spirit. Only through learning to communicate as one mind and with one purpose firmly set can we be guided by the Holy Spirit. Two minds in conflict with each other can't follow guidance that will lead to God. The Holy Spirit waits on our willingness to come together and put aside our separate interests. A Holy Relationship shares what God wants for both of us. We shouldn't substitute a different purpose and make a will that is different from God's will by thinking that our partner is the cause of our unhappiness.

We don't know yet how to let the Holy Spirit decide for our holy purpose. Relationships without this guidance can't achieve the designed purpose. Why? We have to be very honest with our circumstances by admitting that we are trapped in the part of our mind that teaches us that the material world is all that is real. We have become very accustomed to living in bodies. We are very blocked in our awareness of a spiritual reality. We live in a programmed mind that believes its false opinions are true. We seek for comfort, pleasure, and happiness through our identity as a body even though we also experience pain through it. We have many false values attached to being special as well as to not being special. Generally, being body-identified has just become a habit, a rut, and a prison for which we have not yet learned to escape. This false identity is the cause of not being holy.

Holy Relationship has as its purpose, the proper escape from being limited to form. The major question is "How do I know that I am a Spirit, when all of my self identity is centered on being a body?" The answer: our Holy Relationships. The means for realizing a spiritual identity is to follow the guidance of the Holy Spirit. We shut out the Holy Spirit when we fail to set the correct purpose. Without having a correct purpose defined, we resort to the only other possible choices of purpose, which lead us on a path of looking for love in the wrong way. This wrong way is to value the body more than the Spirit. The wrong way is to value separation more than the union. The wrong way is to be right and not happy.

When our partner and we share the same purpose that the Holy Spirit has for our relationship, then we will learn how not to be afraid. Our relationship with the Holy Spirit has never been broken, but we have chosen to focus on goals that differ from the goals of the Holy Spirit. Our Holy Relationship mirrors our inner commitment to find our higher mind.

Asking is all that is required. The willingness to receive guidance as the means to becoming whole becomes easy when we understand how to receive the basic direction that is provided by the Holy Spirit. This higher mind only knows joy and can only lead us toward an inner joy.

The first guideline is to pray together and create an experience of asking the Holy Spirit into your relationship. This is a celebration of unity; it is a marriage of mind. It is a ritual of Spirit and a devotion to healing. This ceremony could be seen as a private spiritual marriage with the Holy Spirit as the minister. However you choose to create the experience is up to you. It can be done in five minutes or can take several hours. You can do it inside your home or outside with nature. Create an experience that you will remember. You can make it simple or elaborate. You may choose to use candles, burn incense, eat, drink, dance, sing, write, read, or meditate.

Tantric yoga has many examples of such ceremonies. Plan the experience before the chosen date. Be spontaneous and open to what happens in the experience. Make sure that you are not interrupted by the outside world. This is not a public affair but an inner sanctum.

The key ingredient is that you and your partner both sense a common joining with a higher purpose where you are asking for help from a force known as pure joy. This third force is in charge, and you both are willing to assist each other in learning how to let this force guide the involvement. Let your intuition guide the experience and write down purposes and any agreements of commitment. (See Agreements on page153.) Frame the ideas in your own words. Express to each other what it means in your own understanding at this stage to be in a Holy Relationship. Discuss how you can best reinforce the awareness of Spirit.

If you choose to be publicly married, then it is an affirmation of what you already know. Let the final say in your Holy Relationship be said by the Holy Spirit and no anger, guilt, fear, or doubt will enter into your communication. To learn from the Holy Spirit requires that you learn to trust, and to understand that trust in a way that you may never have experienced before.

2. Open your heart.

You're with the perfect partner for teaching you how to know your higher mind. Don't substitute another person for your Holy Relationship; include everyone. Have no secrets and hide nothing from each other. Strive to put an end to jealousy, envy and greed, and all the lower emotions of the heart.

Who is not looking for the perfect person? Who is not looking for the person we believe will love us unconditionally and will treat us as we always dreamed we would be treated? When we fall in love, we believe that we have found this person. This feeling is usually accurate for at least the first few weeks, and then something happens and the person is no longer perfect. We find fault with the person, so either we want him or her to change or we are ready to leave the involvement completely.

If we are with a partner who has agreed to make the relationship holy and he or she is committed to a spiritual path, then this agreement is our indication that this person is perfect for us no matter what happens in the relationship. Under this agreement, which is set from the view of the higher mind, the idea of being perfect is different from the view of the lower mind. The higher mind of the Holy Spirit sees perfection in the moment of what we are as God created us. The lower mind sees perfection as a conditioned is behavior that is based on a past experience. This conditioned behavior also becomes a fixed pattern that is required in order to attain perfection in the Future.

Only the lower mind can see imperfections, and it's this point of view that attempts to convince us that we need to get out of the relationship and pick another person who can be more perfect. The lower mind will always persuade us to seek outside of our self for this idea of perfection. When we enter into a Holy Relationship, our ability to trust is very necessary before transformation and healing can occur. Opening our heart is the only way to gain some power over our lower mind.

The Heart is our center, and the physical heart is the symbol of our spiritual center and becomes opened when we decide that we are not afraid to share. If we think of how important our physical heart is to our life, then we can start to comprehend how important our center is to our experiences of love and life. Literally, the heart is our very self, pure consciousness, and our being source. It is our holiness and our truth of existence. To know what we are as God created us is to be in our heart. So, to open our heart means to know what we are as Spirit Self. To let our heart open with another person is to let the person know the Core of Self and when that happens he or she will know everything about us. No private thoughts can exist with an open heart because we are fearless and open. Opening means to reveal or to show.

The true purpose of intimacy is to see all aspects of the self, which is against the beliefs of the lower mind. The lower mind teaches us to close down, hide, and run. The lower mind is rooted in shame so it tries to convince us that we are not acceptable, and we should not be open about sharing our faults with another person. "Hide it," shouts the lower mind, "Only show the good half of the self." Staying with our Holy Relationship and not substituting another person is the best way to bring about healing. Choosing not to heal within the Holy Relationship established with one person will only result in the need to start the process over with the next person. Changing an involvement or changing the form of the relationship should be accomplished with love and happiness. However, if we decide to change the form of our relationship because we are choosing not to heal, then this decision will result in the darkening of the heart.

The Dark Heart

As you begin to look within yourself, you must pass through your darkness, and purify your center. The process of looking into your heart can be painful indeed. You are dealing with the thoughts that govern your lower thinking, which are the core beliefs of being unloved, being unlovable, and being fearful of God. The darkness covers the Light but the Light is always there, just as the sun shines on a cloudy or snowy day. Dark heart energy shows up in forms of greed, envy, jealousy, and possession of another person.

The lower dark heart speaks to you with ideas of "getting," and the more you feel like you are attempting to get, the more the dark heart responds with greed. Excessive need is greed. Stealing is taking what is not yours in consciousness or rightful ownership. Whenever you feel a sense of lack in any form, the lower mind's solution is to go outside of yourself and take whatever you lack. If you become good at taking, then the cycle of lacking and taking continues, and you are always seeking to take more. Continuing to take more never satisfies your sense of lack; therefore, you become addicted to the cycle and your heart center develops a misunderstanding of the purpose of living.

As the heart darkens, the mind turns to performing evil actions. These evil actions occur when one person acts to control another person to the point of harm. Any attempt to control another person and not respect his or her free will is an aspect of darkness and separateness, which produces fear. As you begin to feel more fear, you allow more darkness to be created. In this darkness, you forget the feeling of love. From this state of not knowing love, you make the concept of "wanting." Your feelings direct you to say, "I am alone."

In this darkness, you also feel as though you are not lovable and you are not loved. You then project fears of envy and jealousy onto a person who you choose to believe could steal your love partner away from you because he or she is a better person than you are in some way. You live in a world of many darkened hearts, and most of them are acting out their fears without knowing how to remove or heal the thoughts around their heart center.

The Descent into Darkness

In every relationship, there is a descent into darkness. It is inevitable, even with the partner that you so adore, and especially if you think he or she is your soul mate. In a way, you could say it is a necessary experience because it is part of the purpose for your involvement in this Holy Relationship. It is the requirement of every couple to make this journey. With the help of the Holy Spirit and through healing they make the choice to use this journey as a step towards their miraculous ascension or the revelation of real love. The success depends on how clear they are in defining and living the purpose for that journey. Make no mistake for you must go and face all the danger and darkness that waits.

Before you met your holy partner, you had already traveled and walked in the land of darkness many times, and now you are living with its effects. A part of you is still in the shadow, and this is true for everyone here in form.

You carry its treasures and hold dear to its patterns of belief and habits of living. When you meet a person, you do not see these effects or what he or she possesses from his or her travels. You certainly are not willing to show him or her your collections of fears, for if you did you know that he or she would leave you right away.

In the special relationship, you do your best to conceal the darkness you hold. You hide your darkness often from even yourself, and many do everything they can to avoid it. What belief does your dark self still hold as true? Few have the courage to face it or admit it and join together in order to heal it. For the act of hiding the darkness, I use the term "ignorance." For avoidance, I use the term "denial." Somehow, you believe all of the darkness has gone away because you met a person with whom you share a special love. In truth, you can't hide from the darkness; however to the lower mind, your belief that you can hide from the darkness is the greatest and most effective way it can maintain its belief in itself. I am alone and separate from you. "I am a different self than you," shouts the Ego in the void. From that darkness, you also believe that you can experience a sense of lack and a feeling of being lost. Not only do you believe that you are separate from God, but you view yourself as unworthy and unable to return to your true nature. Who or what will come and find you? How can you be freed from the damage that you have done? Can your partner save you? But, how could he or she? The past love partner did not save you. After he or she left you, you felt more in the dark. Who can see your depression? It is by taking a look at darkness together and bringing the Light of the Holy Spirit into the darkness that you can be freed and released. This process is the healing power of the miracle with the ability to release you from darkness. Whatever darkness you have experienced from your past can be healed with love. First, you must learn how to share that darkness, join in it correctly, and see it for what it is.

You are with the perfect person because he or she is willing to share dark secrets with the understanding that both of you are seeking the purification and healing of your hearts simultaneously. Much of the remaining material in this book will assist you in this healing. It is only through the process of sharing your darkness can Spirit enter into your heart. If you keep your dark thoughts private and hidden from your love partner, then the darkened heart will remain within you. Avoidance is not a good plan, but it is the option that is offered to you by the lower mind as a way of keeping your unloved self-intact.

By choosing not to hold your dark thoughts as private, you are helping to bring the darkness to the Light. You must feel safe to do this process of sharing because you are often hiding feelings of guilt, shame, and disgust regarding past actions of the lower self. The lower self finds more value in hiding these dark thoughts and feelings than in sharing them for the purpose of healing them. Until you learn that sharing is the necessary step in joining in order to heal, you would prefer to keep your darkness hidden rather than reveal it. It is unlikely that your parents ever learned how to deal with darkness correctly. Therefore, you probably did not learn how to heal through the process of sharing during your childhood. However, choosing to maintain the darkness in the heart can only lead to the destruction of the relationship.

When you learn to include everyone in this process, you enter a space where you fear no one and your heart is open. Opening your heart means you love everyone and everything as Spirit created them. When you are searching within yourself for the darkness, you are looking for the "YOU," who you don't love and the thoughts held regarding any person whom you believe didn't love you. When you share the darkness, you will be healing these perceptions through true forgiveness. The open heart is unconditional love. The heart is the key and when opened through healing, God will pour through it, like sunshine through an open window. Clearing your hearts together is the goal of a Holy Relationship.

3. Act as mirrors (equals) and heal each other.

God's children are equal and the same. Neither of you is more advanced on the healing path than the other. Refrain from thoughts of being "better than" or "less than." Be open to being both a student and a teacher to each other. Nothing happens that is not affecting both of you. You're both equally dealing with the same issues. Make choices that promote joining.

The purpose of a Holy Relationship is to provide you and your partner with an opportunity to see each other as the same self. The qualities that you see in your partner must be qualities that are within yourself as well. If you think that you are better or less than your partner is, then you will often project that thought. Through projection, your words and behaviors would relay thoughts such as, "We are not the same or equal," "You have the problem, not me," "My situation or problem is worse than yours," and "I am less important than you." These imbalances prevent healing. Healing happens only when we are the same self, and this same self has joined with the Holy Spirit. You must understand that both you and your partner share in cause and effect. Effects must be shared as the one same self and not blamed on each other as though you were separate.

In a Holy Relationship, you and your partner need to understand that you are in this relationship together. Stop believing that your partner has issues that you do not share, and stop projecting these beliefs. While it may appear at times that you are in the role of a teacher who is solving a problem, and your partner is the student who is learning how to modify a behavior, remember that these roles may reverse at any given moment. Sometimes, you may need your partner to lead the conversation and be the teacher for an idea or change what you are refusing to learn. When you and your partner alternate the roles of student and teacher, you assist each other in finding the equal point of where you want to be. Don't stay stuck on being right and on being the teacher. Admit how you are also a student who has learned from past experiences. Your love of being a student will make you a great teacher.

Take responsibility for your own emotions in a relationship. You and your partner must each take responsibility for the push and pull that either of you initiates within each partner's emotional body. For every response, there is a reaction and for every reaction there is a response. Even the Ego knows this fact and knows well how to upset its partner. The Ego mind demands that happiness be a certain way through a certain type of behavior. You and your partner are more connected emotionally than you may realize. Every emotional reaction affects your partner and every feeling that you feel affects the whole on some level. To say you enter into a relationship without inner conflict is unrealistic. It is also true to say that you don't know how to truly love. To act as if you will always be nice to your partner is "special love." You must admit that you can become conflicted or judgmental at any moment. It is also important to admit that even though you may want to trust your partner, you may lose trust when you move out of the sense of feeling physically or emotionally safe in the relationship.

The Holy Spirit does judge, and it's judgment is for love only. Its judgment is for your release. It judges for your innocence. It sees you as guiltless, regardless of any negative acts you think you have done. Through the process of teaching you that you are the Son of God, the Holy Spirit helps you learn that the world and the body are parts of a dream, and any negative acts that you did to another person were actually done to yourself. This judgment, when seen correctly, will free you from repeating any acts of separation or attacks that you would do against a body.

This Golden Rule you are learning regarding the concept that actions you direct toward another person are actually being directed towards yourself, is such a simple rule, but your Ego self will be unwilling to follow it. The Ego's rule is to treat other people as you were treated, and to add a special form of attack in order to prove that your Ego self was hurt. An eye for an eye is the old law of self-preservation.

4. Create a safe space for sharing and healing.

Start the process by sharing feelings first and be willing to use your feelings as a vehicle for healing. Communication is for growth and healing. Tell the truth about your experiences. Choose to work past the Ego illusions of communication. Don't hold grievances against your partner. Practice forgiveness by not attacking your partner for his or her admitted faults. Admit your own errors, but don't seek out your partner's errors. Don't attempt to correct your partner's errors, and do not judge him or her for judging you.
Whole people learn how to speak about themselves first, and admit the feelings that they are having at the beginning of the conversation. Identifying your feelings first and owning those feelings are skills that you did not learn from your parents. This format is the new approach and may be forgotten until you and your partner have had opportunities to practice it frequently.

When you recognize that your partner is feeling a fearful emotion such as anger or sadness, remember that these feelings are your clue to know that he or she is trapped in his or her Ego. Start to pray for help immediately and do not react with an attack response towards your partner. Also, do not interpret that your partner is attacking you. You do not need to defend yourself in return. Create a safe space that will allow your partner a moment to become sane enough to direct his or her energy toward the Holy Spirit. Often, you just need to be a quiet listener. If your partner is trying to change you, you need to remain at peace for him or her.

In every relationship, either partner can be insane or sane at any moment. Ideally both partners are sane at the same time. When you recognize the Ego is in charge call it "insane." The most unhealed situation is where both remain insane together. Most often that situation is not the case. Don't refer to your partner as "insane." Say instead, "the Ego is insane." You are just referring to a message in the mind. Praying for sanity is praying for peace and acceptance. If the tension is great, it is very appropriate to release it. Throw the sour milk into the ocean. Ask if your partner is willing to release. The Holy Spirit is always willing to have you give away any painful thoughts and will gladly exchange them for joyous thoughts. Mis-perceptions can be exchanged for true acceptance of events that occurred.

It is important to practice releasing anger or sadness through the use of tones and not with words. We have more empathy for other people because we understand feelings more than language. It is difficult to believe this idea, but words do separate us more than feelings do. Our language only confuses us, and our stories are always mis-perceptions of facts anyway. Our reasons for feeling the way we do are invalid, yet we choose to believe in them anyway.

So when you are releasing any feelings based on fearful emotions, like anger or sadness, to the Holy Spirit, use as few words as possible. Use sounds instead. By expressing only tones, you are less likely to verbally attack your partner and your partner is less likely to take your feelings personally. If you have never done this before, think of the sounds that you make when you are crying. Reach deep within your lower self and imagine what sounds the feelings would express if you couldn't use words. Let those sounds come up and out of your mouth without controlling them. Like throwing up bad pizza, the emotional body is sick with toxic thoughts. It requires that you vomit and throw them out. Remember that you don't want to throw these toxic thoughts onto your partner.

When working with your partner in their emotional release session, practice keeping a shield of protection around yourself. A ball of white light is like an energy shield that doesn't allow your partner's emotional garbage in.

The relationship is for healing and is always open to a new insight. Sharing changes will strengthen the process and the more honest you are about looking at grievances; the more you are undoing them instead of holding on to them. Be a leader by choosing to laugh at mistaken perceptions instead of feeling guilty for having them. Allow your partner to have as many healing as possible and have no expectations about how far along in the process you or your partner "should" be. Give your partner the gift of undoing as many fears as he or she may express at any moment. Encourage your partner because each of his or her releases is your release as well. There is no need to pretend any longer that you don't have judgments or errors.

5. See the Is-ness in each other.

Admit judgments for the purpose of correcting them. Don't make them real. Agree to disagree by allowing your partner to have a different perception of the situation. Ask the Holy Mind to judge for you and show you the true perception, which I call the Is -ness. Judgments are the cause for the distorted thinking in your mental thought system. Judgment bends the lens of the mind. Each twisted judgment is a distortion; each distortion is a misperception of Is-ness. Every misperception is an illusion of reality that is the result of a judgment. The state of love is non-judgmental. It is also non-conditional. You are learning in your Holy Relationships to look at judgments for what they are. You are learning not to make your judgments real. It is very difficult to catch yourself judging because you are so used to making judgments. It is very difficult to correct your judgments because you believe them.

We judge ourselves for judging. We judge others for judging. Judgments keep us in the Ego's grip. We judge about 98% or more of what we perceive. It takes a lot of work to lower the amount of thoughts that have judgment in them. Again, by being able to admit that we are judging, we are allowing our mind to look at our judgments. This cannot be overstated. It is the key to change. So many of our judgments go unnoticed, and that is precisely what the Ego mind wants to happen. Judgment splits our mind, which directs us to see other people as separate and different. It is the task of a Holy Relationship to mend all splits, to heal all hurts, and to correct all judgments by not judging.

Whenever you have expressed your feelings, your behavior has been based on methods that you've learned. You also developed a strategy for dealing with the feelings expressed by other people. Your partner has developed his or her own methods as well. Since you and your partner are choosing to be in a Holy Relationship that is healing, you should both be willing to admit that your approaches may be different and neither of you should expect your partner to deal with emotions in a certain way. In a No Loss Relationship, you and your partner learn to adopt the correct method of using the Holy Spirit.

When we moved away from God, we fell into judgment of good and evil, according to the Bible. Therefore, to reverse this fall through the process of learning how not to think with judgment is the way to know God. When a couple practices together, they shift from judgment to Is-ness (true perception). The separated mind joins and they have a glimpse of truth, they know the Oneness, and they know the wholeness of life.

If we live in a non-judgmental state of mind, the Ego vanishes. The Ego hates to lose just like any NFL team. To win is to be right and to judge accordingly. Correcting other people and not allowing them to have their point of view proves that the Ego is real. We are all entitled to our point of view because we all have a mind that "perceives." All points of view prove that we are all individual beings with free will to perceive as we choose. We all also have a non-judgmental perception of any events, situations, and people. We are learning to notice one level (judgmental) and to transcend to the non-judgmental level. If we remain at the judgmental level, then we will retain a perception that is limited. It keeps the mind split and separate. Our judgments disturb our emotional body. Those who constantly judge are very disturbed and can't find peace of mind.

When the Ego judges, it imprisons and repeats the action and the dream. Until you are able to see the dream and the dreamer as one and to see the dream of separation as not real, your thoughts of judgment will lock you into believing that this world is your home. It is madness indeed to believe that your body and the things that rust are your home. You are Spirit, and it is because you have lost sight of this truth that you judge against your brothers and your brother judges against you.

The non-judgmental state of mind is peace. Achieving a peaceful mind is the result for which every Holy Relationship strives. Don't tell yourself to stop judging, yet. Just be aware of the voice that judges. When you hear the judgment, use that realization as a walk-up call to learn of the non-judgmental perceptions that exist instead.

Every moment has a true perception, which is a perception that has no judgment in it. An apple is red. The judgment is the good tasting apple is red. Good implies bad; heaven implies there is a hell. We must repeat this idea again and again that if you have judgment, and then you must experience duality which are the two parts of the judgment. You can't be positive without noticing that you see negativity. No person has ever been totally positive. Even those who attempt it very diligently find that they see negativity outside of themselves. The higher mind wants you to see your judgments, both parts, even if that other part is a reflection from your partner's mind. Remember all minds are joined.

The true perception is the Is-ness. The true perception is what happened. It is just facts. A rose is a rose is a rose. The Is-ness is the non-judgmental state of awareness, whereby what is, IS. The sun produces heat, water is wet, fire burns, rocks are hard, red is red. The Is-ness is what you see with your eyes, hear with your ears, and feel with your senses without any judgment or interpretation of why or how.

Sit before a mirror and just look at your face. There are two eyes, two ears, one nose, big or small, it is just a nose. Sit for more than 30 minutes. Look at the judgments that arise. You know you have to do something about that hair; it looks so bad, so messy. Look into those eyes. Keep looking. Just look. When a judgment comes to the surface, let it go, imagine it is a bird taking flight. Keep looking. Practice until you understand what is the Is-ness of your face. If you can understand it and see what Is-ness is, then you can understand the Is-ness of everyone and everything made.

Everyone and everything is expressing an Is-ness. Like it or dislike it, there is always a just happening event. Your entire past has "Is-ness awareness." If this term is new to you, get used to it and repeat it often until you become very familiar with it. This Is-ness must be valued over your judgment or you will keep your judgment. A judgment is what you add or subtract to an event.

In a Holy Relationship, you and your partner practice the acts of releasing judgment and supporting Is-ness. Is-ness leads to Spirit. You will only see Spirit when you have achieved a certainty of Is-ness. True perception leads to pure knowledge. At the level of perception, you have two choices—judgmental perception or Is-ness true perception. Each choice is a level of consciousness. Within a Holy Relationship, there is a continual movement of awareness towards the Is-ness of each moment. You and your partner will share and admit the perceptions that you have chosen, and then you will ask for help with the task of suspending judgment. You are a free Spirit which means that your will is free to judge, or not to judge.

You can never stop another person from judging or having his or her point of view based in his or her judgments. It is pointless to point to another person without healing yourself first. Being critical is easy to do when you are beginning to learn. You can't make another person wrong if you are at a non-judgmental level. You can call for both of you to move out of that level and remember that if you are seeing judgment in your brother, then you are looking into a mirror. If you hear your brother's judgment at all, then you need to admit that you have the same judgments, even though they may be hidden within yourself. Truly desire to be free of it. Be careful of making accusations. Be careful of being righteous. The "what is" moves you away from words. It moves you into the silence. The inner peace of self is perceived when you choose to look upon Is-ness.

Whatever you have judged, you will be judged. This is an exact law of mind. The Holy Spirit has the power to release you from your judgments and free your mind from being under the effects of your judgments. The feeling is often referred to as grace. A state of non-judgment is pure grace. When you go through life in grace, you may encounter many appearances of danger, but as many masters of Spirit have proven (Jesus, Gandhi, Buddha,

73

etc.), love without resistance overcomes and transcends threats. A No Loss Relationship loses the judgmental mind.

Agree to disagree

We enter into a relationship fully programmed and completely conditioned, unless we have been working spiritually on ourselves for many years. We all have countless mental beliefs, judgments, scripts, and ways of dealing with life's dramas. We all disagree and judge more times than we can honestly admit. By agreeing to disagree we admit that we can be different. We can see our differences as a way to shift our minds towards that, which is the same.

If you find that your judgments or the judgments of your partner lead to a disagreement, then choose to agree to disagree. Allow your partner to have the difference of perception that was probably made long before you arrived on the scene. Attempting to defend your perception during a disagreement will not stop your partner from attacking you or continuing to spout his or her perception.

Choose certain words that can serve as a clue to you and your partner that a fire (fight) is about to break out unless each of you allows the other person to have his or her point of view about a situation. The idea is that you both become quiet and relinquish your positions. Faced with changes, the Ego can be very stubborn and restive. Making the choice to give your partner the right to have his or her opinions is the way to be the most helpful. Don't attempt to correct your partner when he or she is not willing to be corrected. Use a catchy phrase that will remind you that it's not your place to change another person's perception. Here are some suggestions: "Let's see, I have to go remove this board out of my own eye," "Yes, you're right for your perception," "Thank you, for sharing," "What's up Doc.," and, "It's a private joke."

6. Love your partner as yourself.

Agree not to be verbally or physically abusive. Make it a priority to maintain peace within yourself and within your home. Practice the Golden Rule. Do nothing physically to the other without his or her full consent. Proper expression of feeling is to be targeted into the Holy Spirit and not to your partner. Pray together and heal together. Your feelings are the key to healing. For many generations people have been very confused about how to understand feelings. When you listen to the Ego, you will experience a range of feelings. But when you listen to the Holy Spirit, you feel only true joy. Your true self always feels the attributes of Spirit, love, peace, and bliss in Light.

The goal of a Holy Relationship is to end violence and establish safety within the relationship. The partners in every relationship want to experience peace, yet neither knows how to appropriately express the emotions that he or she feels. The goal of a Holy Relationship is to create a safe space to heal. Most people have encountered a situation where someone was treating them in a manner that was physically or verbally abusive. The word abusive is used here not to imply that there was a victim, but to admit that the person involved resisted the behavior and attempted to defend him or herself from the tonality or the physical expression.

Everyone has a built-in comfort level, which varies from person to person, regarding his or her tolerance of emotional expressiveness and physical sensitivities. Whenever you violate a person's comfort level, you create abuse in his or her mind. When you address within his or her level of comfort, which is his or her safety zone, then he or she says, "I feel safe when you speak in this way." However, if you raise your voice above a particular vibratory rate or if your physical actions invade his or her space, then he or she says, "I feel unsafe."

A person's comfort level can be unpredictable. A certain look at a sensitive little girl and she starts to cry; yet a particular little boy may need you to grab him and shake him to get his attention. Being able to determine your partner's zone of safety is very important. It is also important to realize that when you are violating that space, you are activating his or her defenses.

All physical creatures have defenses. When the need to protect yourself arises, no spiritual healing can occur. From the state of fear, you believe you have to protect yourself from harm. You feel threatened and then you judge. It is your animal nature that says, "I could be dinner." Run before being eaten or fight back. Judgment is based in survival, and a Holy Relationship teaches that you always survive and will never die.

A major lesson of life is to teach our self that we are not a victim. We are a living Spirit that is invincible regarding the events that happen in this world. Unfortunately, most of us are unaware of this, so we react with attacks and defenses in an attempt to protect that which we believe is "us" or "ours."
We are all in a process of learning to expand our safety zone. Making it safe to go beyond these imposed limits plays an important part in advancing a relationship to wholeness. Justified anger is based in morality. If we attack in the name of justice we are defending our beliefs in morality.

All acts of physical violence and attack are learned behaviors. It must be unlearned through agreements. When we choose to judge the behaviors of bodies as unacceptable, then we will feel anger. Unacceptable behavior is a judgment made by the perceptional mind. In absolute truth, everything that happens in the physical level must be recognized as acceptable. Why? Because it is a play of form, not reality. A child plays with clay. The parent knows the child is not the clay they are playing with.
Reality is not threatened by what is projected upon it, just as a movie screen is not changed because of light images that are cast upon it. If you project a film image onto a movie screen, and someone gets up and fights with the light images on the screen, what happens to the film in the camera? Our minds do the same thing. We project images and produce movies of violence using our partner as the screen. If we attack another person, then we are not changing our minds. Those who get angry or sad have forgotten what they are because the projector mind has made an unacceptable belief about the behavior.

If behavior conflicts with beliefs, then emotional stress is produced. If our beliefs are in conflict, then we produce emotional tension. This tension is an inner pressure that must be released. The release is often expressed as anger. Anger, when projected at a target, is not healing. Our partner is often the target. Why? Because we trust our partner, and we hope that he or she can help us. We assume that because we are together, this connection is a safe place to dump our emotions, and we need someone to understand our pain. We think that the act of sharing our pain will help us to feel better. Unfortunately, it does not produce the desired healing results.

In a Holy Relationship, we make a commitment not to project anger onto anyone, thus learning that healing can only occur when we learn to deal with conflict with the help of the Holy Spirit. Healing can only happen through joy, never through guilt. Healing happens through correcting the mind that is in conflict. All anger is a false attempt to correct the mind. We think that by getting angry we are causing a change. When we awake to the understanding that change does not occur through anger, we gladly make an agreement not to be verbally or physically abusive.

If you have experienced verbal attacks or physical violence from a parent, then you are likely to repeat that pattern with a mate. If your partner has been verbally or physically abused, then he or she has likely built many defenses. Your past relationships need to be healed because they are affecting your behavior in your present relationship. If you have acted out violently against a past partner, then it is likely that you feel guilty because either your anger was wrong or because you feel that your partner's anger was wrong. Insofar as other people have projected anger towards you, you will want to project anger towards other people. This behavior is a trained response.

An argument occurs when you and your partner make decisions without the understanding that comes from a joined mind. It is likely that you and your partner believe that because your bodies are joined, you don't have to join in your minds. You assume that your partner will understand if your behavior doesn't match your mind's intention. When minds do join, behavior matters very little. Does that mean that you can do whatever you want if your minds are joined? Yes! You will learn that if your minds are truly joined, then you never do anything that would change your purpose. The power of joined minds is love, and love acts for the interest of all.

7. Have no separate interests or ways to end the relationship.

Turn all decisions about the relationship over to the Holy Spirit, and make no major decisions without each other and the guidance of the Holy Spirit. Share the miracles and inspire them to happen. Don't make plans for the future without your partner's acceptance. Create fun and happy dreams. Make happy dreams by giving all plans over to the Holy Spirit to fulfill your desires for you.

To create fun in your relationship, replace romance with the desire to join, and set your partner free from any fantasies that your happiness comes from your partner. Replace specialness with wholeness, and learn to see that you are giving first to yourself and then to a partner who is the same as you. Having no separate interest is the way to know Oneness.

In a Holy Relationship the goal is to learn that joined minds create loving expressions called miracles or happy dreams. You share miracles, and miracles are inspired when two minds give up selfish interests for love's expressions. Happy dreams are created from this willingness to become one in thought and purpose, allowing goals and desires to manifest under the guidance of Spirit. The only requirement to experiencing happy dreams is the willingness to say "not my way."

In a Holy Relationship, you and your partner work to heal dreams by honoring each other's dreams while examining them for aspects of "selfishness" and control. When you support each other, you don't make your partner's dreams "bad." You simply ask questions. Asking appropriate questions leads to wisdom.

When exploring the wants, dreams, wishes, and fantasies, keep an open mind. Remember that you need training in discernment. Here are some appropriate questions: What purpose does this dream support? Is this dream in alignment with all our other goals? What will this goal teach me? What am I teaching others by acting on this dream?

Making decisions

A Holy Relationship establishes new powers when both partners learn not to make decisions alone. It introduces a new understanding about being happy. When we look at our personal plans, we have put them into two categories, major and minor decisions. Major decisions are key issues that come up in every relationship. They always come up when the romantic specialness starts to leave. Key issues are the inner core beliefs that keep you separate. These beliefs are the major grip that the Ego has on you. Major issues include lifestyle, habits, service, entertainment, home, hobbies, education, socializing, personal programming, or anything that gives you a reason to avoid the healing process and continue to establish a Holy Relationship.

Major decisions such as where do I live, should I further my education, should I buy that new car, have a child, make a community contribution, or enter into another relationship all have a common theme of "It's important to my happiness." We do have priorities for happiness that are already established in our mind before we get involved. We have wants and beliefs, which we called dreams. These major (dreams) issues say, "My happiness depends upon X happening. I demand this dream so I can be happy."

When we learn not to make major decisions alone and ask for the support of the Holy Spirit and our partner, then we are saying in essence, "I don't understand my own best interest," and, "my best interest must include my primary purposes." Joining in purpose then extends to major decisions, and when we are joined in mind about our goals, we create in love. This produces true happiness. If we don't consult our partner, we will be reinforcing separation. The Ego will try to convince us that by making a decision alone, we will be happy. This false happiness is selfishness. While we may seem to feel good when we are being selfish, the side effects are devastating. Selfishness is a temporary "high" with a big low. When a major issue surfaces, and I assure you they will, pray together and ask for inner guidance. Teach each other the power of trusting and listening to the Holy Spirit.

Your private mind will try to deceive you into believing that your partner will be happy if you get your way. It will instruct you to go ahead and do what you want without your partner's consent. For example, if you consider the idea of sexual substitution then the Ego is saying, "Why even tell your partner?" If you consider the idea of buying a product, then the Ego is saying, "It's for both of us anyway, so go ahead and buy it." You can learn how to recognize the best decisions when you learn to include your partner in the decision-making process. If you find yourself unwilling to ask about a decision or to talk about a dream plan with your partner, then this unwillingness is called "ego temptation."

The power to overcome "temptation" comes from a joined mind, and you can never overcome a temptation alone. Your unwillingness to discuss a topic is considered a temptation for you, and therefore, addressing it will require your partner's help and the guidance of the Holy Spirit. They will act together to give you strength when your Ego seems to have more force. Be willing to take direction from the joined mind and do not follow what your private mind says.

Following the directions from your joined mind will lead to an internal happiness. All temptations are seeking happiness in outer ways. If drinking alcohol is a temptation, then before taking a drink, ask your partner for his or her advice. Then take a moment for you and your partner to pray together. This required act stops you long enough for wisdom to enter. You need to stop acting impulsively and based on your own thoughts.

Ending the relationship

For every relationship that you believe ended, there was a decision to value "your plan" over the "joined plan." If you think he or she rejected you, then the story is usually told as, "they wanted their way, not mine." If you believe that you rejected him or her then you said, "I choose to leave." Rarely was it a happy joint decision, and if it was, then you may feel as though you and that partner are still together in some ways.

Relationships seem to end because of separate interests. If you and your partner do many separate deeds, even if they are considered minor, then you are causing "minor" deaths. The seeming end of a relationship occurs because of selfishness.

Relationships never end. It is important to seek within your mind to find out the ways you believe you did end a relationship. It is important to examine your mind for the reason that you believe the relationship ended and discover that it did not end. If you think you have ended a relationship with someone or they have ended a relationship with you, then you are establishing 1a belief in your mind about loss. This belief includes any ideas and all objective and subjective thoughts. There can be no perceptions of loss left in a Holy Relationship. The healing of loss must occur to cause true happiness.

If you support a belief that a relationship ended, then this belief enforces that death is possible. A Holy Relationship never supports such a conclusion and neither does reality. The ideas that appear to die are your physical-mental perceptions. You believe the ideas that your sensory perceptions tell you. You support your reasons for ending it. You support your illusion of love by quitting on your partner instead of seeking real love. Don't do anything that would support ending a relationship. Don't believe that your partner can do something that would make you want to end your relationship with him or her.

Under the guidance of the Holy Spirit and the purpose you choose for your relationship, the physical involvement will be established. Physical participation may vary greatly within relationships, so a lack of physical participation doesn't mean that you and your partner are not connected in mind.

Co-dependence is another term for wanting to control the physical and disregarding the mind. Why do people want to control the physical and ignore the mind? We are afraid to look within the mind because we fear that we may be unhappy with our true intentions, if we look hard enough. We may learn that our intention is not to bring a partner physically closer. The more a person attempts to control the events of the physical, the unhappier that person becomes.

Unfortunately, when the mind attempts to control the physical, you bear witness to loss. This feeling of loss is based on thoughts from the Ego mind. The Ego is the only thought system that understands loss and death. When you hear your thoughts speak of loss, then the Ego is speaking. When you hear your mind talk about pain and lack, then the Ego is speaking. You are in a Holy Relationship to hear another voice. The Holy Spirit will prove to you that loss and ending never happen if you give your full attention to joy.

The end of a relationship never occurs when partners are experiencing a true Holy Relationship because both partners never allow themselves to be confused about which perceptions are based on the shared mind and which perceptions are based on the Ego thought system. As long as you and your partner have experienced a holy moment in which you recognized that you both exist in the same mind and you've become aware that the shared mind has no end, then you cannot be misled regarding the end of a relationship. You will not be concerned with how much interaction the Holy Spirit has planned for you and your partner at the physical level because you have learned that you are not the body.

8. Choose to be happy.

Admit that you have expectations and addictions, and be willing to share them in order for them to be healed. Make no demands, rules, or conditions regarding the physical form of the relationship. Understand pure happiness as a way of being.

To make happy is to be whole. Through the act of extending happiness, you recognize your divine nature. Your true self is always happy. The Holy Spirit is the Spirit of joy and learning with its guidance means that you are learning with a joyous heart. Spirituality without joy is meaningless. Wholeness and happiness are the same. Regardless of the term used—joy, bliss, ecstasy, Light, love, happiness—we are all looking for it. We all came to this existence to understand how to get back in touch with bliss and then how to extend this bliss to other people. We seek out relationships to express happiness.

Enlightened masters are people just like you and me who have learned how to make all of their relationships happy all the time. Your unhappiness is based on not knowing how to express the happiness that is at the core of your being. Your unhappy relationships developed when you chose to seek happiness from places where happiness did not currently reside. How do you lose sight of this Light and this happiness? You became uncertain of the origin of happiness. You projected that it came from outside of yourself.

You see yourself as being different from other people, less than other people, and incapable of being loved. You believe that someone else has your happiness or that you have lost your inner Light. A partner who is unhappy and looks to you for that happiness will remain in the cycle of specialness. Sexual pleasures can bond you to a false awareness of the origin of happiness. Sensual feelings will steer the mind to focus on the body.

To have fun is to be childlike. Humor comes from not taking yourself seriously. When you follow the Ego's guidance, you create involvements that lead away from your natural state of being. The Ego wants you to be miserable. The basis of your unhappiness is never related to people or things; it always lives within your own mind.

You need to be involved in a Holy Relationship to prove this concept to yourself. You need a relationship that is based on spiritual principles because the majority of people you meet will be unhappy since they are on their own misguided paths of trying to find happiness in other people and making other people the reason for their own unhappiness. Quite a few people are still asleep because they are currently living with the understanding that people are in charge of their own mental attitudes. Happiness is an internal idea generated by being aware of God consciousness.

9. Enjoy spiritual disciplines with each other

Pray, meditate, and do daily energy practices together such as yoga, tai chi, or massage. Commit to spiritual principles that you can apply to your daily practices. Affirm spiritual truths daily.

Spiritual disciplines are the key to spiritual growth and they help you know the degree to which you are mastering spiritual qualities. Life is for developing mastery and for reinforcing the qualities on which you choose to focus. With every thought, either you are choosing to listen to Spirit or to the lower mind, and each choice is a direction and a practice.

Religion is intended to be a spiritual practice; therefore attending a church, synagogue, mosque, or temple is a way of making a connection to the ideas of that organization. Ideas are meant to be strengthened through practice.

Partners who pray together will stay together. Partners who meditate together will learn how to connect beyond language, which is one of the greatest experiences you can have with your partner. Partners who exercise together will move energy. When you and your partner master the art of moving energy, then you will understand how the mind works.

Adhering to a scheduled practice requires discipline and commitment. Choosing to make a commitment is a method of focusing the mind to maintain direction toward a desired behavior, and then toward a concept, which then escalates into pure thought. A commitment to Spirit is different than a religious concept. Concepts stay at the level of mind intelligence. You can think about God or pray to a power beyond you. This thought process could be considered conditioning, programing, or dogma.

It is habit forming because the outcome is for a certain practice to become a habit. When you suspend judgment, habits are neither good nor bad, yet habits provide you with a method of moving in orbit around a concept or idea as opposed to actually implementing that concept or idea. Habits that lead you to feeling high or feeling low will evolve into addictive behaviors. Routines are habits. You have to ask the Holy Spirit if your routines are healthy and spiritual in nature. Building healthy spiritual routines can only enhance the spiritual relationship.

In a Holy Relationship, you create loving agreements stating that you will practice spiritual disciplines together. When you uphold these agreements, you will be building pathways to Light in the brain. The partners of a No Loss Relationship avoid wasting time on the creation of unhealthy habits. You commit your time to building practices that increase the awareness of Spirit. The reason that you may resist following practices that would bring peace, joy, and love into a deeper awareness is simply that you have old habits that are strongly conditioned into your personality.

We uphold a set of values that are rooted within the thought system of our lower minds that are not aligned with our spiritual principles. These values include our need to seek a false interest in power, pleasure, and attention. Our lower mind has a strong grip on our attention and demands that we follow its lower ways. Following those demands of the lower mind shows up in behaviors such as avoidance, procrastination, fear, doubt, sloppiness, and laziness.

When we are expressing resistance to our lower mind, we will say that we have no will power and no self-control. We catch ourselves breaking promises that we'd made to ourselves regarding the completion of activities that would have been good for us. As a result, we feel guilty and ashamed of the choices that we made because they demonstrated our continued resistance to change. We call this feeling "stuck in a rut." We criticize ourselves for our perceived failure and we think that we are incapable of changing this behavior. Everyone has experienced a situation where he or she wanted to change something about himself or herself or wanted to build a healthier behavior yet, his or her efforts resulted in a reaction that was based on the thought system of the lower mind, which essentially served as a block and stopped him or her from accomplishing the change desired.

A holy partner will help us accomplish desired changes by practicing spiritual disciplines with us and by encouraging us to be focused and committed. A habit takes 40 days to form and becomes established within our conscious mind. When we are building new habits together, we are available to hold each other accountable when resistances arise. If we find that we are resistant to a particular new practice, then do a healing session and examine possible underlining causes. Goals that we set together are called "happy dreams," and they will indeed make us happy when they are worked on together.

Four levels of being are discussed throughout this material: the body, the emotions, the mind, and the Spirit. By having goals or spiritual disciplines for each level and by doing activities for each part of our self, we build a whole and complete person.

Spiritual disciplines for the body include physical workouts such as yoga, tai chi, qigong, chakra exercises, walking or running with mind meditations, and sexual practices that move energy through the centers. Focusing on body exercising alone is not a spiritual discipline unless we are working with energy or Spirit because it may reinforce the concept that we are just a body. Sports or dancing may or may not be spiritual in nature. When practicing physical movements, it is of key importance that we pay attention to the spiritual quality that we are building.

Spiritual disciplines for the emotions include healing practices, emotional releasing sessions, breath work, counseling sessions, and tantric sexual practices of clearing that bring the body into alignment and balance. When experimenting with these practices, choose to master the act of not judging.

Spiritual disciplines for the mind include praying, reading, chanting, singing, and contemplating thoughts regarding truth. Repeating affirmations together and reading spiritual scriptures add to mental powers for a spiritual focus. These practices are so much healthier than watching TV or playing computer games. We should commit to our partner and not to distractions.

Spiritual disciplines for Spirit include fellowship with other heart opening people. We can find this fellowship by attending church, attending a spiritual center, participating in a meditation, walking in peace, being in nature, enjoying a deep sleep, doing creative visualization exercises, or being still together.

When we have developed a spiritual life through a Holy Relationship, we will experience a spiritual power that controls the mind, body, and emotions through a demonstration of divine quality. How do we know if we are becoming more spiritual? We are constant, and our words and deeds are in complete congruence with each other. When we are constant, we are unchanging in nature and steadfast in purpose and affection. Enjoy practicing with our holy partner and we will move back into alignment with Spirit faster. We will save time as we both progress through our practices.

10. Not my will but thy will be done

Determine a purpose for the relationship that is greater than your personal interests. Holiness works for causes that are greater than sensational pleasures, power, or survival. Let the Holy Mind show the way of serving God's plan for humanity.

A Holy Relationship serves the whole. It is greater than the sum of its parts. A special relationship serves only the person who has made the other person special. Two people can make each other special, and it seems as though they lean on each other for a certain period of time. A special interest serves the Ego mind only. It becomes a single point of view.

A Holy Relationship includes everyone. The purpose of realizing Oneness is to understand the fundamental principle that we are all connected and, in some way, each of us is affecting everyone and everything is effecting us. This is a difficult idea to understand from the point of view of the separated mind. The separated mind believes it is private, and its thoughts and actions affect only itself or the person to whom it chooses to focus. The Ego's selective focus dictates the choice of whom and when to love.

To move away from a special relationship and into the awareness of wholeness, you and your partner need to develop a purpose that will serve a cause that is greater than each other. Developing this greater cause will require expanding and increasing your understanding of the Self. Your highest good will is experienced through everyone and everything. "Don't put all your eggs in one basket." When you rely on one person as your source for happiness, then you feel hurt when that person doesn't fulfill your dreams. The eggs represent expectations that you have set for a person, and your eggs break when that person is unable to meet your expectations.

The partners in a Holy Relationship work for greater purposes. Your daily employment is just a break from a need to support your intimate special relationship. A job can be a form of an expanded relationship. A higher purpose includes everyone and has no exceptions. If a higher purpose were to end hunger, then everyone is included because everyone must eat or he or she will feel hungry. Creating higher quality air, helping the homeless, volunteering to help sick people, and working to raise consciousness are examples of selfless service. There are hundreds of volunteer programs and organizations that need healthy minds. Teaching spiritual principles without forcing anyone to be part of a religious sect or dogma is one method of serving a greater purpose. Working with kids in order to improve education is another example. Choosing to participate in any activity that reaches a greater group of people without exclusions is an example of giving to a higher cause. The experience that you want to share with your partners is the method in which you are contributing to the whole. The partners in a Holy Relationship teach other people that you are all one, and you are all working for the same common truths.

Love is everywhere and in everyone. When do you limit it and say, it is not here? Why do you try to hide in a small circle of people who only support your private ideas? The more you teach unified ideas with a unified purpose, the more you advance in realizing the Oneness of life and teach yourself that minds are joined. Don't underestimate the part of your mind that would rather remain in a limited comfort zone.

Choose to teach every person you meet a certain spiritual truth. The truth that you choose to teach may be that peace is a greater force than anger. Every moment is a moment to teach peace, and everyone can learn when you teach that peace is the higher choice. You will have a wealth of information to share with your partner when you contact him or her again. Your purpose is always strengthened when it is shared. When people support your purpose and you support the purposes of other people, the circle of love grows.

Can you envision a planet where everyone understands the definition of a Holy Relationship? All brothers and sisters would love each other as themselves. Everyone would be awake to the awareness of God. Like all spiritual masters, couples who choose to live with a higher purpose carry this vision.

The majority of people have not raised their consciousness above the lower aspects of living or working for power, sensational pleasures, or survival. If you want to raise your consciousness, then be sure to focus your attention on a purpose that is greater than the focus of the Ego. Do not promote thoughts that support the lower interests in life. Promote thoughts that support greater efforts. You will live in the center of consciousness that you support within your mind.

Jesus said it this way, "Where your heart is, so will be your treasure." If your treasure is a drug, then you won't be able to focus on ending world hunger. Let wholeness be your aim, and the lower needs will disappear. The spiritual beings that remember what they are have no need for personal power because their power comes from God.

If your relationship is lost in lower meaningless activities, then simply ask, "Am I doing the activities that God would have me do? Am I experiencing the feelings that God would want me to feel?" The greatest joy that any couple can experience occurs when the partners are doing as God wills. God's plan is quite easy to execute. It starts with being at peace and in harmony with that which is immediately around you. The only requirement is that you give up any personal, futurist plans. The inner voice will instruct you on words to say and actions to do without the need for rehearsals. These instructions will not be based on any selfish motive or judgment.

Deciding to act as God wills requires effortless giving and acts accomplished with great joy. Couples who strengthen their relationships by following this guidance will witness a power greater than their self-centered interests will. The experiences of the relationship and the world are never boring because participating in miracles is extremely exciting. When God is your employer, you will inherit great wisdom. "Thy will be done on earth as it is in Heaven" is a motto for service to humanity. The law of manifesting divine ideas into the Earth plane can only happen through the minds that serve the Holy Spirit.

Complete the exercises for this chapter in Chapter 10

CHAPTER 5

WE ARE ONE

The A B C's of Involvements

How to Spiritually End, Change, or Transform an Involvement

Every relationship you encounter has a purpose and an agreement attached to it. No encounter with anyone occurs by accident. Whether you are referring to one person you meet face-to-face or the hundreds of people that you pass briefly on a crowded street, every encounter arose from a cause. Every encounter, regardless of the degree of your involvement, arises and carries two different purposes for making the connection.
Spirit has established one purpose, and your lower self has established the other purpose. Through an agreement made by you, the connection arises within a set time and space and presents you with the opportunity to choose one of the two purposes. The purpose that you express is up to you. Regardless of the tendency to view encounters as "chance" meetings, all relationships are established through conscious and unconscious agreements made by the personal self, the soul, and your higher Self. Since these agreements are made in the non-physical realms of Spirit, you have already chosen all the persons who you will meet before physically meeting them in form. Discovering the form is an aspect of this miraculous existence.

Every relationship's purpose set in form by time and space has a beginning and an ending. Every form of every relationship in the physical realm, including the billions upon billions of galaxies, solar systems, planets, and creatures must begin and end. All forms are passing away, and an unlimited number of new forms are being brought into relationship with the all. Such is the nature of all form. Such is the understanding of all encounters and involvements you make as you are guided by the Higher Self.

The years or moments that span for each encounter are set by agreements that are made before the connection is made. As you learn to recognize these agreements, you will discover your holy purpose, which defines the part you agreed to play in Spirit's plan to return humanity to complete total love for everyone and everything. Every involvement serves as an opportunity for you to experience either a holy encounter within a real relationship or a reenactment of past disconnections and separations that are based in fears derived from the lower mind.

The roles of the lower self and of the Holy Spirit have been examined throughout this material. Each lower agreement you made formed an illusionary special relationship with your lower self. It must be expressed and acted out repeatedly until it is seen as a call for healing that pattern or agreement, thus changing your mind and allowing you to live out a higher chosen agreement or pattern instead. Relationships of karma occur when a lower purpose was not healed during previous involvements, and through an agreement, you continue to reenact that experience until the fear derived from the lower mind has been healed. Special relationships are karmic in nature because they start off with the purpose of the lower mind engaged. Once a lower agreement is replaced by a higher one, the lower agreement is canceled, released, and it can no longer impose karmic effects.

If karmic relationships are in your dream (i.e. form) mind, then they serve as your teachers and your students. Your responses to your experiences within the relationship determine which purpose is played out. No matter how much you may like or dislike your experience within your karmic relationship, it is serving a purpose. You may even experience feelings of hate. Whether you believe in the relationship or not, it was carefully arranged in the interest of your own soul's evolution. You can use the karmic relationship either as a step for ascending into the higher mind or for remaining in the lower mind.

The one purpose you can establish with all relationships is to heal fear by choosing to love. You are always attracting the relationships that you need for you to make all your relationships holy. Spirit is in charge of all your relationships and has established them for you at your request. Every relationship was given time and space agreements. How long they last and how deep they are meant to be has been agreed upon by all souls. "Agreed upon" means you accepted the part, the time, and the involvement to receive the opportunity to choose love. Holy Spirit is in charge of every relationship ever made since the beginning of time. As long as you have a physical form, you (your soul Self) and Holy Spirit have an agreement regarding whom you will encounter and the purpose each person will serve for you in this lifetime.

The "C" Relationship is Casual

Casual relationships have a set length of time that may be contiguous and last anywhere from one-second to several months. However, it is also possible for the length of time to consist of sporadic encounters that are spread across several years. A relationship is described as "casual" not only because of its short length of time, but also because it generally consists of a brief power of attraction energy that serves a focused purpose. The depth of the involvement is very limited. You would likely recognize a casual relationship by your desire to know "little" about the person, and the "little" information that you observe is meaningless.

While the purpose of the encounter has the strength to govern the duration of the relationship, the depth of the encounter is also a factor. When a fear-based decision is made, then healing does not occur, CO-creation is not implemented, and lower agreements are sustained. No judgment is passed regarding the decisions made within the casual relationship because the parameters are designed to simply provide an understanding of a brief purpose.

When you meet a person on the street, in a coffee shop, or through a friend, the encounter does have a purpose, although the purpose is undetected if your attention is focused through your Ego. Each encounter, regardless of how meaningless it may appear to you, does have meaning to Spirit, and the encounter has been arranged and agreed upon by all souls involved. How is this possible, you may ask? Consider the following: Haven't eight billion people agreed to be in form now? Aren't all minds the same at the level of truth? Aren't all minds similar in purpose, desires, needs, dreams, fears, and wants? Are we not all fish swimming together in the one ocean?

Can the higher mind see all your thoughts? Of course! What moves your thoughts in and out of your awareness? How did you come to have certain dreams, beliefs, concepts, or special interests in which to engage? Who gave you the desire to become a doctor, an actor, or a violent criminal? What is the cause of all minds and your relationship to that cause? Spirit's plan is beyond the human brain and its storehouse of thinking. So, yes, Spirit arranges all causal involvements as well as the ones of greater purpose.

Casual relationships include every person you see, hear, or sense on the street, in a car, on television, in the theatre, on the telephone, etc. All are affecting your higher or lower purposes by fulfilling or denying your agreements. Value every casual relationship and teach only joy to that encounter, and it will be made holy. You are not in control of whom you meet in your encounters nor of the agreements you made before an encounter occurs, but you are in control of your decision to choose whether your response to an encounter is based on love or fear.

You pass a so-called "stranger" on the street, and you stop for a moment and look upon each other, and then you choose love or fear. You smile and extend joy. The "stranger" smiles and extends joy as well. Within this exchange, something is recognized, a purpose is expressed, an agreement is kept, and the moment is holy.

In another scenario, you pass a so-called "stranger" on the street and you choose to feel afraid. Within this fear-based response, you have chosen to judge and confirm the belief system of the lower mind. Your response says, "Stay separate; don't share; move on." If you notice your responses to casual encounters, then they can help you determine if your thoughts and energies are focused in love or fear. The thought system of the lower self wants to minimize each connection to prove that you are alone, you should be afraid of people, and you should remember that people can harm you.

Within the multitude of casual relationships that you may encounter in a day, your response may seem to be automatic choices to repeat the pattern of "stay separate." However, every brief involvement is your testing ground to determine your thoughts regarding what you want to see and what purpose you want to remember. When your next encounter occurs, notice how quickly you can remember whom your brother or sister is to you. Causal dating, also referred to as "C-dating", is a process for learning what is real and what is specialness. The C-dating process can provide you with an opportunity to learn and experience your fantasies, and it can serve as a learning tool to determine your own understanding of reality. When you choose to remain within the C-dating process instead of moving beyond it, then you are choosing not to heal the love-hate cycle, and this choice can eventually become emotionally painful. As discussed in previous chapters, the sexual activity experienced within a casual encounter is often interpreted as true bonding, particularly by women; yet, this interaction is a false bond that can result in confusion and unbalanced, painful feelings. The excitement experienced within the C-dating process is based on an interpretation by the lower mind; therefore, feelings of excitement are not an indication that true bonding has occurred. To touch on a higher purpose and begin the bonding process, the casual relationship would need to transform into a B involvement.

A dating relationship that lasts longer than three months must grow or it will turn destructive. Continuing to repeat causal dating experiences is damaging to the soul because it reinforces the belief system of the lower mind. Even though friendships and acquaintances can be causal and may not develop into a deep connection, they still provide an important gift and an opportunity to respond with love. Trying to make a friendship be a deeper connection than it was meant to be is another way your lower mind keeps you in pain and attempts to prove that you are unworthy of love. Instead of trying to force a deeper connection, choose to accept the natural purpose of the involvement.

Causal involvements are not wrong or bad. They are meant to be great teachers, once the higher purposes are understood. Often the higher purpose of a causal involvement is to increase your awareness of the thought system of your lower mind and allow you to decide if you want to continue with your lower agreement. It may also show you that a brief encounter can be divinely holy. Ask inner questions about C involvements and Spirit will reveal both purposes.

When you decide to review your pattern of casual dating, relinquish any tendency to pass judgment. List what you have learned and what didn't work in areas such as fantasy, communication, intention, and special attraction. Notice how your views and behaviors may surface in other areas of your life, such as employment, special interests, hobbies, or skill learning.

You may ask yourself the following questions: Do you quit easily? Was there no real interest? What trick did your mind play on you? What good came from that brief encounter? How did you benefit from that situation or person? Was the encounter holy or fearful? Was the stranger turned into a friend? Were you content with the duration of the encounter, even if it lasted only for a moment? Was the moment changed because of your special function? Did you recognize the gift of the encounter, even if you have interpreted it as a negative experience? Did you see the body or a purpose? Were there any feelings of pain regarding the involvement? If yes, then how did you hold on to that moment and make it special? What expectations did you set for the casual encounter? Two purposes occur in every meeting; are you able to realize them?

A Course in Miracles states, *"When you meet anyone, remember it is a holy encounter. As you see him you will see yourself. As you treat him you will treat yourself. As you think of him you will think of yourself. Never forget this, for in him you will find yourself or lose yourself. Whenever two Sons of God meet, they are given another chance at salvation. Do not leave anyone without giving salvation to him and receiving it yourself. For I am always there with you, in remembrance of you."* The partners of a Holy Relationship understand that everyone is a reflection of the partnership. They understand that to see the Light of pure consciousness in each other, as well as in each person they encounter, is the purpose of being together.

When two partners come together they are given a chance to recognize the real Self. They understand that it is impossible to see someone else as joyous if they feel miserable inside themselves. They understand that if they feel wonderful, then others will recognize that feeling and will also want to feel it. To save another person is to bring their feelings and thoughts into alignment with pure joy. You can't bring other people into a state of mind with feelings that you don't honestly feel yourself. When a person is pretending to be in the Light, other people can easily recognize this falsehood. When you think you are happy but that happiness is an illusion of happiness, you should understand that, on some level, people are able to detect your false happiness, and their reactions will reflect their confusion.

If you are expressing an illusion of happiness, people will often respond by offering you a problem, which is their way of offering a solution to your hidden unhappiness. This offer may seem confusing, but when people are shaken by an illusion of suffering, their offer is actually an attempt to fix your unhappiness by diverting your mind to a problem that they can verbalize. The real answer is found with the Spirit within yourself.

If anyone fails to see the pure joy in a situation, then he or she is being provided with a chance to heal. If he or she fails to heal, then he or she is given an experience of separation so that he or she will receive an opportunity to make another choice. If he or she continues to choose to remain separate and different, then the relationship is not meeting the purpose for which the Holy Relationship was established. If he or she chooses the option of healing instead of being different, then he or she will be guided to see the thoughts that must be removed from his or her mind. Removal of these thoughts will allow him or her to see the spark of pure consciousness called holiness and he or she will be blessed with the awareness of love.

When the partners of a Holy Relationship acknowledge the option to heal and practice it with each person they encounter, they are essentially teaching with the power of God. Once you experience holiness with your primary partner, you will desire to experience it with others. Once you understand the power in it, you will want to experience it with more people. When you experience it with the majority of the people you meet, you are an advanced teacher of God. Those who refuse to join with you in this awareness are too afraid and will not remain in your presence. As an advanced teacher of God, you will continue to extend Light to a person who leaves you because you know that in the right time and space, that soul will value coming into the same awareness.

If a soul chooses to remain separate, it is only because it values feelings of guilt or attraction to the body as more valuable than the experience of being whole. Free will honors each person's choice. Never doubt every person's eventual choice to remember his or her natural state of consciousness. What 'saves' someone is the remembrance of what they are as God created them. You and your partner become saved by choosing to remember together who you are and what made you. Through this choice to remember, you and your partner have become a Holy Relationship.

The " B" Relationship is the "Bridge" Involvement or the "Best" Involvement

If the partners of a "C" relationship recognize a strong enough purpose, then it can grow into a "B" involvement. A "B" involvement was already destined before the relationship began. If Holy Spirit and you have decided to establish a "B" relationship with someone, then that relationship has a deepening process within it, and the causes for the involvement where predetermined. In the romantic special relationship, it is called "chemistry." In business, it is called a job description. In friendship, it is common interests. In sports or music, it is talent, abilities, hobbies, or special interests. In the classrooms, "B" involvements are realized in your fellow students and teachers who share your interests in particular subjects. In friendship, a bonding occurs that helps you feel connected to your greatest understanding of love.

These individuals with whom you meet and form a "B" involvement are meant to teach you something about yourself and to take you into a different state of consciousness. They are meant to take you deeper into knowing more about the Higher Self and to help you heal the lower thoughts of your inner mind. They are called "Bridge" relationships because you cross from one level to another level. Once you've crossed to another level, the purpose is served and the relationship may either end or change involvement. Holy Spirit has established these relationships for a specific life-learning lesson.

"B" involvements can last from 6 months to 20 years. The time-space involvement ends when the agreed lessons have been learned. Often accompanied by pain, these relationship endings mark the beginning of a new cycle of growth and a new understanding of life. The feelings of pain are due to a change in the bonding and to the difficult task of accepting that a learning phase has reached its peak development. One person may carry more pain because he or she wants to hold on to the relationship even though the limit set in the agreement has been reached.

A "B" partnership means that some growth or ending of Ego can't happen if each person's current behavior pattern remains the same. The partners in a marriage used to remain together for a lifetime. Usually forced to uphold wedding vows, they would often live in disharmony and make little or no progress in efforts to eliminate the thought process of the lower mind.

Today, more agreements with "B" involvements are being honored to replace agreements of the lower mind. The ending of an involvement for a higher understanding or purpose has no negative karma because the real purpose has been served. The honest explanation that you can share with a partner who responds with anger is that you have crossed the bridge or learned all you are meant to have learned from this involvement. Simply said, you did your best.

The partners of a No Loss Relationship choose to perceive that a change in a relationship is not the end or death, but a transformation for new growth. It is sometimes better to change an involvement than to remain in the same old patterns that do not promote growth or healing. Delay is decay.

The partners of a No Loss Relationship can change involvement without expressions of violence or feelings of regret because they share a mutual feeling of acceptance. Even though they recognize that fears may be blocking growth, the partners are ready to admit that they have completed all of the work on core issues that is possible at this time. A change is not a loss but a method of approaching the problem from a different perspective. While it may bring up feelings of sadness to perceive that goals were not attained within the current circumstances, agreements can still be made to support each partner's transformation without additional hatred. While partners are always provided with opportunities to undo Ego beliefs, the "B-based" relationship is not intended to provide all the necessary components for partners to complete the process and undo the lower mind thought system completely.

You have helped your partner more than you realize, and your acceptance of the change in the relationship is required for you to release your partner for his or her own continued healing, possibly with another partner. Chipping away at the lower mind thought system can take many years or lifetimes. If an involvement is not growing or healing, then it is a much better decision to cross the bridge separately and allow Holy Spirit to provide the next steps for both of you. If you can do this consciously, and with unconditional love, then you will truly understand the concept of a No Loss Relationship.

The "A" Relationship is an Absolute Involvement

An absolute involvement is best understood when you grasp the nature of God's love for

89

you and your "A" partner. You usually consider your parents' love for you as absolute and unchanging. You consider many aspects of life as unchanged and absolute, such as water, gravity, sunlight, birth, and death.

The term "soul-mate" refers to a person with whom you share an absolute relationship. Regardless of the state of the involvement or the changes that occur within the involvement on the level of form, you know in your heart that you will always love the person, and you will always want the person to experience his or her highest possible realizations. Your love for a child, a cause, or a career can have an absolute purpose attached. Fulfilling an absolute purpose is your special function in this world. Examples of an absolute purpose could be to always teach peace or to always be grateful. Attributes of Spirit are absolute.

You only have a few relationships in each lifetime that are absolute, but the expression of an attitude based on unconditional love towards another person is also an "A" involvement. "A" is for Always. Within your "A" relationships are those people with whom you bond in your heart center. You are never willing to undo that connection because the person mirrors your true heart connection with Spirit. Your relationship with a soul mate may include some very difficult experiences. You may not stay in agreement and you may not stay together on the level of form, but you are still able to realize the significance of the purpose served in your "A" involvement.

"A" relationships are Holy Relationships that master unconditional love.

"A" relationships are with people you will always love, regardless of the degree of involvement on the level of form, and despite any possible difficulties experienced in your shared karma.

"A" relationships provide opportunities to realize the value of changing the form of the relationship, yet maintaining your heart connection with a person.

"A" relationships are based on connections that extend beyond time and space and carry from one life experience to the next.
Holy Spirit establishes "A" relationships before the Spirit is born into a body. "A" relationships provide experiential proof of never-ending love.

"A" relationships provide a way for every individual to identify with the absolute reality of life.

Your experiences within "B" involvements help you learn how to make more choices from a place of love and fewer choices from your lower mind thought system, which is fear-based. If a person is described as "atoned", then he or she experiences only "A" relationships because all choices come from love and he or she sees life as it is through the involvement with another person. Love is always and forever. Enjoying all forms all the time is absolute love. You can experience absolute love through your Holy Relationship. If you do not feel that you are aligned with your purpose within a relationship, then you can change the involvement. If you do change the involvement, then choose to do it without grievances, regrets, or fear. Know that something wonderful has occurred through the experience of the connection and know that there is no loss.

Trust

Trust is considered one of the most important aspects of building a healthy, Holy Relationship. Without it, no deep transformation is conceivable. Trust makes possible the shift from conscience to spirituality. The majority of couples use trust incorrectly because they use it to prove how unloved they really are.

Trust is an absolute internal focus. Trust is a way of holding the mind in a fixed state of being, still and listening, while spiritual knowledge is revealed. If the mind is not in trust, it's afraid of life. At this stage of human evolution, trust is required. True trust is the door to spiritual knowledge. Blind trust is an intellectual concept that often serves as a training process for moving closer to faith. Even though blind trust is a weaker form of true faith, it is still better than faithlessness. Trust is the most important spiritual quality a couple can acquire, for without it, a relationship can't heal.

Most of us put our trust in the part of our partner that is untrustworthy — his or her Ego. Then, we become unwilling to trust our partner because we believe that our partner has let us down. If we build our trust based on the expectation that circumstances will result in a certain outcome, then we will certainly become confused. If we build our trust, like most couples do, based on promises stated by our partner or based on an expected response from our partner, then we will be disappointed and disillusioned. We will constantly be saying to our self, "I can't trust him or her."

The more we believe others have hurt us, the more we mistrust life. A lack of trust destroys the possible outcomes that could have been achieved through the relationship. When we have destroyed trust, the relationship does change.

What is God's plan for our life and the life of our partner? "I don't know, but I am willing to trust that we will be guided." To build trust in God's plan for our relationship means that we are accepting the challenge of transforming our relationship. Building trust in God's plan means we are learning to surrender our personal plans in favor of a higher purpose. Trust keeps us focused so that we can realize our purpose. A lack of faith in our goals leads to not realizing them.

When we develop a more trusting attitude, we become more open to listening to the Holy Spirit. Trust takes us into deeper aspects of our healing processes by helping us learn how to listen to messages that the Holy Spirit dictates. Trust is about learning how to be a child again and how to develop feelings of being dependent on Spirit. Trust provides the foundation to begin the stages of mastering faith. The act of building trust serves as the essential training method that is necessary to develop the ability to still the thoughts in the mind. When the mind wanders from one fear to another, trust becomes impossible. In a No Loss Relationship, both partners build a trust in God's plan. Each partner is an equal participant in a commitment to heal his or her minds. Trusting God's plan is different from trusting our partner's view since his or her view may be coming from his or her lower mind. The key word is "building" because stepping through a process to develop trust requires time and patience. If partners lose trust in each other, then the relationship may not endure through that process.

The more trust a relationship displays the greater is the awareness of peace. The more the relationship fights, the more the trust becomes torn down. Lack of trust produces disagreements. If we want to CO-create with our partner we will learn to meditate together and make our plans with the guidance of the Holy Spirit. The peace that comes from being in stillness together becomes more valuable than anger. When two individuals trust the silence together, a greater power is generated and a certainty emerges. This certainty enhances a value in faith, CO-creation, and a sense of unity. What more do we want from your relationship?

Trust is essential to maintaining commitment. Without trust, we will question our ability to commit because a lack of trust is a lack of devotion to healing, and if a relationship is not continuing toward wholeness, it will not continue. Remember, if we both set the purpose and ask for guidance regularly, then we are asking for healing and for steady progress towards a Holy Relationship. If progress is not occurring from the spiritual point of view, then Spirit will guide us to change the involvement and approach the issues in another manner.

If we lack a sense of commitment to the relationship, then we have not developed a trust in our partner. Examine past relationships by applying the question, "Did I develop a trust in him or her?" If the answer is "Yes," then I'll bet you are still spiritual friends. If the answer is "No," then attempt to heal that involvement by examining the events that prevented you from developing a trust in him or her. Don't focus on the behavior of your past partner. Examine your thoughts and reactions to the behavior. The purpose of your examination is not to apply criticism or guilt to you or to your past partner, but to clarify your interpretation of the events or situations that diminished your ability to trust your past partner.
Trust will also teach us that if the relationship is real, then we are never out of communication. If we lack trust, then we have created a block in communication. Even if the form changes we are always in constant communication because when we consummated a Spiritual Relationship, we opened a channel of sharing thoughts. The only thing that can block that channel is our fear, which can also be described as our stubborn resistant to wholeness. The holy reminder is that we are of one mind. We can trust our purpose, which is from God. We can trust that our partner is the same as us. As long as we are not focusing on the Ego-based behaviors of our partner, then we can always trust our partner because our partner is exactly like us. We can trust that we both desire the same results. We can trust the Holy Spirit and our unified goal for they are constant. We can trust the methods of healing that the Spirit teaches us.

If we decide to build a building, then we can see our daily progress. Likewise daily trust-building in the relationship means working the guidelines, making clear agreements, establishing times to practice healing methods and communicating in healthy, happy ways. If we decide to tear down a building that we have built, this process takes time as well. We see the effects of that progress as well. When we lose trust and fail to regenerate it, then we will notice indications that we are drifting apart. No one who has built a relationship based on spiritual principles ends that relationship. When spiritual principles are at the core of the relationship, they promote a stronger bond that can take a long time to dissolve. If a relationship was built on unholy interests, then it can still take weeks, months, or even years before the involvement is completely dissolved. A lack of trust slowly erodes the healing process.

A Holy Relationship built under God's plans, fortified by trust, and reinforced by spiritual joy, will not fall. A No Loss Relationship uses trust as the towering platform to see far beyond and above this world and all its petty illusions.
When a couple understands the healing methods that free them from living under the dominance of the lower mind, they receive the creative power that God bestowed upon their holy minds. Then, they can use that power to create their happy dreams knowing that those dreams serve the whole. They learn the power of trusting because they learn the power that comes from joining in mind. They learn the power that comes from listening to a higher vibration of joy.

By examining that which is not trust, we get closer to that which is trust. All mistrust is rooted from the act of our Ego being the controlling influence in your life. We think that we mistrust our partner, people, and past circumstances. We believe that we mistrust our own behavior and how others respond to it. We mistrust that life is leading us toward a union with love. In each of these examples, we are mistrusting something, someone, or some event that is located outside of ourselves. In reality, we mistrust ourselves because we have lost the ability to discern the conflicting messages within our minds. The more prominent mistrust becomes in our thought system, the stronger and louder its guidance seems to be. Mistrust means we missed knowing our Spirit. Mistrust is a wrong perception in our mind and a way of being kept in fear. We will then project that mistrust onto a partner by blaming him or her for something with a negative context. Our feelings of mistrust or blame have nothing to do with our partner. Our feelings have everything to do with our ability to develop our own knowledge of right-minded perception.

When a relationship loses trust, that relationship is already displaying an enormous amount of disagreement and separation, even if the people involved don't recognize it. The purpose of any real relationship is to extend love and peace.

If we believe in the messages we received from our partner's Ego, then we also believe in our own Ego because the messages are always the same. Any trust placed in the lower mind is a sign that we have lost the guide that runs the universe. If we truly believed we could not be harmed, and that all changes in this life were carefully planned for our highest good, how could we not but trust?

The association that this world and our relationships cause us pain is the source of mistrust. We forget that we are projecting our beliefs and stories onto reality by not taking responsibly for our thoughts. It is always our thoughts that cause us pain. By not taking responsibility for our thoughts, we lose the ability to discern whether the source of these thoughts is the Ego or the Holy Spirit. The behavior or response from our partner can only be a mirror that reflects the thoughts in our mind. Our partner is not responding independently of the thoughts in our mind. Trusting this concept is the key to healing, even though we may find it very difficult to believe at times.

Correcting another person without mutual consent is building mistrust in a relationship. Don't play Mr. Corrector to a partner. Don't give them a spiritual "holier than thou" lecture of how to behave. Watch out for a metaphysician who prescribes mental medicine on how to behave. They refuse to take their own prescriptions. If our partner is defensive to our communication it is a sure sign that the attempt to heal was not building trust. Mistrust occurs when our partner admits his or her Ego-driven mistake and we respond with criticism of the behavior or advice on how he or she should have behaved differently. Mistrust grows when we try to make our partner feel guilty by expressing how his or her mistake has caused us harm.

While these are responses that we likely expressed in previous relationships with parents, teachers, and peers, we can now learn how to respond with forgiveness. In our past relationships, we did not know how to build trust, and we did not understand the role that trust has in relinquishing the Ego.

To build trust, we let it become our jobs to overlook behavior and examine Ego thoughts so they can be perceived correctly. We place more confidence in the healing process and less interest in what our partner is doing or, for that matter, not doing. It doesn't work to place trust in our partner's Ego.

Trust is essential to maintaining commitment. Without trust, we will question our ability to commit because a lack of trust is a lack of devotion to healing, and if a relationship is not proceeding toward wholeness, it will not continue. Remember, if we both set the purpose and ask for guidance regularly, then we are asking for healing and for steady progress towards a Holy Relationship. If progress is not occurring from the spiritual point of view, then Spirit will guide us to change the involvement and approach the issues in another manner.

Trust will also teach us that if the relationship is real, then we are never out of communication. If we lack trust, then we have created a block in communication. Even if the form changes, we are always in constant communication because when we consummated a Spiritual Relationship we opened a channel of sharing thoughts. The only thing that can block that channel is our fear, which can also be described as our stubborn resistance to wholeness.

The holy reminder is that we are of one mind. We can trust our purpose, which is from God. We can trust that our partner is the same as us. As long as we are not focusing on the Ego-based behaviors of our partner, then we can always trust our partner because our partner is exactly like us. We can trust that we both desire the same results. We can trust the Holy Spirit and our unified goal for they are constant. We can trust the methods of healing that the Spirit teaches us.

If we decide to build a building, then we can see our daily progress. Likewise, daily trust-building in the relationship means working the guidelines, making clear agreements, establishing times to practice healing methods and communicating in healthy, happy ways.

If we decide to tear down a building that we have built, this process takes time as well. We see the effects of that progress as well. When we lose trust and fail to regenerate it, then we will notice indications that we are drifting apart. No one who has built a relationship based on spiritual principles leaves the relationship without looking back. When spiritual principles are at the core of the relationship, they promote a stronger bond that can take a long time to dissolve.

If a relationship was built on unholy interests, then it can still take weeks, months, or even years before the involvement is completely dissolved. A lack of trust slowly erodes the healing process. A Holy Relationship built under God's plans, fortified by trust, and reinforced by spiritual joy, will not fail. A No Loss Relationship uses trust as the towering platform to see far beyond and above this world and all its petty illusions.

Liar

All mistrust originates from the lies that we tell. We deceive ourselves more than we realize. We lie because the father of telling lies is our Ego personality. Deception (i.e. Telling lies) is the result when we do not truly understand reality as God created it. We have to take a closer look at lying by admitting that we stated a lie and then examining the effects that the lie can have against the movement toward our Holy Relationship. Saying that we don't lie is a lie, for lying is a denial of the truth and a false perception of what happened.

Some of us know and admit that we lie as a defense or as a pathology behavior because of the pain we experienced as children. We have so many ways that we misperceive the truth, thus causing a self-deception of reality. We often rationalize our lies by telling our self that withholding information was necessary in order to protect the feelings of a partner. We also rationalize our lies by defining them as simply an exaggeration or the result of a vivid imagination. We have degrees of lying that range from seemingly less offensive little white lies or little fibs to seemingly major offenses like perjury. Regardless of the degree, a lie is a misconception of truth, and by believing in the lie we essentially develop mistrust in our ability to recognize truth.

It is not the lie that is the problem, but our unawareness of the lie that hurts our trust. It is not the lie that our partner has told that hurts us, but our fear of not knowing the truth. It is not the lie that causes the relationship to break up; it is the fact that we believe the lie to be the truth and fail to see the real truth. No false image has any power except the power we give it. Constantly calling a lie a truth causes us to doubt yourself; then as always, that doubt gets projected onto a partner. If we think we have already lost trust in our partner, then begin the process of forgiving yourself for not being able to know the difference between our partner's Ego and their true heart. If we have lost confidence in our self, then our self-doubt is an indication that we are still in the process of discernment and a healthy dose of self-forgiveness is in order. Lack of trust in anyone is a lack of trust in Spirit. It is a belief that we can be hurt or used. It proves we have forgotten what we are.

At the beginning of making any relationship holy, our mind is constantly under the direction of our Ego; therefore, most of the messages are deceptive in nature. In short, they are lies. This is not "bad," it is a call for healing which is one of the reasons for practicing a 4 H relationship (Healthy, Happy, Healed, Holy). The Ego doesn't want us to know the lies it's telling us. It doesn't want us to keep our word. It wants to confuse us and even tell us that it is O.K. that we have misrepresented the truth. The Ego can totally convince us that the lie is the truth, and the scary part about this perception is that we believe it. The Ego gives several ways to look at a specific event, and none of them is an exact representation of the event that actually occurred. The Ego is a faulty program made up of emotional perceptions.

Let's take an honest look at the origins and effects of telling a lie. The lie arises from the acts of distorting the facts, exaggerating the details, passing judgment on the event, viewing partial information, avoiding the inclusion of relevant information, fantasizing about future events, viewing the past from the perception of a victim, evaluating our self from a low self-image, or harvesting feelings of guilt. All forms of criticism are lies because they are used to accomplish a desired result.

Criticism may be about making personal plans for selfish reasons, telling our interpretation of a story to accomplish a certain response, adjusting our decision on a prior commitment made in order to suit a selfish interest, categorizing people as either better or worse than other people, gossiping or talking about someone's sickness as if it were real, and communicating about the concepts of lack and death in order to enforce the belief in them. Any action taken that serves a purpose other than the actual true perception of an event is a lie. Has this changed your definition of lying? I hope so because expanding the concepts of self-deception can only be helpful.

The partners in most relationships are afraid to admit the lies the Ego makes up. Either the feelings of shame and embarrassment or the fear of being attacked for the error can cause us to hide our mistaken perceptions. This makes the error impossible to correct. If we think our partner is making us wrong for the misperceptions (lies), we won't want to heal them. We fear losing respect or losing love so we lie to ourselves by telling ourselves that it's not safe to admit the mistake. We have been punished for lying, and we fear being rejected again. Yes, another lie.

Create a safe space in the relationship where lying is not a sin or a crime. Guilt and shame are not helpful in the healing process. Without this safe space in the relationship, we will react by punishing each other instead of addressing the real correction. The Ego loves to point to the errors of other Ego's to avoid looking at its own errors. Admitting the ways we deceive ourselves helps us discern between our inner voices.

Trust is not about believing that our partner will never lie to us. Trust is learning that the lie will not hurt us and it can be healed. All our personal problems and doubts come from a misplacement of trust. As the healing process promotes correction, we begin to choose to place trust in the Holy Spirit and not in the thought system of our partner's Ego.

When we choose to tell a lie, we are essentially becoming attached to a fear-based perception of the event. Even though we may think that telling the lie has no personal effect, we will experience feelings of doubt and uncertainty in other areas of our life. Without a willingness to examine the impact that telling a lie has on the relationship, we are increasing our own feelings of mistrust. Until we have admitted to telling the lies and offered them to the Holy Spirit, we will not only continue to believe in the lies and reinforce them, but we will also continue to harbor feelings of mistrust and disappointment which will negatively have an impact on our ability to experience joy. The lack of joy we experience can then have a negative effect on interactions with our partner whom we have appointed to be our teacher. Just as trust is meant to lead us into a greater awareness of wholeness, our lies will lead us into a greater feeling of being alone and separate. By admitting the lie, releasing it, and putting faith in a different message, we learn that true happening is reality.

Five Stages of TRUST

Before being able to admit to our partner that we have lied, we need to feel safe about our partner's reaction. We need to be able to trust that our partner will understand that telling the lie was an Ego-based behavior. We must trust that our partner is there to help us through the healing process as our dark self comes into conscious awareness. The decision to tell a lie is often made quickly and before we've taken a moment to consider the possible impact. We are accustomed to responding to a situation from the thoughts that have been programmed into our heads throughout our lifetimes. In our culture, we learn to quickly respond from the English language voices that we hear in our heads instead of pausing to respond from the voices of silence that come from our hearts.

Stage 1. Do we believe what our spiritual intuition says or do we believe our Ego? Can we tell the difference? The partners of a relationship that is properly built on trust notice the message of the Ego and direct it to Spirit in a way that reforms the message into a laughing matter. This resolves the need for either partner to become defensive. Our partner needs to be able to rely on our love when he or she is facing and addressing the destructive nature of his or her own Ego. Our love represents our acceptance of the fact that each of us lets the lower messages of our mind dictate our view of reality, and the only way we can release alliance to its thoughts is by trusting our partner. When we share something with a partner, and that partner loves us, we make space within our own mind to see a different way of being. The power of joining from loving minds causes transformation.

Stage 2. The second stage of trust involves learning to recognize the difference between an Ego lie and the voice of truth or Spirit, and being able to distinguish messages of fear from messages of love. The partners in a relationship need to work together by verbally sharing the voices in their minds for the purpose of redirecting their minds toward trust. Feelings of trust will then become more apparent. To recognize if the source of the message is Ego or Spirit, decide whether the message promotes a sense of joining between us or a sense of feeling further apart. As we begin to value our Holy Relationship more than our personal interests, we learn to trust that all events and external circumstances, including those we judge against, occur in the interest of our greater good.

Deciding to build a relationship on trust means that each partner agrees to support the other partner through a period of healing. Sharing compassion when mistakes are made is part of the involvement. Like us, our perfect partner is often listening to the messages from the Ego which may direct him or her to tell a lie, which we can address as part of the healing process. These Ego-based messages may also invoke feelings of fear, guilt, and a great deal of general uncertainty.

We know we are going to show and look at all the dark and fearful parts of our souls together. It means we are moving away from the false ways we protected ourselves. It means we are going to teach each other that the messenger of fear has no power in our lives together. So many couples hold such high standards for their partner that they don't allow space for their fears. If we can't share our dark side with the one we love, with whom can we share it? Without trust, we share our dark thoughts by acting them out, consciously or unconsciously. Sabotaging behavior comes from an unsafe feeling that our partner will not accept our thoughts.

Stage 3. The third stage for building trust evolves as partners recognize that their core beliefs are the same and they begin to release themselves together to a higher power. Trust that we are no different or better or less than our partner and that together we both experience more power than we do when we are apart. It is always a joint effort to recognize mutual equality and sameness. If we expect our partner to do this effort without us, then we have missed the point of healing. Always be open and ready to recognize how we both are the same in many different areas of our lives.

Stage 4. The fourth stage of building trust involves the art of listening. When we have learned how to hold our mind in a state where we feel centered and peaceful, then we are in a place where we have the ability to listen to Spirit. While in this place, the voice of the Ego is not dominating our attention. Occasionally the voice of the Ego can attempt to enter into our listening space, but we are able to quickly relinquish it and return to our experience of being peaceful.

Learning the ability to build trust in yourself is the real challenge. Begin by building faith that our higher mind is leading us, and not our lower mind. We fear our lower minds will lead us into more pain and imprisonment, and we don't trust that our inner spiritual voice will guide us to freedom. Guidance from Spirit is followed by inner joy, bliss, and a certainty of purpose.

Laughter is the key way we dissipate pain. If we have lost our ability to laugh in the relationship, it is a sure sign that trust is absent as well. In laughter the solar plexus is moving, which causes a release of control. Trust that the Holy Spirit understands how to accomplish this release of control and we don't. Sadness also causes the solar plexus to move, which creates the need for forgiveness. Sadness can turn to joy as quickly as we are willing to trust the Holy Spirit's plan for our enlightenment!

Stage 5. Stepping into the now moment is the last stage of trust. A trusting mind is focused internally and is unconcerned with what did happen or what will happen. A trusting mind does not hold events of the past against a partner by anticipating that a negative past behavior will recur. An untrusting mind fears that a negative behavior of the past will be repeated and it feels the need to control the future by preventing that recurrence. A trusting mind lives in the now moment and has no concern for the future since the future is in God's hands anyway.

Once we understand the correct method of healing our mind with our partner's help, trust becomes natural, and the guidance that follows reinforces the value of unity. Until we feel comfortable with these methods, which require practice, we will be tempted to go back to old methods of not trusting. Support is crucial at the beginning stages of learning to trust. Support that comes from outside the relationship is as valuable as support from our partner. We may be bringing up some very deep fears that seem too scary, and we may feel that we will risk losing our partner's respect by sharing these thoughts and stories. Practice building trust on the minor issues, and admit when issues bring up fears that are too difficult to deal with right now. Allow yourself time to build trust, but also be willing to feel the risk that arises when we are sharing intimate details about yourself. Being able to deal with the risk will help us appreciate the trust developed.

When a relationship seems not to be working and the couple is disagreeing, trust is often tested. When we think we have failed in a relationship, or are being rejected, it is easy to feel we can't trust. Lack of agreement and rejection are messages the Ego thrives on, and the Ego wants us to believe in failure. We feel we can't trust because we have bought into the Ego messages of loss and grievances. Trust is the way we learn we can't lose because trust leads to a higher learning.

In higher learning, there is no loss, there is only creation. Trust will show us that we are always a part of creation, and to be separate from it is impossible. We release our trust in life when we perceive that a relationship did not provide our seemingly desired results. When a relationship changes, we often feel emotional pain. When we are feeling emotional pain, we can be sure that our ability to trust is being tested.

Life is not testing us, we are testing life. Can we trust it? Do we agree with it? When we feel that we can't trust the changes we are going through, remember that trust sees all change as good. So, which voice are we listening to? If we think the changes are not for our good, then we don't trust life and its evolutionary process. Life's goal is to return our mind to wholeness, However, our personal plans may be to remain separate by clinging to a specific way of living.

Emotional pain is our way of resisting life's goal. If we feel pain in regards to a relationship change, then we can be sure that we are asserting our personal will upon our partner. Remember that emotional pain and sadness need not produce feelings of guilt. Emotional pain is feedback, or the response to a belief that we are less than whole or lacking completeness. This pain is an indication that we need help. Help from the Holy Spirit is always available to those who return to the place within themselves where they trust that all changes are for spiritual evolution. If a professional counselor or another spiritual friend is available to help us release any unexpected attachment, then we need to be willing to ask for the help without self-criticism. It takes great learning to accept and appreciate changes when a part of the mind wants a different outcome.

A nonresistant, non-attached attitude to support our partner's desires is essential to the development of trust. In the no pain, no gain approach to the relationship there is a temporarily perceived sense of gain that occurs when we forcibly express our view as more important or more correct than our partner's view. The resulting pain felt afterwards is part of the price we pay. We often test ourselves when we are working with a desire for wholeness because the feelings of being separate are so familiar, which makes them seem safer. Pain is intended to reassure us that we don't want "our way" because God's way is our path to joy. Our Ego-based thoughts will direct us to blame someone outside of ourselves, and we'll hold him or her responsible for our pain. The Ego-based voice convinces us that our partner is to blame, and if our partner as more important or more correct could accept our view, then our pain will be gone. We are convinced that by keeping the pain we are right, and our partner is wrong. Until we reverse this way of thinking we will be a victim who continues to harvest feelings of doubt and mistrust.

Pain disappears when we focus our mind into trusting what life is. We only will feel pain to the degree that we think it serves us to control life. Emotional pain comes from not being able to trust life. Emotional pain comes from wanting to repeat special past moments with a specific partner. By repeating the specialness experienced, we are listening to the voice of the Ego and believing that we cannot trust living in the now moment.
Never quit on a partner we're in a Holy Relationship with or we will be mistrusting life. Never give up on a partner or end a Holy Relationship. If it is not mutually acceptable to be together in a form based on each person's current way of being, then change or let your partner change. If we are not agreeing, don't fight. Trust that your guidance is showing both of you a higher way. There are 8 billion people in the world, and we have chosen this involvement for a certain learning lesson.

If mutual CO-creating is not occurring, trust that no agreement is an agreement to let the other be free to experiment with what they want. Life wants us to understand how to CO-create. Life wants us to relinquish our selfish plans and our co-dependent beliefs. We are testing trust by playing drama games of attacking and defending our specialness. If we are in a drama game of breaking up and making up, we have lost faith in the process of joining minds for a common purpose. We are fighting for control and our selfishness is producing fear. The fear of losing what we think we want fuels the act of quitting on our relationship. Any form of quitting is a belief in lack and originates from the messenger of faithlessness.

Never change a relationship from a space of anger, sadness, or disappointment. Most people leave a relationship from a space of disagreement. They are running away, and fear is controlling the involvement. I have already said that fear comes from a lack of trust. While it can be appropriate to take some time away from the relationship to recollect peace, it serves no usefulness to threaten the relationship by claiming to end it. If in our deepest meditation we are told to change an involvement and is followed by joy, we should trust it. Even if later we become sad or feel loss, remember the decision was made with relief and lightheartedness. The Ego always attempts to make us feel guilty and regret decisions. It always reminds us about past special moments. The loss of those special moments and the belief we'll never have them again causes us to want to rush back to that old way of relating. The Ego wants to destroy our faith in Spirit. Hard work within yourself can turn those sad messages into joy, thus returning to trust.

Changing the Form of the Relationship is Not Loss.

If the quantity of physical attention changes, remember that we are not leaving the relationship. We can always keep our heart open and be connected without controlling or placing conditions on the other person. Both partners must willingly agree to maintain the connection of the relationship. Otherwise, the connection is not real. If the process of CO-creation does not occur within this connection, then mutual trust and respect free partners to disconnect without a feeling of loss.

We can disconnect physically from a particular partner, but we should never let our mind convince us that we are giving up on the transformation process to holiness. This process is never about the events that occur in this three dimensional world. True faith takes us beyond time and space. If we continue to love and trust while relinquishing any need to control the behavior of our partner or the circumstances of the relationship, then we will not experience pain when we change involvement with a partner.

Believing we can develop a level of trust that supports this concept may seem difficult. A No Loss Relationship is built on learning how to live at this deep level of trust. From the initial involvement, partners begin by trusting in God's plan. As the relationship evolves, the trust in God's plan grows when expectations and demands in the context of this material world are relinquished. All concerns within the partnership are focused on the quality and content of thoughts. Love has no limits so it is only through no limitations set on the relationship that partners will be able to experience the true joy of a Holy Relationship.

Trust that the Holy Spirit is arranging for our encounter with the right partner for the appropriate amount of involvement. We will receive guidance on words to say and actions to take that will bring the experience of true joy that is based on real love. Without this trust in the Holy Spirit, we both will experience a love that feels good, yet touches only the surface level of this material world.

Our relationships can provide a method of transcending disagreements as long as each partner is willing to relinquish his or her part of the disagreement. We may have heard of the cliché "it takes two to make love and two to argue." Each time we have a disagreement with our mate, it is because neither of us has been willing to give up our respective parts. Being able to lay down our perception of a situation requires trust in our partner that he or she is willing to do the same. If we don't have this trust in our partner, then the argument will continue as each partner pushes for agreement on his or her perception of the situation. The purpose of the argument becomes more of a survival technique because each partner is personally identified with his or her perception of the situation. Who is going to lay down his or her weapons first? Our concepts and opinions are our weapons, and our ammo is the words we spit out of our mouths. We continue the argument under the illusion that if our partner does not agree with our perception, then we have "lost" a part of yourself.

When we can trust that we both are complete and whole, then there can be no loss. The illusion of loss is due to our investment in the outcome of the argument and expectations we previously set regarding the relationship. When there is a mutual feeling of trust and no fear of loss, then we both are comfortable with laying down our perceptions, as well as our expectations and being together in silence.

When we focus on our partner's mistakes during an argument, we magnify those mistakes. Trust teaches us to look past the mistakes and forgive our partner. Consider our own behaviors. What lies beyond our own mistakes? When we both share a mutual trust, then forgiveness is not about applying a correction to a past behavior that is seen as a mistake.

Forgiveness is choosing to see the mistake as gone. The past is gone. A behavior can be repeated only by believing that it will be repeated. If a negative behavior is repeated, then we both are better equipped to discuss the situation without an argument and choose forgiveness. The ongoing trust, which is true forgiveness, is shared in our relationship while continually chipping away pieces of the Ego with each occurrence in which the Ego's view is not supported. Each partner must make choices that continue to chip away at the Ego and the darkness. By making choices in our relationship that are based on trust, we are trusting the Holy Spirit to accomplish a whole release within us from Ego, fear to love, and holiness.

The need to change a partner is a reflection of a lack of trust in our partner. Our partner will behave only in the manner that we request. If we attack our partner, then he or she will respond with anger or sadness. If we offer our partner acceptance, then he or she will offer us trust. No one is different from us. No one wants something different than love. Trust will teach us how much we are the same. When we stop valuing the actions that cause a lack of trust, such as disagreeing with our partner's perception of a situation, then we will be choosing peace.

What is the Same and What is Different

When we examine our relationships, it is important to focus on the views and perceptions of each person that are the same and learn to look at the differing views and perceptions as illusionary. An illusion is a "sick" way of looking at someone—an "ill" us. Do we really want to look at our partner in a sick way? Wouldn't it be wiser to choose a healthy way of perceiving a lover? If we take an honest approach to understand how we feel, then our feelings will help us determine if our perception or concept is an illusion or a truth. Feelings often show us our inner image.

Focusing on differences without an awareness to heal with our partner will only strengthen the illusion that those differences exist. If we focus on a difference by attempting to correct it, then we are actually taking an aggressive stance against our partner. Differences must be seen as an illusion and healed in order to share a Holy Relationship with our partner.

The illusion of differences is healed when we learn to give up the illusion and to shift to perceptions shared by both of us that are the same. The false way to correct a difference is to persuade our partner to change his perception. Love has no differences and no opposites. Love is in conflict with nothing. Love waits for mutual acceptance between both of us. This acceptance arises in the minds of our loving partner and us when we choose to value sameness over differences.

In relationships, we reinforce differences by noting that "men are this way and women are that way." When we state that women want something different from men or that women need to be treated differently than men, we are only deceiving our self. At the level of our true essence, men and women do not have different desires, and we develop Holy Relationships to prove that we are the same.

Another false way to deal with perceived "differences" is to develop a strategy to cope with them. It takes a lot of effort to understand differences, to decide how to maintain them as true, and to remember the strategy we developed to deal with them. Each difference the lower mind invents is a way of blocking that, which is the same. One thought system exists at the expense of the other.

Healing our relationships involves finding out that the differences are not true. A relationship is not two parts coming together to form a whole. Parts all have the same common essence. Parts all have the same common desires. Parts all have the same needs. All parts share the same mind. All thoughts exist within the same mind. No part can be outside of the one mind. The greatest realization is love, and love's message is Oneness.

Differences are often experienced as opposites: the opposite sex, the opposite side of the same coin. Duality is always composed of opposites: hot and cold, good and bad, day and night. Every difference invented must have another half. We state that men are opposites of women because we like the idea of differences.

Men are not sexual opposites of women. The concept of sex is the same, regardless of the gender. The hardware is different in size and shape, but it works the same way. Techniques vary, but in sexuality, emotions of pleasure and pain swing for both men and women. It is not possible to understand and communicate differences between men and women in a way that validates that the differences are real. We cannot say, "All men are _____ but women are _____." It is only by seeing the sameness of an experience that we can appreciate and accept the differences. When we are experiencing our sameness, then we are realizing our source and our true essence. If we exclude seeing the sameness that we all share, then we will essentially be focusing on the differences and making false idols within the relationship.

In the need to prove that differences do exist, a woman may say, "We produce children and have menstrual cycles; men don't." A person chooses to see differences by looking through the lower part of the mind, which we have called the Ego mind that is mostly aware of body and behavior. The perceptional Ego mind makes up differences and depends on them in order to maintain its reality. When we listen to the Ego mind, our thoughts will be dominated by hundreds of differences in people daily. If we are trapped in being right about those differences, then we will never "see" beyond that limited perception, and we will always be in an "against" stance. If differences are allowed to block the awareness of Oneness, then they will prevent us from joining.

It is the goal of a Holy Relationship to bring our differences to the place within us where they can be released. If too many differences stand between us, then we will forget the means to love. Each difference is a brick in the wall, and this wall becomes the prison that keeps us confined to our limited world. Yes, women have the hardware to produce the child, but the sameness is that both men and women parent the child from conception to adulthood. The man carries the energy container to provide for the child's living through action.

Most relationships are trapped or stuck in the Ego mind, and therefore, these relationships do not work. Two people who are listening to their Ego minds and know that they are "right" about their perceived differences are choosing to reinforce separation. Separate minds can't experience a Holy Relationship.

Before we get involved in a relationship, we feel separate and alone. We choose to enter into the relationship in order to end that sense of separation. Choosing to focus on differences only establishes that not being in a relationship is better. Everyone desires to end the feelings of being separate. Unfortunately, the method we often use causes an even stronger sense of separation.

So, let us learn to see in a way that emphasizes our sameness. To look for sameness in relationships we must look with a certain type of perception. We must be trained in Is-ness awareness. We must learn to value the truth about each other.

We affirm the following ideas, about what is the same, over and over to each other:

We are all spiritual beings. We are all created from the same source. We all have the same spiritual parents: father-mother God. We are all children of God. We are units of pure consciousness. We all have a spiritual body, a Light body made of spiritual energy. We all have a mind, and that mind is not divided nor does it have parts outside of the collective mind.

The one true mind works the same way for everyone. We all can share the same thoughts. Our range of emotion is the same. We all have free will—the power to decide. We all have focus—a single point of awareness called consciousness. We all have a physical body made up of atoms. We all live for energy and within energy. We can't live without it. Everything we see in the material world is made of atoms and energy.

We all eat and need water. We all must breathe air. All molecules of water are the same. We all grow older. We all are born, and we all pass out of form. We all seek for a higher understanding or purpose of life. We all need the basics for survival. We all need love. In relationships we all want the same thing: love, joy, and security.

If we have not been experiencing these truths, then we have been concentrating on some perceived difference.

How Do Differences Arise in the Mind?

Our perceptions and experiences make up our personality, which is our lower Ego mind. Why do we value our differences so much? We value our differences because we are trapped in our lower mind.

Differences come from the comparative aspect of the mind. The lower mind as the perceiver learns to choose one object over another. The value of one being greater and the other lesser establishes the likes and dislikes of our personal perceptions. This perception is how judgment enters the mind. We choose to categorize any person or object as better or worse, and wanted or unwanted.

We are always trying to keep our likes and discard our dislikes. Our personality is a collection of likes and dislikes. When we meet someone, we show him or her our likes, hoping that our likes and dislikes match. We call this chemistry. It is the illusion of love. What happens when we don't agree? What happens when our differences matter more than our relationship? What if we don't know how to heal these differences?

Differences arise and descend into our lower mind. Judgments work much like a teeter-totter. Our likes are pushed to the surface of awareness and the dislikes are suppressed. We work hard at keeping our judgmental differences apart. A thought, however, is whole, having no judgments of good or bad (like or dislike).

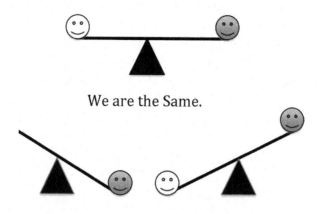

We are the Same.

You, up. Me, down. Me, down. You,

A twisted rubber band illustrates the point. The band can be twisted once to make it appear to have two halves. Twisted twice and it appears as four, but it is still whole when untwisted. Untwist your judgments by bringing them together, and the whole thought behind the perception appears. A relationship provides the means to see both sides of our judgments. Through experiences in the relationship, we correct our concepts of judgments and separation. If we notice a characteristic in our partner that we dislike, then we have an opportunity to bring the judgmental thought together. We can't have one part of a judgment without the other part. Ask for help in bringing these parts together. Ask for help in remembering the conditions that occurred that brought us into judgment and caused us to separate the thought and split the idea into good and bad. Learn not to project our judgments onto our partner that would make him or her represent the other half of our judgment.

When we judge, we split our mind, and this causes us to lose energy. We also lose energy when we keep our judgments private. The effort it takes to suppress thought and hold thoughts private is much greater than we may realize. For this reason, a judgmental person will often feel very tired. Re-collect that energy and use it for a greater purpose. When hidden parts of thoughts reunite, energy is released, and we can live in joy, love, and bliss. Those who highlight their differences go to extreme measures to experience the idea of opposites. When we see someone who swings from one side to the other, it is a clear sign that their Ego mind is making differences valuable. Our relationships become very dramatic when we explore the highs and lows of emotions. We choose to be very emotional because we believe in our perceptions, which recognize differences. Some people like to be dramatic. Promoting drama can be a habit and a way of living that provides excitement.

The problem with extreme differences is that the act of judging becomes addictive and compulsive, like a merry-go-round that never stops. The more we feel the need to be extreme about a perception, the more we need to prove it is true. Extremes lead to violence and attack. A sense of peace and balance is the choice we make in a Holy Relationship. A raging fire destroys and burns the forest. Extreme love and hate leads to destruction.

Why are differences so important to us? We tell ourselves that without them, we could not exist. We would lose our individuality and our unique special self. We are afraid of the Oneness because we fear that it will require a loss of our imagined self. Real individuality is the awareness of both will and soul. False image is low self-esteem; it's a wish to be special and different. It is a selfish pride to be "right" about judgmental perceptions. It is the darkness within and our shadow self. If this part rules our relationship, then it will surely destroy the involvement.

How have we tried to prove our point of view? Do we try to persuade other people to agree with our opinions or beliefs by arguing with them? What if their opinions differ from ours, and they argue with us? How many relationships have fallen apart over attacking each other's differences?

The holy mind sees no differences. For every idea that makes us the same, our Ego makes an equal difference. The Ego mind is in conflict with the holy mind, but the holy mind doesn't get involved with the game of differences. The holy mind is continually reminding us of sameness, but only when we are willing to listen. The Ego mind that speaks of differences believes it must survive, and by being "right" about its differences, it stays alive. When the Ego mind of one person finds other people who agree with its "righteousness," then it believes that it has collected the power needed to remain alive. When it has enough power, it goes to war against the people who seemingly do not agree with its "righteousness." Wars are fought over imagined differences.

The Ego mind wants us to perceive differences in appearance, behavior, and concepts, because that is its scope of existence. Notice the way our Ego mind focuses on these differences. Be honest—are we making the following differences important? Are they causing problems in our relationship?

Differences in Appearance

When applying the concept of differences to the human body, we could list many visual characteristics that might include the body's shape, smell, weight, and design. The Ego mind will even choose certain parts of the human body to make special and particularly more attractive than other parts. Are we strongly invested in how our partner looks? Is the hair too long? Are the legs too short? What do we think about the teeth? Our Ego mind can even narrow the difference to how that part must move in order for us to be happy. Judgments on the behavior of the body can range from unacceptable to perfect, and an expectation is often set for the body to consistently perform that perfect behavior. Hence, we monitor and categorize the behavior of the body as either right or wrong. Then, we criticize behavior that is wrong or does not meet our expectations. The final descent of the Ego mind occurs when we want to possess whatever part we're focusing on because we "like" it. Then, we feel that we must own it from the sense of she or he is mine.
We refer to our partner as "My _____."

Material Things

To the Ego mind, clothing denotes our charm and our possessions are proof that we hold value in this world. Our worth is measured by what we have and what we do. We build fences and houses that represent a fight over property boundaries that don't exist except in our different minds. As long as we continue to support a materialistic view of this world by rating the value of any one thing as higher or lower than any other thing, differences will continue to dominate our perceptions. We seek to be different by owning different things. "My material things make me stand out; I am different from you."

Interest and Hobbies

When we share a common interest with another person, we have both decided to judge the interest in terms of "liking" a similar perception, and this choice in perception will determine our compatibility. This common interest often comes with expectations, such as believing in the same goals and doing things to please one another. Our personalities seem to match—or do they? We choose to be with you because you want to do what we like to do—or do you? Are you doing something just to be different from others? Are our tastes in music or in the arts different? Do you play a musical instrument better than us? Are you more talented?

Concepts, Beliefs, and Opinions

Concepts are learned beliefs; they are opinions we collect. We have made concepts of how we are to be, of what we are to do, and of how we are to feel. We have learned concepts from other people, but we have also developed them ourselves whenever we experienced a situation where we felt the need to make a judgment. We have a concept for existences that we have labeled as "being a parent," or "being a boss," or "being a priest," for example. Each of us has given a concept to every person and every object in our world. These concepts represent a false means for us to reach happiness.

Within every area of life—religion, politics, science, technology, self-esteem, health our concepts differ considerably. We determine whether each concept makes us feel good or bad. Concepts cause us to believe we are different. We choose to fight over our concepts more than we choose to agree over them. Our concepts never let us experience love. Developing a concept is a false attempt to know about any person or situation that currently has our attention. We all want to think that we know the "important" information. When we think we know something about someone, it is best to realize that we have actually created a concept about him or her—we don't really know him or her. Who knows, really? This particular person may have changed his own concept of himself just seconds before we thought we knew him. Knowledge is not a concept or a fact. Concepts change; knowledge doesn't change. Who wants to keep a person in prison by holding that person to a specific opinion or expectation?

Until we learn that our concepts of our self and others are not important and not true, we will essentially continue attempts to prove a judgment made in the past as if it holds validity and purpose. We do not take into account the idea that holding on to a concept can negatively have an impact on our current relationship and our ability to experience a creative future. Couples fight over what happened in the past, and they choose to view the past judgment of an event as an important concept about life. How many couples fight over opinions and beliefs of how things should be in the future? What concepts do they insist must become the future? All concepts must be undone in a Holy Relationship. Ideas are the methods we use to build a special Ego mind. Often, we have so many concepts around us that we won't allow our self to be loved. It affects our ability to receive love if we choose to value our concepts, our behavior, our rules, and our body more than love.

Who makes these differences and then uses them to condemn the one we love? Who makes concepts of how life is supposed to be and points an accusing finger to attack those who disbelieve? Seek not our mate in concepts that have to match ours. Don't let judgment, differences, or beliefs keep us from our purpose. Are we what our brother has made of us? Are we the victim of learned responses from family and social conditioning that continue to dictate how to live and think? How will we respond if those concepts are challenged or attacked? How will we react if another person teaches us that our concepts are wrong? Who are we then—but another concept?

We are the one who makes a "different self." The world can teach us no concept unless we want to learn it. It is simply a trick of the mind to believe we are taught without our willing consent. We say, "I don't like what I was taught nor do I believe it; look what it has done to me. I was a child." Projection of responsibility leads to the decision to blame another person, who will not help us, change an internal mental belief. We taught these concepts to our self and we choose to believe in our Ego thought process. We are never a victim, and we are not a program without choice.

Concepts can never provide real joining even though we think that we feel a sense of joining when we share a concept with another person. We want to experience joining so much that we believe that we must be joining with a person if he or she agrees with our opinions. We think we feel a sense of sameness. Concepts cannot offer real joining because conceptual beliefs exist on the perceptional level, and in order to have a perception, we must be separate from the person or thing that we are perceiving.

For example, one concept says, "Jesus is the only son of God." Millions seem to agree with this statement and millions more disagree. Everyone has his or her own experience of the "truth," which is backed by an emotional experience. Add this memory to others linked with this statement, and we have a "special belief" and a concept about God's son. We decide to agree with this belief if we perceive that it will bring us happiness or security. If we agree with this belief, then we will dislike a person who does not agree. In a subtle way, we will dislike our self for not experiencing joining with the person who disagrees. Our concept has placed a wedge in our relationship.

Not joining is always some form of pain. We are more accustomed to the pain experienced when we do not join than to the bliss we would experience if we did join. We prefer our pain and separation simply because we are used to it. We fight over concepts because we believe that if we defeat another person, then we will feel less pain.

Our self-concepts reach more to the core of who we think we are than even our bodies or our behaviors. Our self identify is wrapped in self-concepts. Our concepts are so closely guarded and protected by our defenses that we can hardly admit that they're only perceptions. Evidence of our defense system appears when we express our need to "be right."
At the expense of being happy, we voice our opinions and make up the concept that if you don't agree (a request to join), then we will leave you. Rejection and abandonment are beliefs in loss. If we are experiencing loss of any kind, it is because we believe in a concept of which we are unwilling to release or examine.

Focusing on an outward behavior serves as a distraction and leads us away from examining our long-held belief or concept. The real joy in a relationship is found by learning to admit concepts and judgmental perceptions for the sake of releasing them, not reinforcing them. Let's learn to see our past concepts as one way, not "the" way of perceiving. They never served us with joy, and they cannot protect us. If we continue to value our concepts, then we will see the world accordingly. The world can only reflect what we believe. If our differences are keeping us at war in our relationship, it is because we would rather keep them than learn to release them. Cherish the love—not our own specialness.

If we believe we have lost love, then we will cling to our perceptions because we now believe that our perceptions are all we have. When we are experiencing a Holy Relationship and there is a change with the physical partner, we will naturally bring doubt to perceptions. We will question any desire we have to hold on to perceptions.

Looking at differences is not the problem. Holding on to differences and regarding them as true, right, and real is the problem. Learn to recognize differences as simply a perception that is based on a learned image and a desire to be special. If we see a difference, call it an "opportunity to find love." Remember that we had a strong Ego mind upon entering into this relationship. We are learning how to undo the Ego mind and the pride that prevents us from experiencing true happiness. This process of undoing is a primary purpose of a Holy Relationship.

When we understand how to heal differences, we will laugh together and experience true joining, and we will know that our differences offered us nothing valuable. Until we learn to have a healing experience, we will always think our differences matter because our differences offer us a false sense of being powerful.

Remember that the Ego part of mind doesn't want to be seen. If it can point to our differences and make us fight over them, it believes it wins. Winning is maintaining existence to the Ego; its self-existence is all it cares about. Learn to say, "This is just an Ego's view and not the view our Spirit sees."

Have fun looking at differences. Don't be heavy about them. Keep the conversation light and simple when we are admitting differences. Remember not to make our partner wrong, and do not attack him or her in any way for perceptions learned during past experiences. The past is not where we want to live. When we release a difference, we are bringing our mind to the present moment. Each time we succeed in healing a difference and in recognizing the Oneness of life, we strengthen the purpose of our Holy Relationship.

The couples that learn to go beyond perceptions of differences live in harmony and peace. What they experience is something akin to: "We agree to disagree," or better put, "we agree that our disagreement will not disturb our agreements." The Holy Relationship sets clear agreements of purpose and values that lead toward union. Everything else is dissolved. All differences disappear in the light of love.

Be willing to let go of your concepts, the images you hold, and the ideas that you think the world has taught you. Use your relationship to disprove your differences, not to reinforce them. The more you find that you are the same, the greater the love will be and the greater the expression of joy will burst through you.

Unraveling the Oneness

It is not possible to perceive a difference with another person and not create an image within "our" mind. One of the errors is that there is such a thing as "our mind" that differs from "their mind." If our relationship is to be holy we must learn not to make a difference between minds. There is only one mind. Sometimes, this idea is difficult to understand, but every person that is in our life is a reflection of some thought-image that exists within the one mind. We can say, "I'm not like him or her," but the truth is that if we see it in them, it is within our own mind as well.

We are angry or sad depending on how we judge thought. Without judgment we are in a state of constant joy. So let us learn to put our judgmental perceptions of difference to rest.

Here are the steps to unraveling the difference:

1. Recognize that we are not at peace or experiencing love with our partner. Notice that we don't like the way we feel when sharing a point of view or story.

2. Ask for help from our partner and Holy Spirit.

3. Admit that we are locked into a perception of being right about a difference and that we have a judgment. See both sides of the judgment and the circumstances that surround that judgment.

4. Make a clear choice to join with our partner and put our love first. Be still.

5. Inwardly release the need to hold on to the difference.

6. Feel the surrender and the joy of releasing.

7. Share the thought that we are releasing, and admit any false concepts we perceive.

8. Affirm the truth of our sameness and source with our partner.

9. Make an agreement of CO-creation with each other.

If we follow these steps in our relationship, then there is no opinion, judgment, or concept that will control our emotions. We both will be ending differences and experiencing the true beauty of life. In this way we prove love is real.

In a No Loss Relationship, we are learning to undo the awareness that we are here, and you are there, and we are different. I am teaching that the feelings that I perceive in me are the same feelings that reside in you. The partners of a No Loss Relationship are not afraid of being whom God created. We see creation as it is. We do not judge creation.

If a relationship is in trouble and changing form out of anger, resentment, or rejection, this change is occurring because the partners have learned how to reinforce differences. The partners have made those differences real as if they represent the truth. Each partner has decided to be right and values his or her difference so much that each partner wants to make the other partner feel guilty for not thinking the same way. Choosing to heal is the way to change our mind about these differences so that the unity of love can be restored.

We seek healing because we no longer want to live with our differences, and we some-how realize the cost of retaining our differences. There is no difference that happiness can't correct if we are willing to forgive. We can enjoy any difference if we perceive it correctly. If we call someone "wrong" or "evil" because of a perceived difference, then we are refus-ing to forgive. With this refusal, we are choosing to prove how separation can protect us and how war wins over love. The partners of a No Loss Relationship do not view the act of giving up differences as a loss.

Complete the exercises for this chapter in Chapter 10.

CHAPTER 6

BODY OR ENERGY

Since all intimate relationships start off as special, we must admit that we are mostly attracted to the physical body or parts of it. We may be attracted to part of the person's emotional temperament, but we are blind to most of it at first. If we are attracted primarily to someone's physical appearance, which is often experienced as "lust," then we will not be able to see his or her emotional body. In addition, we will not understand how to relate to it. Lust is limited to physical perception. As we become more involved with a partner, we become more inclined to look beyond his or her physical appearance.

Being connected physically is not love. We can hold hands, but that connection does not represent being joined. When we are extremely attracted to someone by reason of physical beauty, then we are not seeing a connection to his or her Spirit energy. We can never know the heart and soul of a partner if our attention stays on the perimeter of form. We may state that we like his or her personality, and we may like the excitement we feel when the person is near us. Yet, these feelings are not an indication that we are joining or truly relating to his or her use of energy.

We will have no choice but to destroy the relationship if we stay at this level because our thoughts will always be focused on judging his or her behavior and the words he or she speaks. We will never get to the cause or the source of the feelings and behaviors that need to be healed within yourself.

We end relationships because, on some level, we can't live in the disease of not joining. Bodies never join and personalities never join. If joining at the level of the body or the personality is the focus of our relationship, then we will never feel satisfied. If the purpose of a Holy Relationship is to experience Oneness, then an unholy relationship is based on not joining and making form real, which is the same as making separation real. Within the unholy relationship, we will then be living in a constant state of emotional fear.

A major reason that partners in most relationships don't stay together is that each person is relating only to the behavior and ignoring the feelings that occur within his or her partner's emotional body. Transcendence teaches us to move through the physical body to see the emotional body; we must also move through the emotional body to see the mental body and beyond the mental body is the real essence that is our partner. We can't move to the emotional body of our partner if we remain at the level of lust. We can't move to the mental body if we deny the feelings of our partner. If we project our feelings onto our partner, then we are not able to correct the judgmental perception that is occurring within our mental body. It is not until we are able to arrive at a true perception of our mental images that we can know holiness. Each level of being is like a veil that hides or blocks our essence.

Our Lower, Second Brain

The main purpose of a Holy Relationship is to shift the focus away from the physical, and more towards the spiritual. We must learn to join and relate to each other while we are in these bodies. This learning process can be the most difficult and confusing part of becoming one. Partners will develop an emotional understanding when they move into a desire for a higher level of involvement, which becomes apparent when there is a willingness to learn how to heal together.

The judgmental or emotional body is less dense than the physical body and resides within our second brain, which is also known as the lower brain. Brain cells extend throughout the whole body. These cells can reflect stored memories. The lower brain is made up of cells that hold thought and expand throughout a network of nerves that run through our spine and stomach. Nerve cells are very similar to brain cells in that they reflect thought or store thought. Every cell has intelligence and there are many types of memories stored within our cells.

Personal experience constitutes one type of memory; institutional responses are another. Autonomic memories direct the autonomic nervous system to maintain the proper functioning of the body, which we also refer to as health. We also have soul memories. These combined memories are the reason that each of us is unique as individuals, yet the same as one Self. Few people are able to relate to their emotional self correctly and few people are able to understand the capacity of their second brain. We often refer to it as "intuition" or "a gut feeling," but we seldom listen to it. Those who perceive themselves to be very intellectual are likely ignoring the activity that occurs within their emotional brain.

Every person has an emotional body that is within the physical body. Emotion is energy moving. Energy moves in response to judgmental thoughts. Every person has energy moving within and throughout the physical body. Emotions are like the waves on the surface of the ocean. Sometimes the ocean can be very stormy and other times it can be only slightly wavy. Think of your relationship as a boat from which you and your partner navigate the emotional sea of life. Before emotion, there was stillness. Stillness is like a lake, calm as glass. Stillness is experienced when all thoughts are non-judgmental. What would an experience be without any judgment? Peace.

Within every relationship, you experience stimulation, which results in some type of emotional response. Emotions determine our temperament, which then establishes our tolerance for one another. We make decisions to judge perceptions as valuable or invaluable, good or bad, and right or wrong, which constitute our ability to relate harmoniously with each partner.

True intimacy requires connecting with the emotional body and with the mind, and then reaching for the soul and being one with the pure Self. True intimacy has little to do with liking the same things or looking good. True intimacy has nothing to do with controlling a partner's emotions or finding him or her unacceptable. True intimacy requires that you understand healing through the act of supporting each other in order to achieve the healing that is needed.

Share feelings first and be willing to see the relationship as a vehicle for healing. Communication is for healing only. Notice the mind that chooses illusions of communication. Don't hold grievances. Practice forgiveness by not attacking your partner for his or her admitted faults. Admit errors but don't seek them out. Create a safe space for sharing and healing.

Your feelings are the key to healing. For many generations people have been very confused about how to understand feelings. When you listen to the Ego, you will experience a range of different feelings, yet when you listen to the Holy Spirit you feel only true joy. Your true Self always feels the attributes of Spirit, love, peace, and bliss in Light.

One purpose for a Holy Relationship is to heal the emotional body. It's difficult to feel safe to show your emotions until you are in a relationship with a person in whom you can trust. The act of falling in love may seem to make it safe for you to share your innermost thoughts. Within this sense of safety, you may release your restraints a little and show the hidden side of yourself. Every person has a hidden Self that is hidden because it is perceived as the cause of some pain. A healing relationship is the vehicle to bring that Self to the surface and cast light and joy upon it. It is the act of looking upon it which facilities the healing. The response from the healed Self is one of joy. It is unreasonable to think that the act of falling in love is an indication that you do not have issues that need to be addressed. Regardless of the amount of compatibility you feel at the beginning of the relationship, another stage will evolve which will include the process of healing the emotional body. Every person's emotional body is out of harmony. We have not yet learned how to avoid the onset of the imbalance of the emotional body.

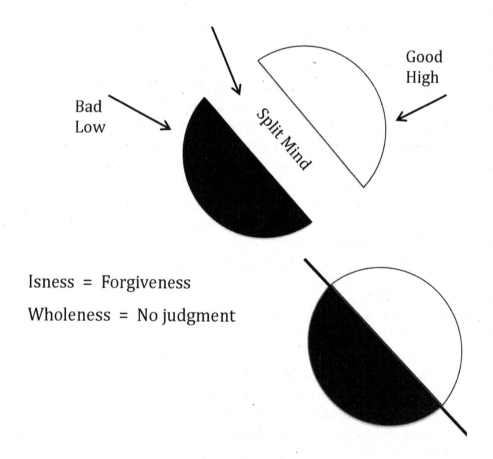

To heal an emotional wound, you must bring back together the thought that was split. Feelings are doorways to the past. The past memories, which hold suppressed emotions, are the cause of every person's problems. In the present there never is a problem. If you could stay in the present without judgment, then you would never experience a conflict over anything. The reason that you are unable to stay in the now moment is because your emotions are blocked.

You can't have a positive without a negative or a good without a bad. When you have one part of a judgment, then you must have the other part. Healing with joy takes away the judgment and helps you to bring the good back into bad and the bad back into good. Regardless of the nature of the event that you have experienced, that event has a judgment attached to it; therefore that event needs to be healed. You have thousands upon thousands of these memories storied in your Ego mind. Most of these memories are hidden in the unconscious Self. You are unaware of them until another event or person stimulates your awareness of them.

The judgmental memory thought has an electromagnetic charge, and this charge is referred to as feelings. Some charges have a lot of energy behind them. When you get very angry or very sad it is because a high amount of energy is attached to a particular memory. By getting in touch with the feeling, you are building a path of communication with un-healed thoughts from your past. Learning how to release the energy charge from those memories is a lost art. You were probably taught by your parents, peers, and teachers to control your feelings or suppress them. Few people know how to release feelings to the Whole. Few people know how to invite pure joy into a past memory. When the energy is released properly as opposed to being projected or suppressed, the thought that was split in the past is able to come together naturally. When both sides of a judgment have been accepted, an inner peace prevails.

No thought that you have of the past is neutral; some degree of electromagnetic charge exists. It wouldn't be considered a past event unless you had placed some judgment to the thought.

Sharing Feelings

To begin sharing your feelings with your partner appropriately, start the process by choosing to take ownership of your own feelings as opposed to projecting them onto your partner. Allow your partner to own his or her own feelings as well. Be very careful not to tell your partner how he or she should feel. Correction of an error in a thought system can only occur within the mind of the person who is experiencing the feeling that may need to be healed.

Sharing feelings means that you feel them without analyzing the situation. Begin the process of sharing with the statement "I feel _____." where the adjective used is only one or two words.

Then, take some time to be with this feeling. Tune into your body and notice sensations that are just within the body awareness. Tightness, heaviness, color, shape, and images can all be used to describe a feeling. Feelings are not understood in language but language points to them. When a person uses many words to describe a feeling, then he or she is often choosing to avoid a feeling.

Notice the sensations of the body while you are sharing your feelings.
Anger causes_____ (e.g.: my jaw to tighten).
Sadness and Depression make my _____ (stomach) feel _____ (nauseous).

This sadness makes me think of _____.

People who avoid the sensations of the body will often become sick or contract a major illness such as cancer, arthritis, kidney issues, etc. Emotional disease can be the cause of physical health problems along with being the cau se of a relationship break up.

If you choose to skip the emotional effects and resort only to your mental reasoning or intellectual explanations regarding a conflict that you and your partner are discussing, then you will never be able to address the real cause and you will not solve the problem.

A woman will often coerce a man to talk about his feelings. Even though a man will often oblige and talk for several minutes, he may not be identifying his feelings unless he is attentive to his emotional body. The head thinks, the heart feels, and both the head and heart are responding to memories.

The manner in which you currently express your feelings is likely based on behaviors learned from past experiences or from other people. You have also developed a strategy for dealing with other people's feelings. Your partner has learned his or her behaviors from the past as well. Partners who are communicating within a healthy relationship that is undergoing a healing process are willing to admit that learned behaviors may differ and there are no expectations for a partner to deal with emotions in a specific manner. Partners involved in a No Loss Relationship learn to adopt the correct method of using the Holy Spirit. Communication is for the purpose of healing. Developing a safe space to explore feelings will set the foundation to allow more intimacy and honesty into the relationship.

The Holy Spirit knows how to balance the energy if you will give the feelings to the Whole. Your part is to learn to release your attachment to learned behaviors and to honestly admit that you are looking for a higher way. As both you and your partner learn to trust the process of true sharing, then you will understand how important it is to openly discuss feelings and the past events on which they are connected. The value of admitting any past perceptions and judgments will become more apparent. At this point, the person sharing his or her feelings may feel very vulnerable. As his or her partner, you don't want to judge, advice, or correct your partner's behaviors or thoughts in any way.

Study the illusions of communication and you will learn how your behaviors can affect your partner's healing process through the addition or reduction of energy. You and your partner can take turns. When it is your turn to feel, then really feel, and when it is your turn to be a good listener, be great at it.

How do we make the best use of emotional energy?

The most beneficial methods of utilizing our emotional energy occur when we share feelings without judgment, balance our feelings, open our minds to new insights, learn the value of being still, and allow ourselves to receive guidance from our higher Self. The universe abhors a vacuum and will fill any void if you allow it. In our minds, we have convinced ourselves that we are more comfortable with lack than with having it all. We have convinced ourselves that stealing a little is better than having it all. We think that by demanding something from another person, we will get our share. Most people are unaware of how energy is received, so they live in a cycle of repeating the mistakes they learned from their childhoods and old patterns of unworthiness.

Learn to schedule healing sessions with your partner to discuss issues and share feelings instead of choosing to hold onto beliefs regarding your upsets and grievances. The past is gone. When your partner shares as a form of releasing very strong feelings, then the most helpful response you can provide is to be still and to direct your mind as well as your partner's mind to the Holy Spirit. This response, which is an act of forgiveness, will allow a higher mind to clear the past and correct the feelings for you. The healing session is not about solving a problem. It is about dissolving a judgment. This initiative is very important work. When you have learned how to support your partner without offering corrections or judgments, then your relationship has reached a major milestone in the task of becoming One

If you experience a situation during a healing session where you respond with an outburst of emotions, then this response is an indication that you are reacting to a grievance that you have held for a long time, and you can no longer contain the energy that needs to be released. As partners progress in their abilities to trust and share for the purpose of healing, they learn that holding on to emotional thoughts only hurts the person who holds them by robbing him or her of the joy that could be experienced through the act of healing. Most people hold on to their judgments because they never learned how easy it is to release them. Releasing is joy; holding is pain. Which would you rather have? You developed a behavior to hold onto your perceptions because you learned that it was improper to express feelings, and because you began to associate the act of releasing feelings as a weakness. Hence, recall the statement, "Men don't cry."

The act of releasing energy to the Holy Spirit can be audible or silent. Spirit will teach you how to release in any situation, and under its guidance, you will know which method is appropriate. If you were in a relationship with a supportive and safe partner who knows how to be helpful, then why would you want to release emotional energy any other way? If you have reason to believe that this process would frighten someone who is unfamiliar with releasing feelings, then choosing the methods of releasing silently or releasing through inner visualizations can work wonders for this endeavor.

The relationship is for healing and for providing opportunities for new insights. Changing your method for sharing feelings will strengthen the healing process. When you take an honest approach to identifying and addressing your grievances, then this effort is an indication that you are more interested in undoing your grievances than holding on to them. Be a leader by laughing at your mistaken perceptions instead of choosing to feel guilty for having them. Allow your partner to have as many healing sessions as possible, and do not set any expectations on your partner's pace, time frame, or rate of progress on his or her healing process. Give your partner the gift of undoing any fears that may arise at any moment. Encourage your partner on his or her healing process knowing that each release for him or her is also your release as well. There is no need to pretend that you don't have judgments or errors any longer.

It has been asked, "Isn't it possible for the partners in a relationship to do too much processing and working on the problems?" I have heard many a man say, "This relationship is too heavy and too intense. Leave me alone and let's just watch television." Remember that anything done with the Holy Spirit is fun and very rewarding. Healing done by the Ego's thought system is a drag, and the false accomplishments result in no desire to continue healing. If you are not experiencing the rewards, and you feel inundated with too much self-examination, then review your process and confirm that healing is coming from the Holy Spirit.

If your relationship is falling apart, then nothing is more important than healing, certainly not another rerun on television. Television is our Ego's finest tool for maintaining avoidance and numbness. If you feel safe within the healing space, understand the importance of healing, trust the sharing process, and recognize your partner as being truly supportive. Then when you need to be healed, healing will be given. Beyond healing, you and your holy partner will leap into creating happy dreams.

As you practice sharing and communicating, you will find that with each day, you become happier and happier. There is nothing greater than the experience of forgiveness in a relationship that understands its meaning.

A No Loss Relationship is fearless in what looks upon from within and without because it understands that all events and situations will be healed, and patterns changed from fear to love. In a No Loss Relationship emotions are your friend, and you do not take them out on your partner. Emotions are your teachers, who point the way to intuition of how to heal what was judged from the past. Those that can master their emotions together stay in love.

Wide Ranges of Emotion

All human beings have access to the same range of feelings; therefore we are all capable of experiencing the feelings that reside within that established range. This range of feelings has limits, just like our eyes have a limited range of view, and our body has a limited temperature range for survival. When we are experiencing emotional pain, which is an indication that we have extended beyond the comfort level within our range of feelings, our ability to communicate effectively may be impaired. If we fail to recognize how feelings can affect our ability to communicate, then we will miss the opportunity to provide healing. Our feelings, if understood, will provide a pathway to address unhealed events. Events that have been judged, improperly perceived, and discarded into the realms of darkness need our healing love. When we choose to deny or to dissociate from our own feelings or from our partner's feelings, then we will fail to see the issues at hand, and this choice removes us from our ability to serve in our purpose as healers.

The Ego mind produces emotions that range from rage to sadness. Emotions that are produced by the Ego mind are called fear. Fear is much like a pendulum that swings from the side to side. One side is rage or madness, and the opposite side is sadness or depression. Each point along this pendulum of emotion represents a volume level. For example, the point closest to the center on the side of madness can be expressed with a seemingly low intensity of "I am a little upset," and the point that is furthest from the center represents a seemingly high intensity of "I am in full anger rage."

On the sadness side of the pendulum, the seemingly low intensity may be expressed as "I am a little disappointed," and a seemingly high intensity may be expressed, as "I am very depressed." If we express a lot of energy through the Ego, then we are functioning at the extreme intensity level on one side, either depression or rage. We control the intensity. We control the direction of our energy. We choose whether to listen to the Ego and react along the pendulum of fear, or to listen to the Holy Spirit and react with love while remaining centered.

The problem is not that we have an Ego. The existence of the Ego is a fact. The problem occurs when we allow the Ego to project its beliefs onto our partner. The problem is not that we feel anger or sorrow, but that we choose to project those feelings onto another person in an effort to rid ourselves of the stress we experience when we have those feelings. The projection may seem to produce temporary release, but the Ego has deceived itself into believing that it has ended the stress and conflict. We must learn that accusing another person of our emotional pain is a method of projection, and it does not resolve the stress and conflict.

When we react to a situation with physical violence, then we have chosen to listen to the Ego mind, and it has gained control of our body. People who respond to a situation by physically acting out their inner rage are functioning at the mercy of their Ego. The insane belief that physically controlling a partner into obedience will produce love is a false use of power. The reason that the Ego wants to destroy our partners and us is that the Ego's beliefs are not eternal.

Those who repress their own feelings or blame another person for their own feelings are falsely dealing with their own events from the past and are making those events more fearful than the events would have been had they been addressed directly. When we avoid addressing our feelings for the purpose of healing them, then we not only postpone the pain, but we also believe that we are reducing that pain by passing it onto another person.

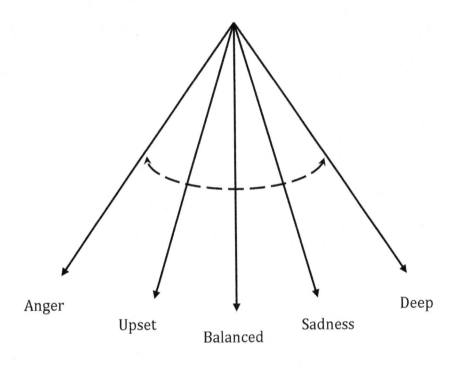

Anger   Deep

Upset   Sadness

Balanced

EMOTIONAL SWINGING BACK AND FORTH CAUSES DISHARMONY

Feelings such as sadness and anger may be perceived as very unacceptable to one person yet is very normal to another person. When a person perceives these feelings as normal, then he or she is also likely to perceive these feelings as a necessary component to the validation of his or her own existence. There are many ways in which we have learned to improperly deal with our own feelings.

While one method of expressing feelings may be considered normal within one relationship, that same method may be considered unbearable within another relationship. The varying views of a method for emotional expression may sometimes be based on cultural differences. For example, Italians and Spaniards may have a tendency to be very loud and boisterous when expressing their emotions. If a person does not share this method of expressing emotions, then he or she might feel uncomfortable when participating in a conversation.

To simplify our ability to address the wide range of possible feelings, they are defined below and numbered on a scale from 0 to 10. This scale provides us with a method for measuring our feelings. While we may be able to verbalize our feelings with the appropriate words, we may not always be able to adequately express the intensity of our feelings with those words. This scale is designed to assist us with matching words and emotional intensity.

The Range of Feelings

0 = stillness, death.
Absolute 0 represents an awareness of infinity in the direction of fear and could be described as a snake biting its own tail.
1 = indifference, numbness, avoidance, and fear.
A denial of emotions or stuck in darkness.
2 = depression.
Sluggish to no movement.
3 = uncertainty, doubt, indecisiveness.
Slight mental activity with no action.
4 = sadness, deep to mild.
Movement in the emotional body, crying pains.
5a = defenses: guilt, shame, blame.
Physical avoiding to hiding or self-protection.
5b = attacks, anger.
Small upsets to rage, physical activity begins to express itself.
6 = pleasure and/or pain, self-gratifying sensations.
Felt in the emotional and physical body.
7 = acceptance and gratitude.
8 = happiness.
Humor to pure joy.
9 = love, bliss.
10 = divine awareness, cosmic consciousness.

Absolute 10 represents an awareness of infinity in the direction of love.
Most psychologists have very elaborate systems for diagnosing clients. However, this method is simple and doesn't "label" someone, for we are only interested in healing. Emotional wellness means that a person is operating within the range of 7, 8, or 9. When a person is considered to be "coping with a situation," he or she is operating within the range of 6 or 7.

When a person is experiencing any dysfunctional emotions, which correlate to darkness, he or she is operating within the range from 5 to 1. The absolute rates of 0 and 10 are outside the possible range for the human experience. Within the human being's comprehension of infinity lies the inability to feel pure death or to know the absolute knowledge of God.

When we choose to communicate our emotions without placing blame onto our partner, then we are choosing to operate within the higher states on the scale. As human beings, we are entitled to feel our feelings because our feelings cannot exceed the range that God gave to us. Just as the limitation on our vision prevents our eyes from being able to see gamma rays, the limitation on our range of feelings prevents us from being able to experience feelings that would exceed this range.

When you use the scale above, you will become more aware of your feelings and the degree of tolerance in which you respond to your feelings. At the same time, you will become more aware of the degree of tolerance in which your partner responds to his or her own feelings. When recognizing feelings, it is important to consider not only the degrees of tolerance, but also the temperament of your responses to feelings.

For example, suppose a person is experiencing sadness at level 4 on the scale and he has a low tolerance for sadness. He may express his low tolerance level by responding with outbursts of crying and wailing. On the other hand, if his partner feels a high tolerance for sadness at the same level, then he or she may respond to his or her own sadness by just displaying a frown or becoming very quiet. Outer expressions may differ, but the awareness of the need to heal those feelings is the same. A person may be described as either mildly depressed or severely depressed, but in an absolute sense all depression is the same. The manner in which a person expresses anger or sadness does not change the level at which he or she is operating on the scale. When it comes to healing, a person is still addressing a fear whether the symptom is rage or mild irritation.

The concept to understand is that a person who has a high tolerance for anger is not any more healed than a person who has a low tolerance for anger. In other words, a person who responds to feelings of anger with just a frown has not healed his or her deep-rooted fear any more than a person who responds to feelings of anger with ranting and raving. The frowning person may seem to have things more "together," but he or she is operating at the same level on the scale and simply masking the feelings that a person with low tolerance would actually express when responding to anger. Only the Holy Spirit does the healing, and our relationships serve as the vessels for that healing to occur. When our fear is blocking our willingness to heal, then we need to recognize our response as a lesson and a call for healing.

Every level on the scale represents an array of responses that are based on low-to-high rates of tolerance. Our tolerance, our temperament, and our method of dealing with feelings determine our ability to accept our feelings without apprehension. We are very individualized in our tolerances, and we have a special attraction to certain feelings that we perceive as desirable. Healing requires that we take responsibility for what we feel and how we express what we feel. We need to honor our own free will as well as the free wills of other people when we choose methods for expressing feelings. No one just "gets" angry without a reason. When we feel angry, we are responding to a belief that something outside of our self has caused us to feel angry. When we choose to place the responsibility for our feelings outside our self instead of taking the responsibility our self, then we essentially perceive our self as a victim.

When we consistently operate at the lower levels of the scale, then we become increasingly imprisoned in the Ego thought system, and it is easy to become locked into a behavioral response that is based on a particular level of high or low tolerance. Even though this behavior is based on the insanity of the Ego thought system, we begin to perceive it as acceptable behavior not only for us, but also for anyone else. When we operate at the higher levels of Light, then we are free.

When we say things like, "I just can't stand to see you cry," or, "don't get angry with me," then we are essentially saying, "Stop feeling that sadness or anger because I have a low tolerance for the feeling that you are expressing." We are attempting to take away the free will that this person has to express his or her feelings in the manner of his or her choosing.

On the other side of the coin, when we are more accustomed to expressing our feelings outward, then we may find it difficult to accept a person who represses or hides his or her feelings. This inward path of expressing feelings is often apparent in people who may also be described as introverted, shy, and self-critical. They tend to deny their feelings or bury their feelings inside themselves.

Whether we choose to direct the expression of our feelings inside or outside of ourselves, neither choice will allow us to address the need to heal our inner fear. When we choose to balance the expressions of our feelings, then we can begin to heal.

The more we choose to identify with the feelings that are expressed by our partner, the greater power we generate for healing. Defining our feelings through the range of feelings scale and identifying our tolerance level will allow US to practice the act of balancing our expressions of our feelings. The goal of healing is always the same: to teach yourself that nothing can harm you.

When we choose against the perception that another person's expressions of feelings is an attack, then we are promoting healing. While this choice in perception may seem easier said than done, it is a major factor in our ability to help another person heal. When we operate from the Ego thought system and interpret a person's expression of a feeling as an attack, then we are quick to react with our own feelings, and we often believe that it is our mission to change how the person feels. The partners who become involved in this "attack and defend" interaction within a relationship are focused on playing a Ping-Pong game or a hot bomb game where the interest lies in defining one person as the opponent or the enemy. This game often becomes very intense. The "attack and defend" game can be very explosive and destructive. When one of the partners recognizes that this game is taking place, then you can pray for help. You can pray in order to ask for ways to be supportive.

When we use the scale to help us understand our feelings, then we can choose a higher level on the scale in order to communicate at a critical moment. If I knew, for example, that my partner tends to react with a low tolerance for anger (5b) and is often very verbal, then I could choose to respond in my usual defensive method by becoming sad (4) and having a high tolerance by saying nothing and burying my feelings inward. Or I could choose to remember that my partner and I really want the same result, which is peace (8).

In a Holy Relationship, partners make agreements to become more conscious of their inter actions to recognize the games that might be played and to learn how to end those games as quickly as possible. Strategies are developed that will help to resolve the game if it gets out of control. Asking for help from the Holy Spirit is the only defense that will result in a positive effect for both partners. When partners take an active role in listening to each other, then this choice can often serve as the key to ending the conflict.

When the feelings of partners are not in harmony, then each partner can take this opportunity to expand his or her feelings beyond a self-imposed limit. Any uncomfortable feelings that arise, like wanting one person to stop crying, is an indication that a limit has been imposed on the expression of a feeling, and a fixed tolerance level is impairing a person's ability to respond at a higher level on the range of feelings scale. This experience of uncomfortable feelings becomes the tool that will allow both partners to expand and grow beyond the limitations of that condition.

Temperament

Each level on the Range of Feelings scale can be further defined by tolerance. The tolerance levels are high, coping (neutral status), and low. This scale may list words to describe each of these levels, but it is important to be able to reference them as high, coping, or low so we can chart our awareness of our need to heal.

1 = Indifference, numbness, avoidance and fear
High = unaware of the fear, the numbness seems normal, spends lots of time feeling alone and distant from others, always separate.
Coping = aware of the fear, hiding but doing little about problems or causes, avoiding communicating or sharing, denial of effects of problems.
Low = trouble admitting feelings but still taking minor actions, others can tell that he or she is avoiding dealing with issues at hand.

2 = Depression
High = staying depressed for months, not dealing with daily issues.
Coping = aware of being depressed but not seeking help and little is changing.
Low = getting medication and advice but not practicing much of what they are being told to do.

3 = Uncertainty, doubt, indecisiveness
High = no goals, no purpose, no spiritual practices.
Coping = doubting sometimes, hoping but procrastinating, stalling, indecisive.
Low = asking for advice but often from the wrong sources, making choices but not following through. Little to no risk taking.

4 = Sadness: deep to mild
High = holds sadness in and doesn't let others see it, cries often, deeply saddened by many perceived losses.
Coping = expressing sadness to loved ones but not resolving the cause of it, not finding forgiveness.
Low = mildly sad, frowning, pouting, or denying the feeling of sadness.
5a = Defenses: guilt, shame, blame
High = very protective of self and others, feels lots of shame or guilt.
Coping = argumentative or stays in small groups that share beliefs and opinions.
Low = blames partner to make him or her "wrong," holds onto defenses but keeps them more to him or herself.
5b = Attacks: anger, small upsets to rage
High = expresses opinions easily and often, keeps an appearance of being mildly upset or

holds anger, can be self-critical.
Coping = expresses anger with self-justification.
Low = unhappy with feelings, ashamed but seeking help while looking for correct methods to deal with the emotions.

6 = Pleasure/pain, self-gratifying sensations
High = addictive behavior to wanting to be punished.
Coping = finding balance in both pleasure and pain.
Low = looking for new ways to find pleasure (spiritual methods) and learning to source the true causes of pain.

7 = Acceptance and gratitude
Low = practicing more and more.
Coping = finding more reasons to be grateful and forgiving.
High = singing, praising, practicing being in the Is-ness often.

8 = Happiness/humor to pure joy
Low = humor, laughter, joking.
Coping = enjoying both inner and outer joy.
High = constantly happy, unperturbed by things or people.

9 = Love, bliss
Low = glimpses of bliss, deep meditations, brief moments of revelation.
Coping = glimpses of bliss happen more and more, longer periods of uninterrupted peace.
High = awareness of always being One with God; enlightenment.

Notice that the order is High to Low for levels 1 through 6, and the order is Low to High for levels 7 through 9. This difference in the order is due to the change at level 7, which represents a shift from darkness to Light. When moving through the darkness levels of 1 through 6, a person's healing process would progress from a higher darkness to a lower darkness level on the chart, yet once the person has shifted to the Light levels of 7 through 9, his or her healing process would progress from a lower Light to a higher Light level. For example, when you are at the lowest level of depression, you are about to leap to the next level, which is (3) uncertainty. Our goal is to transcend the lower levels of darkness completely.

In Chapter 10 is the chart that will help you track your feelings and your partner's feelings. The task of documenting feelings needs to be a joint effort. Share your thoughts about each other's feelings, but be careful not to chart a partner's feelings on his or her behalf. Remember that it is not under your authority to define how your partner feels or to experience his or her feelings for the purpose of healing them. Thank goodness!

At first, the task of charting feelings is difficult and most people will notice feelings of resistance and avoidance, but the effects of perseverance are worth the effort. When the partners of a relationship are experiencing trouble with communication, such as not sharing ideas lovingly, openly, and without judgment, then they must admit that their feelings are out of harmony, which blocks their CO-creative process. The reason that most couples lose the feeling of being in love is because the lower, or dark side, of their personalities takes on an active role in the relationship. Most couples respond to this dark side either by unsuccessfully trying to cope or by unsuccessfully dealing with each partner's feelings. Through the practice of charting feelings, partners can begin to learn where they are in the healing process, and they can follow guidance to direct them to where they want to be.

We must be gentle with ourselves. Someone who has been in depression for quite a while is not going to leap into level 8 and remain in a high awareness of that level overnight. In the absolute sense of a miracle, we have no resistance to healing, but the concept of being happy all the time can seem quite frightening when we are accustomed to our darkness. Loving someone is often about being willing to go through the process of healing and accepting the time and effort it may take. The process certainly gets easier if we have the correct methods and the help of our Holy Mind.

We must be careful not to label a partner based on his or her feelings or to use the marks on our chart in a negative manner. We don't want to limit our partner or refer to him or her with a name that implies a negative perception. We don't want to give meaning or assure our righteousness as to where we are in relationship to one another. We need to learn to look honestly at our position on the chart and choose to move to a lighter level with the help of our inner teacher.

When we approach the task of charting our feelings as healers, then we are not afraid to acknowledge our position on the chart, and we honor our partners for their positions on the chart. We also know that our partners may be our teachers at any time, and they will honor our positions on the chart. As healers, both partners know that any level of darkness does not limit their healing process. They can practice the feelings of not fearing the darkness by not judging or condemning any person's position on the chart.

When utilizing the chart during a conversation, for example, you could say, "I notice that in my awareness you seem to be expressing a low tolerance for sadness." Your partner could reply with either, "I agree," or, "No I feel that I am at a high tolerance of defensiveness," or whatever statement would explain his or her feelings at that moment. This framework of charting provides you and your partner with a starting point for relating to each other without placing blame.

In a Holy Relationship, couples are not afraid to share their feelings. The partners of a special relationship have little to no understanding of how to deal with each other. Once the initial strictly romantic stage has somewhat dissolved and disharmonies begin to arise, the partners' only recourse for interaction is to act out the dysfunctional patterns that were learned during previous relationships. We know by now that every special relationship must transform or it will die.

Partners that spend time together healing their emotions will find they enjoy the process of experiencing each other's temperaments. Couples who notice that they are making progress and finding ways to move out of the darkness become much more tolerant of each other.

It is only when we have a negative views of being stuck, or when we believe that our partner will remain limited, do we give up on our partner. Each time we choose to grow and improve our understanding of feelings, we are strengthening the bonds of intimacy. Real intimacy must pass through the physical and heal the emotions. You and your partner will enjoy a happy learning experience.

The partners of a No Loss Relationship heal together knowing that when a healing occurs, both partners become lifted. Within the connection of a No Loss Relationship, no limits are placed on the expression of feelings and partners share a desire to support each other in efforts to reach for Light. A No Loss Relationship means that the partners experience no difficulty in dealing with feelings, and there is no need for one partner to control the other partner. Control is given to the Holy Spirit.

Manifestation of Ego Defects:

1. Trust
Lack of taking responsibility for situations.
Extreme planning.
Indecisiveness.
Anger toward someone or higher Spirit.

2. Honesty
Dishonesty, cover-ups.
Shutting out others.
Failure to admit faults.

3. Tolerance
Perfectionism.
People pleasing.
Tolerating sexual abuse or loss of personal morality.

4. Gentleness
Expressing feelings explosively.
Incorrect expression of anger.
Wanting the other to change.

5. Joy
Lack of passion or commitment.
Physical or mental illness.

6. Defenselessness
Embarrassment.
Inappropriate social behavior.

7. Generosity
Helplessness.
Envy.
Inadequate or unfulfilled sex life.
Financial problems.
Irresponsibility.

8. Patience
Controlling the reality of others.
Score keeping.
Arguing about facts.

9. Faithfulness
Self-centeredness.
Making others special or more equipped to make decisions for you.

10. Open-mindedness
Jealousy.
Wanting someone who has your value system.

Grievances

A grievance can be defined as any moment when we are not feeling a sense of peace, and the thoughts in our mind are focused on a sense of lack or an inability to exist attentively within the present moment. When we hold on to upsets or any negative beliefs regarding an event, then we will experience emotional pain, which we will either suppress or project onto another person. It is very acceptable to say, "I have a grievance," followed by "Help, Holy Spirit." The call for help is the correct way to instigate a healing.

Grievances come from the thought system of the lower mind. They show you the imbalances that reside within the emotional body. Watch for them and admit them. Do not minimize them, analyze them, or deny that you have them. Recognizing and addressing grievances requires an effort to constantly observe your behavior for indications that your Ego thought system is directing you on a path to anger or sadness.

Your decision to hold grievances means that you are choosing to believe in your judgment regarding an event in which you perceive that you experienced a loss. You are choosing to keep the perception of loss locked in your mind. When you choose to hold grievances, then you are also choosing against bringing them to the healing Light within. A willingness to see a different view of the grievance will clear the way for Spirit to enter. Sharing any new perceptions and admitting the faults of your Ego are acts of honest expression that are never threatening to the partners involved in a Holy Relationship.

The concept that we most desire to learn in our Holy Relationship is that we are not separate, and that whatever happens in physical form happens not by chance or accident but by an order of thoughts from a mind that is whole.

The R's: Right Relationship with Reality

Understanding the Atonement, Relax, Release, Reflect, and Reveal Revelation of that which is Real.

A Holy Relationship has as its purpose, the practice of being centered in the Atonement. The Atonement is your perfect, centered self with another perfect, centered self in the Absolute Reality of the one perfect Self. The real Self is revealed to those who are in the Atonement. Spirit desires to reveal itself as much as we desire to be with our Holy Relationship. To reveal means to show or to be known. Knowledge of Self is the major purpose of being in a Holy Relationship. Knowledge is not explained in words nor is it a concept or a perception about a thing or situation. True Knowledge is God Self and anyone on a path to Spirit is seeking to know, not perceive or think about.

The first **R is for Relax**. Relaxing is the key to start being ready to receive. If you are not relaxed you are tense in mind, emotions, and body. Tension becomes a problem, and the sign that the mind is locked in fear. Conflict is two opposing forces, and reality has only one causal force. The body follows the mind, and if the mind is locked in conflict and resistance to what is, no peace can be experienced. Peace is a great gift to any relationship that seeks it. Peace is necessary to receive divine qualities.

The first step to any meditation practice is to learn to relax. Yoga postures teach the body to relax through contemplative stretching. When you take time to relax the body, the mind goes in the direction of peace. Make learning to relax a priority in your relationship and enjoy relaxing together. Why is healthy sex valuable? Because the result is a relaxed union or a climax that releases tension.

Most of us need to start with relaxing the body because we are so body driven or outer driven in our doer self. If you are externally driven, learning to relax is relief.

The first step to become one with Spirit is to relax into now. If you are aware that you are in the future or the past or unaccepting this moment, you are out of the Atonement. Emotional balancing is peaceful as well and doesn't have highs or lows commonplace in drama-filled relationships. Relaxing emotionally is finding the balancing point of non-judgment. Being in past and future thinking processes is seen as mental stress and inner pain. Relaxing the mind is not holding onto mental beliefs which move you away from your center.

The second **R is the Release**. The moment you are truly relaxed you feel relief, or release, or a letting go of fear, or inner tightness, or pain called stress. We release in many ways what does not serve us, such as the carbon dioxide, the waste from our food, the sweat from our skin, tears from our sadness, or vomiting up poisons, or coughing or sneezing. Both physical and mental release is important to practice. Practice squeezing your hand, or any body part. Tighter, even a little tighter now, and now let go and release the pressure of gripping. Feel the release. Now hold a ball in your hand, squeeze it, then let the fingers relax and become very loose. Watch the ball release from your hand. Feel the release. Notice the tightness and then the release by your command. Practice this with all your body parts, tightening then releasing, then noticing the inner feelings of release. Mastering how to release is very helpful in a relationship. It's the core idea of 'not my way' but 'Let go and let God.' The Ego always wants to grip us in its controlling ways. The more uptight we are, the more the Ego wins and keeps us out of the Atonement. The mastery of letting go is releasing thoughts or giving them to Spirit.

Releasing feeling is taught throughout this material. Couples releasing together the unwanted feelings from the lower mind, cause the beginning shifts out of fear into love. Couples that release correctly together stay joined together. True releasing is sharing and produces some type of joining. Inner tension keeps us in conflict, and struggle blocks our CO-creative processes. Practice something as simple as breathing together, and be in the same breath process. Watch each other release the breath jointly.

Few understand that the emotional body and the mental body have their respective ways of releasing as well. These bodies need to release toxins as much as the physical body does. Emotional release is done with tones. Mental releasing is done with words or images through the imagination. All releasing requires understanding and power directed in the correct ways. Just as the physical body has holes for releasing, so do our inner bodies have openings where releasing can occur, which are called chakras. Blocked chakras occur because you have been holding grievances and dark thoughts within these inner bodies for quite some time.

Learning to release inner dark thoughts through the appropriate chakras is a part of the healing process learned in a Holy Relationship. Cleaning out the fear thoughts is called purification of the soul. Releasing is a blessing from Spirit, and inner wisdom from Holy Spirit will teach us if we're ready to be free of fear. In a No Loss Relationship, a couple constantly releases together, both physically, emotionally, and mentally, so that the adjustments from fear to love are achieved.

The third **R is Reflect**. Like the moon reflects sunlight, so does inner reflecting allowing us to see signs of Spirit. We see the reflections of what we think. We shine in darkness and in Light. We are mirrors of each other, and what is reflected off our souls is seen as perceptions of who we are, as well as glimpses of our true nature. Reflections show both the darkness and the Spirit. The moonlight shows us shadows and helps us see what is there. Only by recognizing what we are reflecting to each other can we admit and accept what thoughts are there. What is in the shadows is starting to be seen, be not afraid. Admitting reflections shows us our starting point, bringing us to the place of honesty and deepening of choice.

Recognizing the true Light starts with reflecting, or observing, and making choices of letting go and shifting to acceptance. The eyes reflect the physical, and the true mind, which we are learning to recognize, moves beyond the physical taking reflection from different levels of vibrations. The inner eye, your spiritual lens, is what reflects thoughts. Shifting to true perception is the goal of the Holy Spirit, who asks us to reflect on our understanding of what is real and what is not. We must learn to discern between illusions and what is true.

Fear images only have the power we give them. Snow melts with the heat of the sun, as darker images disappear by the brightness of Light. Illusion is seen through reflecting on the nature of the deceptions. What is not seen or understood is called "ignorance," and it keeps us in the dark. Be clear and present and still like glass.
Ask to see. Ask to see the reflections of each other's true self move us closer to Absolute Revelation.

If we never had a mirror, how would we see our face? So too if we never had feedback on a type of behavior, how would we know if its right or wrong? Reflecting on effects helps us see the causes as a way of starting the deepening process of knowing. Reflecting on our partner's strengths and weakness alike shows us how to support each other's growth. Reflecting has nothing to do with criticism or attacking behaviors, for the glass just reflects, never judges. Reflecting listening is a skill taught in current couples counseling as a way of really hearing our partner. Correct reflecting of issues causes us to move toward healing and the next step of revealing. Quietly reflecting with softness shows what is working and what is not.

We are seeking correction, not punishment. We are seeking Atonement, not fixing a problem. We are seeking to experience revelation.
The fourth **R is Reveal**. What is revealed to us by Spirit is called revelation, or sometimes called enlightenment. To bring Light or understanding to a person or situation is the Atonement. When we are attracted to someone we think we know them, and as the relationship progresses we find we know very little. If the relationship is devoted to holiness, true revealing of our partner is experienced.

What is shocking to most couples when the revealing starts to happen is they become shocked at what they find, and often this turns on the hate side of knowing or they hate what they find out. Hating or liking what we think we know about someone is the same. It is not true knowing or revealing. It is a perception of something being reflected in the Ego thought system. If we heal correctly then Revealing is from Spirit, but some revealing can be of the Ego at first, which is meant for purification of thought. Revealing fearful thoughts or seeing deeper into lower mind thinking is part of the purpose of a relationship, so keep asking for healing.

By the content and energy of the revealing and true reflecting can we see the quality of knowledge we seek. Karma is the idea of cause and effect, not good or bad.

Revealing is not always pleasant as we face karma or causes that exist in our soul and that of our partner's. But remember, it is by owning and looking deeper into our very self that we reach its center. Just like unpleasant dreams can frighten a child or scary movies can be believable, our inner revealing can show us dark thoughts. It's not all wonderful images within, but we are not alone and can be helped by Holy Spirit. Thus, we may need to return to the beginning of relaxing, and releasing, and reflection on what is real. Mini cycles of processing are like a washing machine that spins out the dirt and cleans the thoughts.

God revelations do occur and are certain to be experienced when forgiveness is complete. When we both have mastered forgiveness and released the Ego thoughts by reflecting Light in the darkness that we are both resting in the Atonement and feeling true love. Then Spirit is welcomed, and God revelation is received. You know you know. You are knowledge. The Absolute Self is present. God speaks or shares knowledge of Self to Self. You both have arrived together, and your relationship is blessed and holy.

There is no greater experience on earth than a Holy Relationship where two walk as one. Whatever they ask for is given, and all they create is manifested for the glory of the all. Their souls are bonded for all eternity, and in eternity are they now.

A No Loss Relationship couple practices the R's with each other regularly and repeatedly. They respect and revere each other for the purpose of revelations.

The final **R is Remember**. We are here only to remember our true nature.
Each day, each hour, each now moment calls for us to remember who we are as God created us and express our divine revelations. Each sharing is an act of Love. Always remember our partner who agreed to walk with us.

A No Loss Relationship is the relationship that remembers there is no lack because of the Atonement. The Atonement is the answer for all problems and will correct all misperceptions of fear, lack, or death. The Atonement shows us the no death state of mind.

A No Loss Relationship shouts, "There is no death."

Remember what is Real.

Complete the exercises for this chapter in Chapter 10

CHAPTER 7

ENERGY IS EVERYWHERE

Three Types of Energy

Energy can be categorized into three types. The first type we call darkness. The second is action. The third is Light.

Energy that becomes dark is fear-based. It is dense and lethargic. People who have allowed their energies to become dark will experience symptoms of laziness, procrastination, depression, doubt, uncertainty, and fear. Dark energy is like having heavy weights all over your body. This dark energy comes from soul karma and the act of constantly judging life. The second type, action, is lighter and promotes action and self-expression. When energy moves, form follows. Highly energetic people, people with bubbly personalities, and people who seem to be on the go have high-active energy. Active energy can come from not taking life seriously or from not being self-conscious. "A" type personalities run businesses, run families, and remain very active in community events.

Type three is luminous in nature and it is the energy of inspiration and divine realization. All religious teachers and people who practice prayer and meditation tap into this type of energy. This energy is untouched by human experience and it is pure and free of judgment. Learning to understand the three types of energy will allow you to make choices regarding the type of energy you want to experience and cultivate. Once you have learned how to recognize the energy types, you want to support each other in efforts to choose Light and to avoid being stuck in darkness. Action energy is required to move you out of darkness. To experience luminous energy, you simply need to meditate and contemplate it. Ask and you shall receive the energy you most desire to experience.

Energy is everywhere. It is totally available to us in unlimited amounts. You are the only one who deprives yourself of it. You block yourself from it, and you attempt to implement false methods of obtaining it. You deplete your reserves and drain your tanks. The word "tired" is simply a term for "running low on energy." You fill up your gas tank when it says "empty," yet you seldom fill up your Spirit-body when it feels depleted.

Only the pure mind can join and experience Oneness. When the partners within a relationship never reach joining, then they will begin to experience pain and discomfort, which will eventually lead to divorce. The prefix "dis" means, "Two kept apart." Remember that the emotion of fear will keep you and your partner apart, split, and different. You cannot correct fear with more fear. Splitting the mind more doesn't cause joining. By admitting that a split has occurred and addressing its cause, you allow the mind to look for connections. You connect by recognizing that you are the same.

Love is the Divine emotion that causes all relationships to return to the awareness of wholeness. Fear is a separating emotion that comes from the judgment to move away from love. Emotions move in two directions, toward love or toward fear.

Energetic Connections

Our emotional energies connect through both fearful thoughts and loving thoughts. Couples' emotional bodies are connected by similar thoughts and cords of energy that join those thoughts. Because our emotional bodies are invisible to the eye, we seldom recognize that all energy is connected in some way. Energy connections are made to join our judgmental bodies, like tubes or pipes connecting two tanks of water. Energy connections can be used either to manipulate other people or to join with them. The Ego, focused on the physical, gives no credence to what happens when two people exchange energies. Energy connections are felt by the psychic and are totally visible in the Spirit world.

Love-based energy connections are light, colorful, and elastic in nature, while fear-based energy connections are seen as dark, dense, and tight. Cords are formed when two people have sex, fight, express anger, laugh, cry, communicate about similar interests, think about the same ideas, and have truly loving experiences of the heart.

We know we are connected; our intuition tells us so. The phone rings and we know who is calling. Even though our partner may be miles away from us, we know what he or she is feeling. Mothers often know when their child feels hurt or suffers an injury.

One client could sense that her mate was having sex with another person, and she confronted him before he had a chance to reveal this information to her. She confronted him without expressing feelings of jealousy or anger. She just pointed to the fact that they share a bond at a level that is deeper than the physical level, and this bond allows her to sense his experiences. Couples in a committed relationship can sometimes think the same thoughts at the same time. Often, one partner may know the thoughts that his or her partner is thinking.

Women have a greater sense of the importance of feelings because women are more rooted in the lower brain, whereas men exist mostly in the upper brain. Men are typically trained to stay away from their feelings. A woman has a natural instinct for bonding and knows that sexual contact causes an energy connection. She also understands energy "intuitively" and loves romance because of its bonding effects. Men are mostly oblivious to this fact; therefore men think they can have sex that is free of any bonding effects. A woman unconsciously recognizes the positive and negative effects of energy bonding.

On the negative side, an energy bond can be the cause of a great deal of pain at times when you feel you have been rejected, when you suddenly make behavioral changes, or when you and your partner divorce. It causes the pain that we feel when someone dies. The pain that you experience feels as though someone is tearing the fabric of your soul. You feel the impact because it affects the energy connections and your joined emotional bodies. Energy cords can be fear-based if the thoughts that two people share are rooted in physical limitation. Connections that are fear-based consist of physical dependencies. When the partners of a relationship share primarily a physical interaction, then the energy cords are tied through behaviors that are based on control and limitation. These fearful energy cords create restriction.

Fear-based connections tie two people together with a common agreement to live in a fixed, limited way. Hate bonds people together, and anger connects them with dark cords. In a codependent relationship, which consists of controlling behaviors and rules, partners will regularly make fearful agreements. Partners become energetically connected through a willingness to share any thought or action. This act of agreeing may occur either consciously or unconsciously. Examples are "Let's run away together," "Let's be afraid together," "Let us fight together against the world," or "Let's just have casual sex." A relationship that has fear-based connections is full of control issues and games that make the relationship feel like a prison.

Men (and often, women) are very fearful of entrapment. They do not want to be controlled. They have commitment issues because they have previously experienced fear-based bonding with their parents. As human animals we make more fearful memories than true loving connections. A relat ionship can easily become a cage.

Those who never learned how to connect to a family have an emotional attachment deficit. When this deficit is played out, it is referred to as a fear of commitment, but this view only touches the surface of the issue. The origin of this deficit occurred during improper bonding within the family, specifically with the mother. The reason that an improper bond developed is not particularly the mother's fault, because it is possible that the soul of the child had chosen to be born into a family in which he or she had already planned to leave.

In early development, a mind can learn how to detach quickly from energy connections. Then, the act of detaching becomes a habit. Children of divorced parents learn about detachment because they often feel pain when the energy cords that bond their parents begin to break. Most people have ties with their parents that are still causing pain, and they are unaware of the magnitude of the effects of those bonds. The effects can be very subtle if you have buried or denied them, but they still exist and continue to affect every relationship you enter.

Unfinished issues with parents always show up in current relationships because thoughts and patterns are played out repeatedly until they are healed. Count on your mate having many strings that he or she has not dealt with because few people know how to heal or release these binding energies. While some bonds created through energy cords can have negative effects, some bonds provide positive effects. When partners share in a healing process, the emotions play a major role, and energy cords are not seen as a threat but as a way of feeling closer to a partner. We are all much more connected than we realize. Something inside each of us knows that we need to join. Something inside each of us knows that we need to seek real love.

Having judgmental emotions will attract the very person or situation in which you are judging into your experience. People whom you hate the most are also the people to whom you can be the most bonded. This is why you "think" about them. Do you wonder why a battered woman continues to return to the same person for more abuse? She is energy-attached to fear-based connections. A greater degree of special love will lend itself to a greater degree of special hate. The more that a person feels "high" as a result of a special love, the more pain he or she will experience as a result of the loss of that special love. The degree to which a person feels attraction and pain is due to the bonding that has occurred through energy cords.

When partners are connected through a fear-based bond, their relationship consists of a lot of arguments, a lot of drama, and many running away from the relationship only to come back with an even greater need for the attachment that the relationship provided. Fear emotions are addictive and compulsive.

You've probably felt these pains in your stomach when a relationship goes through stages such as breaking up or arguing. Most of us who have changed a relationship and continued to feel a deep desire to be with the ex-partner can testify to that feeling.

131

Emotional pain comes from messages that say, "You can't have." Emotional sadness that is felt due to a "split up" reminds us of our bonds and the special moments that you shared with the ex-partner. Special thoughts come to your awareness because the judgments are not balanced. By making a judgment that someone is special, you limit the love that you can receive, and you declare that love has to come in a specific way. It is just a mistake in your thought process, but it can still cause tremendous pain.

Fearful thoughts become very toxic since they are not supplied with love energy. Our codependent arrangements seem to supply enough energy to the thoughts until the agreements are changed. Then, a deficiency occurs that is much like food turning poisonous or rotting.

If you eat a piece of bad pizza, then your stomach detects that the pizza is not healthy, and your stomach regurgitates the pizza. You are attempting to do the same thing when special love moments turn toxic. If you hang on to these memories, then you will feel sicker. Even if you feel like you don't want the relationship to change, on some emotional level, you believe that you have to "get rid of" something.

Thoughts of loss or "not having" generate painful feelings because the Ego is improperly attempting to "get rid of" your partner or the Ego believes that you are being "gotten rid of." It's the thoughts that are the problem, not the partner. It's the judgmental thoughts of specialness that cause the pain, not what your partner is doing.

The Ego's beliefs in loss and lack manifest as perceptions, and the Ego deals with these perceptions by projecting the loss onto another person as opposed to dealing with the inner cause of the belief. The Ego is accustomed to set amounts of energy that it believes come from a relationship. Your emotional comfort zone is often congruent with the amount of attention or nurturing the involvement offers you. When you limit the amount of nurturing you can receive, then you deprive yourself.

Fear-based energy connections limit the way you take in energy. Love-based energy connections are unlimited and never deprive you because you know that the proper way to receive energy is from Spirit.

When you are whole and complete, you are aligned with the entire universe, and you can receive energy from everyone. In a fear-based special involvement, you focus on only one way of "getting."

Emotional pain comes from the belief that you are being deprived of something. If you think that your partner is the source that provides you with energy (i.e. happiness and love) and your partner stops providing that energy, then you experience a feeling of withdrawal. This withdrawal is much like the feeling that an alcoholic experiences if he or she delays taking a drink for a long period of time or a smoker experiences when he or she delays smoking a cigarette for a long time.

A codependent relationship can be just like an addiction to alcohol or drugs. This is why most relationship-based groups are founded in 12-step work. One person's "drug" is his or her partner. The fear-based energy bond causes the need for the "fix." Being connected to someone that you believe treated you badly isn't the problem; the problem is being ignorant of the ties and not knowing how to deal with them.

The withdrawal method of recovery for co-dependence is the same method that is used for recovery from any drug addiction. You must learn to abstain from the attachment and disconnect from the substance, form, or behavior. When the fear-based emotional energy connection is broken, then the person can return to the sense of being centered and find new ways of connecting (joining) to a partner. If a fear bond is maintained, then a love bond cannot occur. The fear bond must be denied and broken. Either love is present or fear is present.

Why do many people have such a difficult time getting over another person?

There are many strands of energy that connect our emotional bodies. When we speak of fond memories of special moments together, then we are referring to tiny energy cords that connect us to our ex-partner, and these cords can be seen if we look at our self at a psychic level. Love bonds can create connections; however many bonds with partners were originally connected as a result of a fear-based thought.

People have told me about situations where they suddenly felt sad or angry for no reason, yet when I examined their emotional bodies, it was easy to see how their energies were still connected to ex-partners, and they were still sending emotional signals even though they were no longer involved in those relationships. When we think we are in love, we want to share emotional signals, but when the relationship changes, it can be more practical to cut the fear-based cords.

It is very difficult for the human animal not to feel some emotional grief when a relation ship changes. Provided we are honestly tuned into our feelings, the less grief we feel, the better indication of progress we have that our "inner work" is successfully healing and balancing our emotional connections. Daily mediation helps to lessen the grief felt after a relationship change because we can make adjustments as needed. Forgiveness is the key. When we learn not to attack or defend, then our emotions will be centered and attuned to wholeness. If we feel emotional grief, then be gentle with ourselves, ask for help, and remember that working on ourselves was the purpose of the relationship. To transcend the programming that we've established through the animal Ego, we may need to experience several involvements. Seeking the correct counsel will ensure our success.

The act of cutting energy cords is seldom explained and most people think that it just takes time to "get over" someone. Time doesn't cut energy cords—you do. Denying or forgetting a partner doesn't release either of you; it only means that you will someday be rejoined physically to work out differences and judgments and to find new ways to join. Some energy cords are karmic and so deep that they join at the soul level and can't be undone. The term "soul mates" represents a situation where energy cords connect one soul to another soul, and this connection can never be broken, regardless of how much the partners of the relationship may seem to struggle. You have destiny cords and destiny dreams that you planned long before this physical experience, and you are now playing them out. Destiny cords explain why two strangers might meet and act out a violent experience. Destiny cords may also be responsible for the attraction that two people have to meet and fall in love to heal a shared experience that wasn't completed in a past life.

Cutting Fearful Energy Cords

Thoughts are ideas held within the mind. Some are fear-based and others are divine. Fear-based energy cords that connect us to old patterns and old ways of relating need to be cut, discarded, and dissolved. They are like jungle vines that hold you down and keep you trapped.

Your first step is to identify these fear-based energy cords. Then you need to look at how you made them by recognizing the judgments you have made and by owning your behaviors that established the connections. These steps require that you get in touch with your feelings and learn to assess the thoughts and memories that exist within these feelings. Feelings of darkness lead to energy cords. Learning to work on the emotional body is simply a matter of going to that level of energy. Your energy body is much like a garden where flowers and vegetables are growing, yet weeds can grow as well. Your feelings allow you to recognize the difference.

Once you have learned how to look for it, you will be able to see energy. You can feel energy once you have learned how to align your focus correctly. In this alignment, your focus resides some distance from the body, yet still within the physical body. When you practice the task of focusing correctly, then you will be able to know the difference between fear and love. Remember that you have a master gardener available to you when you address the Holy Spirit. Just ask for help.

Energy cords and thoughts are buried in and throughout the mind. You must dig into the Earth of your mind. When you find a fear-based cord that you know is not serving you, then pull it, cut it, or burn it by using your imagination and your inner strength. Visualize yourself in the act of pulling or releasing a cord from your inner body.   Sometimes, you can actually see the cord, feel the density of the cord, or feel the pain that occurs when you remove the cord.

In many of my sessions with clients, we act out fun mental games of blowing up cords or pouring acid on them, or extricating the weed-like cord and throwing it in the trash. The more energy you put into growing these cords, the more energy it may take to release them, so the use of sound, breath, and emotional expression are all helpful.

Cords can be seen as points of lights or energy waves, and they can be recognized as special memories or shapes of darkness. Recalling a picture of the person with whom the cord is attached or witnessing a certain event will allow you to get in touch with energy connections. Focusing and breathing into your stomach will help you get in touch with messages that come from your emotional brain. Any part of your body that feels restricted, tight, or painful is clueing you in to a fear-based energy connection.

The Types of Darkness

Your mind is all-powerful and all cords exist by your decision to have them. You had the power to make these memories or impressions and you now have the power to remove or dissolve them. Fear-based cords are connected to a memory. When judgmental energies are balanced, then the memory can be released from the unconscious. When power is taken from the source, the cord withers. Stop attacking or defending behaviors and events. Look within yourself for the source of the energy connections and identify if they are fear-based. Remove all judgments, and you will feel a sense of great relief. Your inner guidance will then impart to you a higher understanding and present the spiritual lesson that you and the other person connected to the cord needed to learn.

You can never lose. You can never be deprived of anything. You are whole and complete as God created you. The only way you can experience lack is by your own selfish acts of controlling other people. When you give up these acts, then you can return to wholeness. Your emotional problems stem from your unwillingness to release these fear-based memories and their respective energy connections. By not releasing emotional patterns, you repeat the same issues with another person.

The partners in a No Loss Relationship make the choice to replace fear with love. In a Holy Relationship, partners focus on making energy cords that connect to Spirit instead of making fear-based cords that center on a desire to control each other. Partners in a No Loss Relationship not only learn how to release the dark binding cords, but they also learn how to open themselves to the energy source that is unlimited. The easiest way to do this is for partners to teach each other that real love is freedom.

When examining the states of darkness, remember not to let judgment cloud your understanding. When the mind crystallizes thoughts, the process is analogous to removing the juice from an apple. The Light (energy) essence is sucked out. Darkness is no more bad or evil than thick mud or rock is good or bad. It is what it is, and the cause of darkness is absence of Light. The action one takes with darkened thought forms might be termed as "evil" because it is an attack upon another darkened form.

Evil is a term that is grossly misunderstood. If you call a person evil, then you are project ing your own hate. No soul is evil. A soul may misuse darkened energies to perform acts of destruction, but the soul is always free of the energy when it learns that the darkened energy no longer serves a purpose. To call the action evil and discern that the soul is still as God created it is to know how to be truly healing. A moral stance against evil actions is appropriate, but to attack a person and judge him or her is not to know immortality.

You may choose to call "sin" an act of evil, but be careful not to say that the energy is evil, for you will miss the mark. Energy is what it is. It is the absence of luminous energy that is misused or acted out that is called evil. The Self that is Whole is never changed by its actions. Action will attack or action will produce miracles. Be a miracle worker, not a "righteous moralist." You are here to learn that you can always call upon the Light and add back the energy that you have allowed, through your ignorance, to be taken away. Happiness is the Light energy. When added to darkness, it transforms or restores the thought and expands it to its real nature. What is lack, but the removal of Light? What is loss, but the awareness that spiritual energies have been taken from a thought? In truth, energy can shift or be taken but never lost, and energy is infinitely available, provided you know the source of it. The partners in a codependent relationship think that energy comes from each other, but the partners in a Holy Relationship understand that energy comes from God.

Fear

Fear is a false evaluation about reality that is based on the judgment of a form as destructive. We use sensory information to judge objective forms as harmful and destructive based on our survival instincts as well as our personal beliefs. Fear thoughts govern most of the Ego thought system.

Dense thoughts (fear) produce unfulfilled dreams. Who judges that we don't get what we want? I'm sure you've heard the term "emotional baggage." Someone can have hundreds of these darkened fear thoughts within their emotional body, just as someone could have thousands of toxic particles within their physical body. Most people don't acknowledge that they are living in a state of fear, and they choose to mask the fear emotion. This decision becomes a big problem in relationships.

When fear is well masked, it is described as a state of numbness or indifference to feel-

135

ings. We also attempt to minimize our fear by calling it a variety of names, and by believing that fear has different degrees, such as hot, semi-hot, or lukewarm. Fear is fear. Regardless of its apparent degree of intensity, the purpose of fear is to keep us separate. When you accommodate fear, then you are responding with a type of energy that makes you feel unsafe and not happy.

The first step in the correction of fearful emotions is to admit that you're in a state of fear. Any attempts you make to minimize or deny fear will cause you to project problems onto your partner instead of choosing to look inside yourself for a path to healing. Healing is the process of changing the mind from a perception of fear to a presence of love. Fear will block your ability to realize love's presence.

Animals recognize our fear and respond to it; like us, they run or fight. They run from our fear because they sense the aggressive aspect of the energy. The human animal is very capable of "sensing" fear but seldom admits it. Learn to recognize and to know fear, and we can't let the Ego tell us that it is something different, because if we believe in the lie that the Ego relays, then no resolution is possible.

Throughout this book we constantly deal with how to change from fear to love. If you are having any problems in a relationship, then it is because of fear-based emotions. The family of fear includes guilt, anger, sadness, and grief.

Guilt

Guilt is a form of fear because we are afraid that we won't get what we want or because we have behaved in a manner that resulted in another person not getting what he or she wanted. We make others feel guilty because we have lost our ability to create. Guilt and shame are used when we attempting to control the behaviors or thoughts of another person. Guilt is a form of rejection and like all forms of fear, it has an element of separation. Guilt rejects its opposite. We all feel a deep sense of guilt in that we feel separated from love. We act out these feelings by trying to make our partner feel the guilt that we feel. We can call it criticism, blame, or even disappointment. We have all projected our expected behavior onto our partners.

Guilt is overcome by admitting our hidden expectations and by releasing our attachment to any special outcomes. We must accept the situation exactly as it has happened and be willing to accept situations, as they will occur in the future. Guilt is not overcome by making our partner live the way we want him or her to live. Guilt is not overcome through a comparison that we make between our self and other people. Like all fear, guilt is healed by facing it and by bringing the split part into conscious awareness.

Guilt feelings are the preservers of time. They induce fears of retaliation or abandonment, and thus ensure that the future will be like the past. For this reason, the undoing of guilt is an essential part of the Holy Spirit's teaching. As long as we harbor feelings of guilt, then we are listening to the voice of the Ego, which is telling us that we have betrayed God, and therefore, we deserve punishment. Any belief in punishment is false, and it is only because we believe in it that it exists. Like any belief system, it is true for us because we give energy to it.

Guilt serves as an attack on our relationship by hindering love. Those who feel guilty will always condemn, and by choosing to value condemnation, they are nurturing separation in place of unity.

A major step toward a Holy Relationship is to see our partner as "guiltless," which means that we do not set any expectations that could be projected onto our partner. By learning not to make our partner "guilty," we become free from making demands upon our self as well.

Anger

Anger is energy that is stored inside us from repressed, split thoughts. When half of a thought is repressed, the energy builds up like an energetic charge. Each split judgmental thought (like, dislike, etc.) builds up emotional power and must be expressed somehow. We all know the power of a single atom when split; we also know the power in a judgment when split—it becomes an attack.

Anger is used as a method for controlling other people as well as oneself. Anger is simply the Ego's way of attempting to get what it "wants" by having a specific plan for happiness. The energy that builds up must have an outlet to escape being trapped or repressed in the lower mind. Those who are angry need only to learn how to control the method of release without expressing a form of judgment.

The false way to release anger energy is to project it onto someone or something, which can include yourself or your body. We attack with our anger hoping to change something, someone, or some circumstance. The source of our anger is our inner judgmental thought. However, most people think the cause of their own anger is based on something or someone that is outside of them. As long as we continue to justify anger, our healing can never occur. The correct release of anger is always to the Holy Spirit. Only Spirit can supply joyous energy to a split repressed thought. The Holy Spirit puts back the juice that we previously subtracted.

Anger can range from mild upset to rage. Here again, we must learn to see all anger as being the same when it comes to the need for healing. All forms of violence, all dramatic acts, and even mild upsets represent energy that needs to be released. Without a release, we are in pain. It feels like our container will explode because we experience the pressure. With all fearful emotions, we become accustomed to the methods of relief that we practice. Angry people are just hurting units seeking healing. Anger becomes a habit, an addiction, and a way of feeling better, but it never heals our mind. We only condemn ourselves because our judgmental thoughts remain in our mind. These destructive thoughts will eventually cause physical disease if they are not properly healed.

Sadness

Sadness is the reverse of anger. It is an inward attack. It is a belief in the state of being a victim, and it upholds a state of emotional fear that believes that loss is real. Sadness promotes loss and grief, which are used to maintain the belief that we won't receive what we want.

Sadness, like anger, is a way of releasing repressed energy but again, the release isn't complete and is self-destructive. Those who use sadness to get what they want enjoy playing the underdog or the victim. All victims want to be victimizers. All sadness calls for retaliation.

Grief

Grief believes in loss. Grief is the concept of not getting something or losing something that has been taken away. In reality, nothing real is taken away, and we are not deprived of anything. Loss can only occur in the physical reality and in the mental belief system. Feelings of grief are an indication that we value the physical more than the spiritual.

I am not saying that grieving is wrong or bad. Crying is not the problem. Believing the messages that sadness promotes is the problem. Grief is necessary and must happen to the degree that we made someone or something special. We can always measure the energies as the same: four cups of specialness = four cups of grief that come along with it.

Sadness and grief can be helpful if we invite the Holy Spirit while we are expressing our feelings. It is better to express sadness and anger correctly than to go numb and only live in our head. Holding on to grievance will prolong the healing. It is better to feel emotions than to repress them. Many a repressed feeling has led to depression.

Depression

Depression occurs when an enormous amount of crystallized thought is pressed into the lower mind. The more we judge, the more we crystallize thought.

Negative thoughts are like dumbbell weights: hard to carry around. The more fear thoughts we carry around, the harder it is to move. Dense mental energy pushed against the material body makes the mind stuck in a limited way. A depressed person is trapped in his or her own lower thinking process. Our lower minds become black holes. The more we limit thought, the harder it is to get out of bed. We hide from life because life is attempting to show us the effects of depressed thoughts. Anti-depression drugs simply cause a floating experience of chemical reaction that pushes the depressed thoughts away from the body. These drugs act as lifeboats, in a way, by preventing you from sinking. Unfortunately, they change nothing in the way we think; they do nothing to teach us to swim.

Most doctors don't have sufficient time to help heal patients because of the high volume of people seeking treatment and because of the amount of effort that it takes to encourage a person to look within him or herself to find the true cause. Our medical doctors today are often unaware of the true process of healing, and they do not have the time to teach a healing process when it is quicker to prescribe a drug. Chronically depressed people have chemical imbalances, as well; therefore, a prescription drug may be an appropriate aide. All fear causes chemical imbalances at some level in the body. These imbalances are the causes of all sickness.

To be treated chemically is not necessarily the problem, as putting a bandage on a cut is not wrong—it can be useful. In our relationship, if we and/or our partner are considering taking drugs to treat an emotional ailment, then don't reject the idea just because we are starting to find methods of healing. As the healing of the relationship occurs, we will know inside that it is not necessary to take anything outside of us to make us happy.

Balancing of Emotions

In the beginning of getting reacquainted with your feelings, it is appropriate to call fear by other names such as guilt, anger, or sadness. By accepting the decisions that you made in your past when you gave meaning to these different names, you can now begin to decrease your use of these names. As you advance toward the state of complete healing, you will narrow the list of names to just "fear," seeing it all as simply darkness. For advanced healing, you move from darkness to Light and you need no gray areas or middle ground. Learn to advance by only choosing between fear and love. It is much like a light switch.

The balancing of emotions allows you to transcend fear. When your emotions are not balanced, each partner plays off the other and each partner reacts in a manner that will maintain the imbalance. This decision causes the relationship to descend into deeper pits of selfishness and darkness. The relationships you will encounter in these lower realms are filled with projections.

Projections

One of the ways we stay stuck in the darkness is by not noticing our projections and their effects. The mind is so tricky, and we are so used to projecting that we have forgotten how to take a closer look at what we are really doing.

Projection (the movie) never changes the mind (the film). Learning to recognize the difference is a major growth process. Projection never heals because the memories are not changed, nor is the judgment. If we disliked a movie, we can't change it by watching the screen; we have to change the film in the projector.

Projections do nothing to our script. We project because we are attempting to avoid our painful emotions. Projection is an incorrect method to relieve pain. If we use projection to correct other people's behaviors, then no correction of guilt will occur in our mind. If no correction occurs within us, then we remain in pain and fear.

Stop the projector and become more centered by listening to what is happening inside us. One-way we notice our projection is by eliminating the "you" messages: "You don't have time for me," "You are so angry." This pattern keeps us from looking at the "I." Own our feelings and speak from the position of "I": "I feel sad because I want to see more of you," "I feel upset when I observe your behavior."

Understanding the 4 D's

Because I teach there is no F (failure), that leaves only D's in the grades of human relationships. The four D's explained below are The Dent, The Damaged, The Destroyed, and Death—The Void.

Examine your relationships and evaluate them honestly. Look at what you have made throughout your past experiences, all the way back to your birth. Be glad that you are now experiencing a relationship with your Holy Partner and the Holy Spirit. Travel fearlessly together. Learning about the causes of your fears by looking at perceived separations is how you become able to make greater choices.

The Dent

The first layer or level of going into the darkness is called The Dent, which is not only the experience of pain and suffering, but also the duality of pain and suffering which is pleasure.

You can't have pain if you don't have pleasure. All pleasure and pain (outer directed) toward the body is Ego driven, forcing you into the darkness.

We all seek pleasure, power, and special attention (to be singled out for specialness is fame), and these desires arise from the voice of the lower self which instills a belief that we are lost.

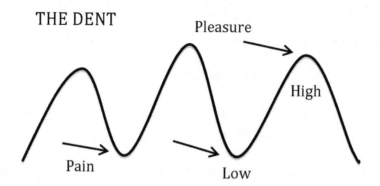

THE DENT — Pleasure — High — Pain — Low

If another person physically hit you, then the force would cause a dent in your flesh, and the brain would call it pain. The brain calls it pleasure when the force is directed toward desire within the darkness (body). The Dent is a sensation or a feeling of either pleasure or pain that is associated with a body as the cause. As you studied the 4 S's, you learned of the causes of moving toward and getting trapped in the darkness.

If you feel pain or grief over the loss of anyone or anything, then a part of your soul has been darkened by the dent of that specialness. Undoing the dent involves the process of accepting change and moving into creation correctly. Remember, the emotional body is similar to the physical body in that it reacts as a reflection of the laws established within and of the physical body. You enter into an emotional body as well as the physical body while bringing your soul into this human condition.

The brain mind is new, but it is quickly filled with continual past attractions of the collective shadow Self. Every high causes a dent in your Soul fabric, as does every low. The S is the symbol of light waves varying from highs to lows. The ups and downs caused by judgments start the process of becoming dented, and then eventually damaged. Dents become the ruts in your conditioned mind or the habits that form in your addictive behaviors. Dents create patterns in your feelings. They establish your levels of temperament and tolerances for pain and pleasure.

Any feeling experienced, other than deep peace, was originally established by a judgment made that resulted in a dent. Dark thoughts have density and are under the influence of gravity, just like people and planets. The darker the density of thought, the greater the dent is within the fabric of your soul. Partners in a No Loss Relationship are able to heal false body identifications, keep the denting to a minimum, and prevent a deepening of the descent into the darkness. It is through these practices that partners will experience true joy.

The Damaged

The next level or layer of descending is called The Damaged, also referred to as the wounded or the broken people. In a similar way that the impact from a sharp knife or bullet or even critical words can penetrate our physical being, our heart and emotional body are damaged from the impact as well. Dark thoughts are energy forms that we throw at our self and project onto others. They cut and separate. The result is a broken self. Who has not attempted to love and felt a wounded heart?

A damaged soul is one who has attempted to love deeply, but each attempt missed its connection, thereby fragmenting the soul causing duality such as Good vs. Evil. The results of the damaged soul are expressed not only through its inability to trust, join, share, or create, but also in its inability to feel connected as though it were a part of something. The results also have a negative impact on the soul's ability to give and receive. Mostly, the damage blocks our awareness of our higher self. All damage creates scars, which are also known as impressions, and these impressions serve as a foundation for fear thoughts and more darkness. These fear thoughts are the treasures of a wounded Ego self, often expressed as the need to be "right" about an opinion, belief, or self-concept.

A damaged Self can still function. It still wants for things. It still seeks for relief. It can still take things away, and it can certainly pretend to be someone who it is not. The damaged Self can still make up wonderful dreams of specialness. It maintains itself as well masked and for the most part, it can function appropriately in the world. Seven out of ten people you see are living from a damaged self 75% of the time. This percentage may even be higher. In the face of these statistics, remember the miracle by choosing to tell the truth. The miracle can heal the damage.

The damaged Self is portrayed through a person who we refer to as the liar, the thief, the con artist, the addict, the workaholic, the victim of a broken family, the bankrupt person, the bipolar person, the one sided politician and the lawyer. A damaged Self may also be portrayed as a spiritual teacher, if the person's goal is to attain self-independence at the cost of another person. The greedy businessperson, the glamour queen, the prostitute, the slave, the debtor, the partner who walked out on his or her family, and the list goes on and on as we recognize the evidence available of the damage done by the lack of love. Depression is an indication of repeated damage, and the latest divorce rate reflects a representation of how deep the wounds have been.

Examples continue in the following list: the angry man: the bitchy woman; the woman who feels forced to be a man; the man who is unable to feel; a person who is careless about our planet; a person who will grab for all he or she can get; the obese person; the bulimic person; the weak person; the lonely person; the person who lives in a state of doubt, worry or fear; the person who lives in great fear of the future; the person who uses a relationship with a pet to avoid having to relate to people; the person who chooses to fuel an argument for personal gain; the person with insomnia; the person who is unable to quiet the mind; the person who is often sick; the person who avoids intimacy; the person with a pattern of shallow relationships (i.e. starts quickly only to run away quickly after grabbing some sex); the person who believes that every person of the opposite gender is all messed up; and the person who chooses to remain single for years and believes that there is no person with whom he or she could share a relationship. How numbed out is the damaged?

And, more examples: the person who stays in a loveless marriage; the person who is too independent; the person who is codependent, and the person who fluctuates between independent and codependent behaviors. Please add your awareness of being wounded to this list as you recognize it in other people and in yourself. Do not recognize your own damaged Self from a place of guilt, blame or shame, but through the acknowledgement that you must be able to see the damage and accept where you are in the process before you can ascend out of the darkness or heal it. Have you found yourself within this list? If yes, then fear not. Remember that you have the option of the miracle available, which you can extend by telling the truth. Every human carries some charter defect; therefore you can say, "We are all in the darkness together."

The partners of a No Loss Relationship do not focus on past damage, but on the relief of healing through miracles today. The partners of a No Loss Relationship admit and own the damage through forgiveness and the desire to seek peace. The only way to heal is to steer your efforts away from judgment, blame, and any negative feelings regarding events from the past.

The Destroyed

The Destroyed refers to the junk land of continuously damaged souls known as Hell. This group represents the souls who remain in darkness past the point of repaired functionality, and the existence of the Light is so dim that all hope seems to be completely lost. All faith in Spirit is diminished, and only the physical world has value or everything has no value at all. This level is one where the focus of the mind can only see itself as one mind against everyone and everything, and it will often react with a strong attack toward anyone who attempts to bring love. This category includes people labeled as the criminal, the murderer, the rapist, the sociopath, the neurotic, the mentally ill person, or the insane person. This group represents people who inflict harm repeatedly or engage in acts of hatred toward others and are referred to as evil.

Often ready to commit suicide or kill another person, the minds of these people are trapped and bonded with a loyalty to the Angel of Death. They make dark thought forms, called demons, and want the destruction of all those who oppose them. They live not only in fear of God and for the actions they have done, but they also live in complete denial of the existence of love.

When darkness is so deep and the void of connecting seems impossible, the soul is lost for a lifetime, and maybe for 4 or 5 lifetimes. Fear not, for each soul receives 1,000,000 chances to enter a body. Yes, evolution occurs throughout billions upon billions of years. The people who are categorized in The Destroyed group believe in oblivion and complete unconsciousness which results in a continual want for death. They seek only to be a taker or to be a destroyer. Those who have been destroyed, must destroy. Those who are destroyed have a tendency to live in extremely large places, live in prison, or live alone in a dark, cluttered home. The hate they feel is all consuming. They only think of themselves as being locked in the darkness of not knowing the true Self.

You can pretend that this level of existence is not in your awareness, and you can pretend that you are not a part of the collective lower mind. Yet, with today's technology, this level is unavoidable. Just watch the news. Just wake up a little and you are ready to be a teacher of Spirit. The hands of the destroyed are killing millions upon millions. The partners of Holy Rela tionships and the advanced teachers of Light are the answer.

Is the miracle available to the destroyed, the darkest souls around? Indeed it is, but often it is rejected, and it requires a very advanced teacher of Spirit and the plan of the Holy

Spirit to save them. There is a plan for their salvation, and we must only offer compassion and peace and ask for our part to play. We can only seek forgiveness. Any encounter we have with a destroyed soul is our chance to be the advanced teacher…the Christ, the Buddha, the Krishna, or the Mohammed. If destroyed souls see the Light and accept it, then all sin is released and they can start the process of ascension.

Death - The Void

The final and last stage of darkness, while you thought it could not get worse, is Death, The Void. Entering the complete void without any love is eternal death, which is without any feelings or thoughts. Returning to God while in this stage is the end of suffering. Soul death is being totally absorbed into the void.

This is a revelation of truth that if a soul 100% denies the existence of love and Spirit and values death about all else, then it is received into the void Self: God.
This can only possibly occur if God accepts the soul as totally empty of Light. This acceptance would require millions of lifetimes and is a total return to God in reverse, and a surrendering of all knowledge of the Son of God, which is your Individuality. No failure is experienced. The Void is God.

Death of the body is a discard of form and the release of the atomic matter that holds the identity of the lower Self. When the soul releases the body, it enters into the Kingdoms of Light or it chooses to continue to travel into the kingdoms of darkness, or it chooses to return to a body. It is a little bit of all three, for 96% of us. In physical death, the soul does not change a single thought of Light or darkness but is given a glimpse of what is real. That glimpse is grace, and can be experienced in each moment of death. For death and grace are the same, like two sides of the same coin.

Each day you die a little, and each day you face death. Each day you can also receive grace. Death and grace are of Spirit, and they allow the understanding of creation and the natural existence of continually creating. Grace that is recognized with death is resurrection.

Jesus, the man who received grace completely and purified all dark thoughts within his soul, achieved complete enlightenment, which is also an acceptance of individuality within the Light of God Self. All spiritual masters choose to accept their Light body rather than value darkened thoughts, the body, possessions, or attachment to possessions.

The purpose of a Holy Relationship is to join with a person, to share in grace, and to become One so love is known. Grace in death is the door. Death, the final release that is done at every level, is what you truly desire to return out of darkness and to become a creator.
The void or pure darkness is absolute God Self, the womb of God, the great embrace, and this is why there is nothing to fear. There is only God. The problem is not darkness, but our perceptions and our choice to treasure the darkness.

If you and your Holy Relationship can experience grace together without fear, then you will know your true Self. Through the process of healing and walking into death together with the Holy Spirit, all knowledge is restored to you. True death is not to be feared, but welcomed with grace as being one of life's greatest experiences.

Each one of us has walked and been through each of these three levels or layers of darkness and have come up and down the ladder, in and out of the awareness of love. Which one of you has not sinned? "Who among you can cast the first stone," speaks Christ.

Death in grace is the answer…or complete freedom from dark thoughts is a return to love. It is perception about darkness that makes us feels separate, not darkness in its absolute nature. The void need not be feared if we know grace. Grace is given already to us. Now we understand that the dark night of the soul is the awaking process of remembering who we are.

Now we understand death as rebirth. Death is never a problem; in actuality, it is the gift. The real problem occurs when we cling to the destroyed and never release it to experience death with grace.

Death is life when it is not feared. Fear is the holding or the attachment to a dark thought. Fear is the refusal to enter into death completely.

As Saint Francis said, "It is in dying we are born into eternal Light."

Surprise! Surprise!

How do I get this death with grace when I am in so much fear and hold on so strongly to fear? Bid welcome to your Holy Relationship.

The Way Out of Darkness

All acts of attack come from judgments. All peace comes from not judging. Many people will fight for family, country, and religious beliefs in the name of righteous judgment. We fight for ideals and imprison those who we perceive as having different views from ours. This is because we feel threatened by differences.

To heal is to make happy, and the key to balancing the emotional body is to learn to bestow joy onto crystallized thoughts. Change the dense thoughts from within and, don't expect others to do it for you. Only true happiness heals by restoring the energy the judgments have removed. It's an inside job.

Darkened fear thoughts must be given a dose of happiness, but not the type of happiness that is perceived to be derived from another person. The type of happiness that is dependent on another person is really darker than we may realize. It is dark because there is a misperception of where the healing comes from. It's a major step to learn that we are whole. Happiness does not come from outside of us. It can't be associated as coming from our partner or from a special moment that our partner has provided for us. The majority of relationships live as if happiness comes from the other person, and for this reason these relationships are codependent.

As our physical bodies take in food from the outside, we become nurtured and energized. The emotional body must also be fed, but from the reserves of energy within called Spirit. This is a great lesson and few understand it. So often, couples try to steal energy from each other or drain energy from the relationship by becoming "takers." A taker is very needy, and the actions of a taker make the relationship high-maintenance. A taker is a person who views his or her own needs and wants with a higher importance than his or her partner's needs and wants. Whether knowingly or unknowingly, the taker is a seeker of attention, and his or her behavior is manipulative and selfish. A taker has forgotten the meaning of being a giver. He or she has forgotten the understandi ng that a giver is a receiver. Taking is the Ego's strategy of correcting lack.

"Taker" and "caretaker" are looking for each other. Takers are emotionally wounded, but the counterpart in the relationship, the caretaker, is also playing out a wound by secretly taking energy from his or her partner's already lifeless emotions. The need to care serves as a mask for the need to feel important and worthy.

Based in an existence of low self-esteem, they each suck energy by enabling the other person to remain helpless. The job of caring must include giving to yourself from within. Caring is a very tricky thing. If you are the caretaker for an emotionally wounded person who is throwing his or her emotions on you, then be careful not to kid yourself into believing that you can handle it or that you are truly helping the person to heal. You are being drained because you are choosing to settle for a mere small amount of attention, and the taker is not progressing on a healing path. Emotionally sick people steal energy, and then they drain themselves. They have not learned how to replenish energy in a correct manner.

The Ego can certainly use caring to defend its position of needing to stay involved. The modern word for taking energy is suck. "Mean people suck" is a popular bumper sticker. Watch how you seem to care for someone and examine your motivation to be sure you are coming from a place of healing by helping in the process of your partner becoming whole. Partners who become involved in an "enabling relationship" are a step away from ongoing drama. Two people who think they want to remain dependent on one another because each partner fears that he or she cannot be happy or whole without being emotionally connected to the other person use "Enabling relationships" as a strategy. You "care" to maintain your special attraction to them.

A relationship can only work to the degree that both partners heal and keep their emotional bodies light. Are you happy? You are happy if you have been working on having a light and balanced emotional body. The happier the person, the lighter their emotional body is. Happiness is the key because it is energy in its purest form, and because it cleans up and balances your emotional body by adding the energy you lack. The cleaner your emotional body is, the less judgmental you will be in your relationships.

When you choose to judge, it is only because you were taught that the act of judging is an acceptable and necessary behavior. You forgot that the choice of listening to your non-judgmental self is an act of your true Self that is based on acceptance and happiness. You wanted to take on the values and judgmental systems that were exemplified by your loved ones. You chose these values and judgmental systems, and now you have chosen your partner. Everyone you know represents a reflection of your own emotional health.

The partners in a Holy Relationship understand their need to share feelings with each other. You know that you have two ways to deal with feeling—to react (attack or defend) or to heal. The partners in a Holy Relationship accept the tasks involved with the process of healing, knowing that involvement in a relationship is required to heal the emotional body. You need the mirror and the support that is provided in a relationship to look at your judgments.

The partners of a Holy Relationship learn not to attack or defend. Each partner catches himself or herself in the act of passing judgment and asks for correction and healing. The partners have also learned how to choose to release themselves or each other from any blame when one of them has mistakenly repeated an old habit of attack.

Releasing feelings and thoughts is the response that is opposite of judging. Attacking and defending is a circle of non-communication because no joining can occur when your mind is in either of these states. You slowly learn to recognize these states of mind that the

Ego chooses and replace them with a choice to be loving and accepting, and in this way, emotional connections are preserved.

The 4 G's to God: Grace, Gratitude, Giving the Gifts, Glory

God

The moment a soul can recognize where it is, becomes the moment of return to choice. Denial is one of the Ego's greatest methods for keeping you in the D's. Denial prevents you from looking at dark thoughts, and avoidance keeps you from being released from them. No matter how much or at what level of darkness you have entered, there is always an answer. Nothing is impossible with the Holy Spirit and the awareness of grace. The partners of a Holy Relationship must practice being in grace together. It's a very easy thing to experience. Even if you are not in a Holy Relationship, you can ask for help in experiencing grace. Ask and you shall receive what is real. Grace is a spark of truth in the soul of every soul. Grace is the call, the Light within. Find it, know it, and seek it above all else, and you are saved. Hold on to grace no matter what you are currently going through, and you will see the truth and be set free. Stand in grace with your partner, and recognize it in both of you. You are never alone. Love has given you the grace to recognize what is the same in all.

Practicing Grace

The first step is to admit that you are in darkness, and you are seeing and feeling its effects. Make a statement of the darkness and describe its effects. For example, your statement of darkness could be, "I feel alone," and its effect could be, "no one cares" or "I don't want to go on with life."
Step two is to ask for help. Call on your holy partner. Call on someone who is spiritual. This person could be a teacher, a minister, a friend, or anyone who you know will hold a higher view of truth for you.
Step three is to pray together in order to know grace, which is a form of asking together. It is through the act of asking together that grace can be received. If you do not know of a human person that you may call, then call out to the angels, spirit guides, or any concept of the Holy Spirit with which you can identify. Think of pure joy and remember what it means to be happy no matter what has happened. Make no mistake about this step. You need to join with some deity or some person because you come to truth when you are together with another and never by yourself.
The entire concept of darkness is that you are separate and without Spirit. Without some type of joining, you don't have the power to receive grace. Those who pray strongly and honestly by themselves will connect to a higher deity and can be given grace. Just thinking of your holy partner can cause a connection that will allow the reception of grace. There is great value within a Holy Relationship because partners know each other at a level that is beyond the level of form, and this connection allows them to receive grace at will.
Step four is to surrender and be still. Allow and release. Be here now. Feel a connection

with your Holy Relationship. Release all thoughts about the past. Do your best to stop thinking about the issues of fear. Stillness is a feeling of peace, and release is a feeling of being lighter.

Step five is to bring a state of acceptance. Acceptance is grace. Acceptance is a state of being with the Is-ness. Forgiveness is acceptance. If you realize that you are listening to the feeling of grace, then know that you are at a turning point. You are moving toward Spirit now. The past is gone and finished, and its effects are as gone as you can accept that they are gone. Grace means that you are able to listen to joining again, and you are open to the idea of creating. You and your partner can now start to make agreements that serve the greater good of all. You can accept that you are saved from the past and can see Light. You can be happy now.

Step six is action and honesty. Do what you agreed to do through your commitment and unity. Like a seed, your ability to practice grace will grow one step at a time. Enlightenment is like co-creating through a process, and like evolution, it works for everyone. Your act of arising from the darkness is your purpose, and you are able to help many people by never forgetting who walks with you now.

Step seven is about repetition. Repeat steps one through six as often as you can. Remember that your walk out of darkness has meaning for other holy companions. Living with grace becomes a familiar and desirable feeling to experience. It is one feeling that you would say you couldn't live without experiencing on a daily basis, and indeed you would be right. For without grace, there is no awareness other than darkness. Within the presence of grace is all the higher knowledge revealed.

Gratitude

The moment you feel grace is the moment you can feel real gratitude and pure happiness. It's the proof that you are feeling a great spiritual quality. It is the cultivation of gratitude that gives you the reassurance that you are on the right path.

Grace and gratitude are the same spiritual essence, but gratitude can be extended toward a person, place, or situation. Gratitude is strengthened through the process of sharing it. Do you feel gratitude for everyone and everything that has happened in your life? If not, then be sure to practice forgiveness with your holy partner and see if you can unlock the fear and replace it with gratitude. Again, always be willing to ask for help.

Gratitude is an emotional thought that lifts you from the darkness. Pure joy is gratitude. A depressed person just needs to feel a little bit of gratitude. Then he or she needs to make attempts each day to feel more gratitude as it grows. He or she needs to make a list of all the things for which he or she is grateful. You can't have your cake and eat it too, and you can't have depression if you have gratitude. Constant gratitude is a spiritual practice. If you seem more attracted to your depression than the practice of being grateful, then start small. List only one or two things, and these little steps will help you progress. Practice often with your partner. Make it like eating, three meals a day or five small meals throughout the day. Feed yourself because it's good food for the soul. Darkness is down while gratitude is up, so seek to be lifted and learn to feel the shift. Small little shifts in attitude are the key.

The partners in a No Loss Relationship have much to be grateful for. Assist your partner in practicing gratitude, and remind him or her of your gifts to each other. It is your decision to practice the AAA's (Acknowledge, Acceptance, Appreciation) mind method daily, even hourly. That helps you never slip out of gratitude. A true spiritual relationship is always lifting up.

Giving the Gifts

In the greatest awareness of wholeness, life is the gift. You are life, and life itself gave you all of its qualities and nature. If you are not grateful for life itself, then you have slipped into darkness and are seeking relief. You are probably feeling grief or loss. Something needs to shift or change, and of course, I teach that it's the mind that needs to move from fear to love. Love is life. Love recognizes life for what it is.

You are God's gift to life, meaning, you CO-create with life through sharing your gifts and love. You are a co-creator with life itself through a knowing of what creating is. This is the purpose of life: to create. All that you see around you are your creations. They are your gifts to yourself.

Forgiveness is the process of shifting the mind from Ego to Spirit. The mind that is trapped in darkness needs to learn the act of forgiveness to come out of its separation from Self and from life.

There is only one way out, because there is only one way in. You have to go out of darkness the way you came in, through the mind that perceived in darkness.

Forgiveness is the way out of that mind. The very word forgiveness speaks of the way, but forgiveness is so misunderstood. Forgiveness is seen as a way of pardoning a mistake. In the lower view of forgiveness, the mistake is still seen as real, true, and harmful to yourself or to the ones you love. Darkness is the idea of form as real, and you need a gift from Spirit to see that idea as a lie. Forgiveness is really not a pardoning but a gift received to learn that form is not real or that form has less meaning than you have given to it. Forgiveness is for a gift to be given to you (no one else). Forgiveness is for you, as you are the one who needs the gift or the replacement of darkness for Light. Forgiveness is not for the one who you believe harmed you or trespassed against you. Forgiveness is for you to have a revelation.

The revelation is always that you are still as God created you and nothing can harm your true Self. The gift is receiving grace, gratitude, and pure joy, which can only show you who you are. Give the gift of forgiveness to yourself often so you can give it to others. Receive the gift by giving it. Give, give, and give, because Spirit is nothing but the totally of all giving. It is impossible to out-give God, and the only way to know Spirit is through giving.

What is forgiveness? Forgiveness is the ability to receive a gift so you can give what was missing. It is a quality of the No Loss Relationship to teach that nothing was ever missing, and the Now provides opportunity for you to Give. Give something away to keep it.

Partners of a No Loss Relationship learn how to give gifts of appreciation and how to acknowledge joy, so that fear is recognized as not real. The AAA's (Acknowledge, Acceptance, Appreciation) mind method of transformation brings the Miracle and lifts the score-card from D's to A's. Happiness is your Holy Relationship through love. The path out of darkness is shared, and what was destroyed was reborn into eternal love. God is love.

Energy Bonding

Energy bonding involves thoughts of love. The bonding that occurs in our Holy Relationships is the glue that leads us toward eternal love. This bonding effect lasts long beyond time and far beyond space. It is also the motivation that keeps us committed and devoted to a relationship. It allows souls to know each other from lifetime to lifetime. It is the energy that allows us to use our intuition to know what is happening to our partner, even though we are not within close, physical proximity.

Deep within the soul, we all have an energy cord that connects us directly to God. This is love in its purest form. Find it, and we will never be lonely again. Energy bonding leads to Oneness. It is the glue that makes the difficult times easier to endure and the good times even more rewarding.

When energy cords are based in freedom, they take on a more elastic quality and allow more openness into the relationship. The outcome of a successful Holy Relationship is a bonding that is eternal.

Do you really want this with your partner? What does it take to achieve it? You can no longer pretend that you are happy without being involved in a Holy Relationship. You have to truly desire and work for it.

Let Us Learn to Teach Each Other:

"In the name of love and being with you, I agree to feel what you feel. When I take upon myself to feel what you feel, I also have to take responsibility for my reactions. I am not to hide my feelings from you, and I choose not to project my feelings onto you. You are not doing anything that I have not asked for. I asked to experience your emotions. I asked to take on the healing process with you. I am not a victim of your feelings and voice tones. I am healed as we heal together."

Learning more about these energy cords is essential in developing a healthy relationship. Learn how to increase the truly loving connections and eliminate the fearful ones. Strengthen the connections that make your relations whole and cut emotional bonds that inhibit your growth.

Love is freedom; fear is imprisonment. When real love enters, you are set free, and you can't be bonded in any physical or mental way. No demands or measures of control are necessary.

Learning How to Balance

Balancing the judgmental (emotional) body is a major step in every relationship, and the success of the relationship depends upon both partners doing his or her part.

All true healing starts in the judgmental body, not the physical. To balance an emotion, we must learn to see the truth of any event or person without our judgments. This is not an easy step to learn and will be met with much resistance until it is felt to be a joyous experience.

To balance a judgment is much like balancing a teeter-totter; you must be centered in the middle. Visualize a teeter-totter. You are sitting in the middle, not on one end or the other.

If you favor one half of a judgment more than another, then you will tip the scales. Unbalanced energies that repress a thought will make it impossible to heal. A repressed thought is held lower in consciousness (pressed into body nerves and/or cells), and the higher split-thought is projected onto the screen of your conscious awareness. Your teeter-totter spins as well because, in the mind, there is no ground. This is the reason one moment you are in special love and the next in special hate, and then back again. You keep spinning in drama.

Another reason that you prevent yourself from being able to move to the balance point is that the mind projects thoughts and believes that the projections are real. You are looking for the balance point in positions where it is not and this continued pointless search keeps you off balance. Learning to find balance requires that you spend time with yourself. Most people get so distracted with outer toys that they forget how to return to balance and to their center. You can't return to a state of wholeness unless you understand your center. The importance of being centered is the reason all the great teachers emphasize the need for us to practice some form of meditation.

Acceptance is the key. Learning to accept both good and bad, like and dislike, and not take sides is what allows the mind to balance. Invite the Spirit into any issue that seems off-centered, and it will help you achieve balance by showing you how to accept all aspects of an issue. If you are focusing on the outer, say your partner or an object, then you can be sure you are imbalanced. You are out of balance if you experience any feeling other than peace. Peace is an attribute of a balanced mind. Inner joy is a quiet, peaceful vibration. A unbalanced emotion lead to all the destructive behaviors that dysfunctional relationships produce. Constantly correcting behavior increases the imbalance and tips the scales even further into addictive behavior. Bipolar personalities are up and down. All dysfunctional personality types are dealing with the runaway effects of imbalanced energies.

When ideas are balanced, judgment disappears because each half returns to the other and becomes whole. All imbalanced thoughts produce some pain. When you learn to find the source of the pain, then you will be directed to the balance point.

The first clue for finding the source of the pain is that it is never outside of you. The next clue involves feeling your body. Really get into communication with your physical aches and pains. Each neck ache, back pain, knee, or stomach discomfort is attempting to show you where a repressed judgment lies. Putting your full attention on the pain allows you to enter into the energy that exists behind that area. When you move beyond the body, then you enter into energy. When you go within energy, then you move toward thoughts and ideas. Don't worry about doing this the "right" way. Focus and ask for help from your inner Spirit. Peaceful listening allows you to shift to the level of thoughts.
Most people have been sold antidepressants or some form of relief medicine. They haven't been taught to go toward the pain. Their Ego mind wants them to avoid the pain, and this avoidance is how the Ego keeps them off-centered.

When a split thought is brought back into alignment balanced, and then seen as whole, the healing effect generates Light. The healing function of a Holy Relationship produces spiritual vision. You see creation exactly as it is. You have true perception and knowledge without judgment. This Light is pure ecstasy and the joy you have always been seeking.

The partners of a No Loss Relationship lose the judgmental mind. Each time you practice the behaviors of your non-judgmental self, you learn more about the power of a No Loss Relationship. You take on the role of being a spiritual teacher in a world full of fear and evil. The strength and support of a Holy Relationship prove that you can transcend and live in a non-judgmental state of consciousness. The proof emanates from the practice. You don't have to teach it to the world until you both teach it thoroughly to yourselves. Until you fully understand the power of the Holy Relationship, which may take years, you will not know how to prove the effects of a Holy Relationship to an untrusting mind.

Power Struggles

One of the main reasons we get into emotional disagreements is because we enter into power struggles with the ones we love. It can start with our parents, or it could have started when we thought God was mad at us. It starts when there is a separation of wills, akin to: "I want what I want," and you want something different so our personal wills struggle believing one is going to win at the other's expense.

Power Struggles are witnessed throughout the animal world as creatures fight for dominance. The need to survive makes us strive to be strong. Even puppies become stronger by play fighting. In the animal world, with physical power comes mental dominance, and in all animal communities a ruler emerges. A leader is often challenged by the younger members. If they can gain power over the older leader, they have the right to the females and rule the pack. In the human world, bar scenes and corporate offices often play out these themes. Physical power is gained by conquering.

Power struggles on the emotional level can be played out by bringing up the past and attempting to control the future. Emotional power comes from the desire to play God, by executing the power to judge and to rule. This type of personal will power exists at the level of the lower mind, and the Ego is King.

Intellectual power struggles are played out in a game of who's right and who's wrong, and often involve mental wars of pre-conceptions and opinions. Intellectual power is gained by gathering allies who support one's point of view. Power struggles take place because we believe what we desire can be rejected or denied by someone more powerful than we are. Power struggles promote war, fighting, and verbal battles, and they are the destroyers of unity. Judgment always plays a part in power struggles, and the mind is convinced that one's desire is better or more important than the other's. Power struggles focus more on the judged perception than the potential opportunity to CO-create.

Power struggles between otherwise loving couples occur because of each other's past learning. We have experienced or witnessed so many of them that we think they are normal. Power struggles occurred between us and our parents at a very early age as our parents asserted their authority and strength to lead us into adulthood. The "willful child" attitude is the manifestation of the strong Ego that denies authority and wants to do it its own way. When we have an argument with someone we perceive has more powerful (a boss, a parent, a spouse) the real issue comes down to who we "think" is in charge. We want to believe that we are the author of our own life, and no one has the right to instruct us or tell us what to do or say. The idea that we are in charge and are running the universe according to our own private wishes and demands, is a delusional thought system. During a power struggle, we think the situation is one in which our adversary is literally fighting us for control and power. We also form an inaccurate vision that we could lose in the struggle and must fight harder to win.

We fool ourselves when we don't see how we all have an equal part to play. In the healthier view of wholeness, each person is doing his or her part with an equal amount of willingness and power. They are given exactly what they've asked for. For example, we've asked to be the child just as our parents agreed to play the role of parents. We've signed on as an employee willing to let the owner of the company play boss. Maybe we've agreed to be the shy, reserved partner with an outspoken, more aggressive mate. An even harder situation is to accept the fact that we agreed to play the victim and asked another person to play the perpetrator.

Each time we enter into a power struggle we are matching our personal will against the will of the Creator. No one has ever really won a power struggle, for each time we play one part, we are at the same time asking to play the other part. No one can just be a leader and not have a chance to be a follower, just as each victim will reverse roles and act out being the victimizer. The Creator allows each soul to play all parts until they volunteer to be a peacekeeper and end the struggle.

In absolute truth, there are no power struggles because we are the author of the thoughts and feelings we create. Both parts of any power struggle from the view of the higher mind have been agreed upon. We can admit that we are living in a lower state of mind and ask to transcend into wholeness. The game of power struggles is a misunderstanding of how the mind works.

Power struggles are meaningless when seen for what they are. If in our minds we think someone has more power than we do, remember that we are the ones who have created this thought. Envy of another's position means we are not accepting that we agreed to play our part in the matter. We have chosen to experience every role we put ourselves in.

Our use of will is a source of our power, and those who have forgotten how to use the will are powerless indeed, as they become passive and the "wisher" of dreams. Feeling powerless, they trick even themselves by struggling to get others' power. Why would we want the power stuck in a limited container, which resists and doesn't want to share it when we could have the power that exists in the whole universe? It gladly wants us to use it, because there is so much of it.

It's important to remember that in a healthy relationship it is appropriate for one to lead at times and the other to follow. The leader in a Holy Relationship is simply the one who has gotten free of the restriction placed upon them by the lower mind. The follower is the willing partner who doesn't object to letting their partner be the leader for a period of time because they can admit that the lower mind has gripped their attention.

The leader and the follower are gladly willing to exchange roles, as neither is better than the other. The secret to maximizing progress is to accept that at times we will feel more trapped in our judgments and fears than others. We will feel powerless and helpless in letting the lower animal part dictate our situation. When this happens the first instinct is to fight for control or run away. A good leader will not retaliate and therefore, escalate the power struggle for it takes two to struggle. Nonresistance is the greatest defense.

If we want to do something different fro m our partner, it doesn't mean that we can't agree. Wholeness has nothing to do with controlling the physical, emotional, or mental aspect of our self. Also under the guidance of love, there can always be a win/win, no-loss creation. Sometimes it takes years upon years for a couple to end their power struggles, but it can be done as quickly as they realize that struggling against each other is ultimately defeating themselves. Ending the animalism Ego thought system only requires willingness

152

to choose peace instead of conflict.

Be the first in your relationship to recognize that a power struggle is occurring. Be the first to forgive, and apply the AAA's. (Acknowledge, Acceptance, Appreciation) Be the one who stops playing the game of verbal Ping-Pong. Practice the guidelines for co-creating, and ask for what you really want. Save yourself time and frustration by working on yourself, and worry less about your partner.

In a No Loss Relationship all power struggles are quickly given up because no thought of lack of power is ever perceived. Lack of power comes from looking outside of yourself and judging that another has something you don't. If you only realized who and what you are, you would know that you inherit and hold everything, including all power. God didn't create these ideas of lack, you did.

Gain real power by controlling your own thoughts. To end emotional power struggles, accept all emotional expressions as a call for healing. Enjoy the roles of being both a leader and a follower. Learn about and commit to healing your emotions. To end intellectual power struggles support another's personal opinions, and avoid joining one side of an argument. In the presence of unconditional, healthy love, all judgment is automatically suspended. When judgment is suspended, acceptance replaces conflict. Through your Holy Relationships you learn how to transcend the human animal programs, and power struggles are gladly exchanged for co-creative happy dreams. A healthy couple practices these guidelines and in doing so, is successful in promoting creativity, personal strength, and happiness.

Complete the exercises for this chapter in Chapter 10.

CHAPTER 8

UNIFIED GOALS
Agreements for the Body, Mind, and Spirit

Trinity: It Takes Three

In Christianity, God is seen through the view of Father, Son, and Holy Spirit, which is referred to as the trinity. In Hinduism, God is seen through the view of Shiva, Vishnu, and Brahma. Metaphysicians talk about the ideas of Cause, Thought, and Expression.
Most of us think that just two make up an intimate relationship. In reality, a relationship is always made up of three—the expression coming from the two people is what makes a relationship. Each person adds something to the moment, and what come from it are the expression, the miracle, and the newness of creation. This triangle is the symbol of expression experienced in relationships.

What comes from love comes from male and female coming together, positive and negative joining, like the pistol and stamen creating new flowers. From mating to the birth of galaxies, every living thing has a yin and a yang that causes a new creative expression. This is a universal law, a law of evolution, and the purpose for being. The miracle is always present, but we sometimes fail to recognize it. When we learn to look for this expression in each moment of a relationship, the partnership has an element of creative excitement.

When we don't see this third creative aspect, our Ego is controlling us. The Ego only wants us to look at the past. It avoids change and denies creative expression. We have problems and disagreements in relationships because we are not looking for something new. Instead, we are looking to repeat the past.

Another reason we don't notice it is because we are not joining together—we think we are, but our Egos are preventing us from truly joining. When joining occurs, new creation happens. If this creative expression is seen clearly, joy is recognized as well. For the energy of newness is joy. When two people share ideas, a new way of expression occurs. Most business people understand the power of brainstorming; used effectively it can produce all types of fresh ideas.

The reason most relationships fail is because the joy is lost in the involvement. If we want real joy and love in our relationships, look for the trinity aspect-partner, our what, and—us we can CO-create together—and we can't look at each other as separate units with opposite points of view.

We are a miracle and so is our partner, and in the beginning of most relationships we recognize it because we are excited about new ways of expressing our love. This is the true romantic phase. As the relationship continues we forget to express and produce miracles. We instead find fault and attack. When our relationship has issues or problems or it seems that we are growing apart, remember it is the expression/miracle involvement that will keep us together. If we forget this third factor, then the battles between each other are what seem to win.

How many miracles have we seen today? How much creative expression have we recognized as a result of our joining? It requires a conscious effort and an "on-purpose" attitude to focus on joining and enjoy the results. We are mostly asleep and forget to look. Many books are written about keeping the roma nce and passion alive in the relationship. Many authors give suggestions of things to do or how to act—instead of how to create. Creating miracles is the greatest joy any relationship can experience.

There exists within each of us a state of creative potential—a spiritual essence. This state of being is within the atomic level of form. During our most playful or meditative state of existence we have touched it. We may or may not reach it when involved in sexual activity. I say this because many couples make love from the level of the Ego and miss the opportunity to go to the Light together.

The main point is that our partnership is learning how to return to the creative level of existence. Doing so is the most rewarding aspect of being in a Holy Relationship. Couples who learn this secret are never bored with each other, and they do not devalue each other. Those who never reach this state are constantly restless and unhappy in their relationships. We are a child of the creator—like the creator, we can't be happy unless we are in a state of creation. This state can only be maintained through joining.

Are we aware of how much time we spend being separate, trying to change our partner or being alone, working to survive? The alternative is joining for the purpose of creative expression.

Understanding the nature of reality requires the help of the Holy Spirit. This powerful idea is what brings us back to our true identity. It is the first triangle relationship in creation, and in the absolute sense, the only triangular relationship. By letting Spirit guide the relationship we recognize our true relationship with God.

The path of the Holy Relationship is a very fast way of awakening to our true reality and highest potential. Never underestimate the importance of our partner and the Holy Spirit. This process of joining in mind together is the fastest way to return to our natural state of mind—to pure creative potential.

The Principles of Joining

1) The mind is open; no thoughts are hidden, and no opinions are kept to prove a point of view. We are willing to change our interpretation of a situation when we notice it is causing separation.

2) Voice tones are in alignment with the Spirit of joy and gratitude. Learn the tones the Holy Spirit teaches. Atonement is a single vibration that brings beliefs into alignment with peace.

3) The past does not hinder us, nor do thoughts of the future. Real joining brings us into the present moment.

4) Differences are released and similarities are affirmed.

5) Joining occurs in the mind, beyond the body's behavior.

6) Receiving is giving, and giving is receiving.

7) Sharing has no concealment and no private thoughts.

God has no secret communications. Everything of Him is perfectly open and freely accessible to all. By learning to receive from God and then give to our relationships, we establish a link that is a joining of the minds. The Holy Spirit only gives what can be given to all and leaves no one outside of its communication. We can't splice communication, for that would be siding against a part of God. Since all peoples are of God, what fool sides against Him?

A goal of the Holy Relationship is to end all separation. If we communicate in such a way that we exclude someone or something, we are not communicating as God communicates.

A Holy Relationship is based on spiritual purpose, goals aligned with Spirit, and loving agreements. The partners in a Holy Relationship learn how to let the Holy Spirit guide their purposes, goals, and agreements. The partners have learned to set aside their separate interests and look for guidance that serves the whole. A purpose is never-ending and reflects an awareness of God. The purpose of any true relationship is to know God for in the absolute truth, we are only in a relationship with Spirit.

In a Holy Relationship, goals are firmly set and kept clearly in mind in a unique way. They are "unifying" goals that are set by the Holy Spirit. Worldly goals set by our Egos lead to personal pleasures and selfish interests, which in the future provide separation. A unified goal refers to a constant way to direct our mind toward God. A unified goal is the special function of the relationship, the prime objective, and the behavioral practice that results from the relationship.

To have a goal is like climbing a ladder—we have to take it one-step at a time. To be 100% at peace with God, all the time in every situation, and to be a perfect reflection of this Light here on the Earth plane is an absolute purpose. We need to understand the "means" that will provide us with a realistic method for learning how to achieve this purpose. In absolute truth, we are never separate from God or from our partner. Our sense of having problems comes from false beliefs that we are not connected.

At our present stage of development, we cannot demonstrate all qualities of God all the time. This anomaly is the reason we need the Holy Spirit, and it is also why we need to set goals that will allow us to become aware of the qualities that we actively demonstrate. By learning how to express and extend one attribute of God, which becomes our unifying practice, we develop our understanding of God's presence. To attempt to laugh inside at all your troubles and to ask for help when necessary are two tasks that are attainable with lots of practice. Learning how to be joyous is the way to know God.

For example, a unified goal could be for partners to always practice forgiveness towards each other, regardless of the behavior conducted. Another goal could be to find peace in every situation or event. It could be to learn to be grateful for each problem and to see God in every problem. There are many specific unifying goals, and each couple should find the ones that work for their specific involvement, and describe the goals in their own language. We can also have personal unified goals. I have a personal unified goal to teach myself to be joyous. With every situation that I choose to be joyous, I am reaching toward my goal of being joyous constantly. Then, through the practice of being joyous, I am unified. Our unified goal connects us to our personal purpose, and we become a living example that demonstrates our unified goals to other people. We teach the behavior that defines our unified goal to other people by making a decision to prove to our self that we can achieve this goal.

Deciding to define and practice a unified goal is a method that brings unity (joining) to a moment instead of separation. Give yourself some time to be with your inner Self, and find your inner most idea of Spirit that feels right to you. Ask for help in finding the way that God best shows itself to you. Your best reflection of a divine attribute of Spirit will usually present itself to you in a way that you find very familiar. Once you've identified a divine attribute, consider it your unified goal to express it constantly and practice teaching yourself and others that you can reach this goal, even in situations where it may seem unattainable. By deciding on your unified goal, you are reinforcing the power of joining, which will help you and your partner know your highest purpose.

Some of the Unified Goals Others Have Used

To be peaceful.
To be joyous and happy.
To be accepting and forgiving.
To be in agreement with others.
To be in the Now moment.
To be grateful for problems, which create growth.
To be honest and open.
To be generous.
To renounce material greed.
To see a different point of view.

The partners of a Holy Relationship learn to choose a unified goal with one direction. If it seems that you and your partner are not choosing the same direction, then healing is required. While you and your partner can be powerful enough to manifest your material goals, this effort is about defining a unified goal. Remember that true happiness comes from doing God's purpose. Set the Goals of the Holy Spirit to lead us to happiness.

To teach peace in every situation.
To work for the complete healing of all of humanity.
To heal others by sharing spiritual truths.
To sing and dance in joy and laughter.
To undo past associations and programming.
To release the past by reinterpreting loss as gain.
To offer unlimited miracles to whoever comes into your experience.
To be a teacher of non-judgment.
To teach that we are joined in each situation.
To learn to extend appreciation and gratitude to God for the experiences we are having.
To reinforce our special unifying goal and teach us our unique purpose.
To show us the answer through miracles for our partner's problems.
Teach us to recognize when we are not in the Now moment.
To teach us the goal is to "know thyself," and there is nothing else to seek.

Your spiritual calling is to devote yourself with active willingness to live your unified goal, and to teach yourself that this devotion will lead you to love. To love yourself is to heal yourself, and your healing occurs through even the smallest choices and decisions. The difference between Spiritual goals and material-mental goals is that spiritual goals are attainable in the Now. Material goals not only focus on a future gain, but they also require growth, effort, and often, money. Spiritual goals are about returning to a state of being that has always existed. Even though you may have forgotten how to return to Spirit, Spirit is always present, and all things are unlimited and given freely. The problem does not reside in the act of "doing," but in your willingness of "being" able to receive. If your minds are properly attuned to receive, then you can express any spiritual attribute.

The partners of a Holy Relationship live by and for awareness, not acquisition. To acquire is to possess. The awareness of Oneness is never attained through the possession of things. Holy partners must go through a process of undoing a thought system that is based on the idea that it is the role of one partner to supply that, which is needed to fulfill any wants or lacks that are perceived by the other partner. It is a partner's job to support, not to supply. If a partner takes on a false job of supplying you with anything, then it can only lead to dependence; and while this may feel good and noble, it will result in the crippling of the relationship.

Limitless Creativity

A major stage of development in a happy relationship is when partners reach the creative level where they can create together. Most people remember very little of how to live on the creative level. We settle for the attainment of things. We hold on to a single home, a car, and a pile of stuff that we call "ours." Then, in our hopes of getting more "stuff," we believe that we are creating. We fight over stuff. We feel angry when stuff is taken away, and we feel sad if we don't get our stuff as quickly as we think we should. We mistake it for love and we see ourselves as victims in life if someone overpowers us and steals our stuff. We measure our own worth and compare ourselves to other people by the amount and type of stuff we possess. Using money and possessions to measure your creative potential is hardly an accurate way of assessing your understanding of creation. Yes, we live in a material, capitalistic society.

"Seek ye first the kingdom of God, and his righteousness, and all these things shall be added unto you."

The awareness of spiritual abundance and Oneness is far more valuable than acquiring material property. Creativity is working with thought and inner images. The manifestation of thought is the material world. To change our mind about the world is to change our thoughts about what we value. We set goals according to our values and that which we consider to be important.

The upside down perception that money is more valuable than the act of creating with others must be changed in a Holy Relationship. Limits within the mind must be exchanged for the concept of seeking the unlimited. Whenever we seek a limit (which we do quite often unconsciously), it is important to share how that perception is affecting the relationship. What is a limit? What is everything? A million dollars is a limit, and so is having a new car. In awareness, having everything means living in the moment, owning nothing, and being open. When we possess, we form a limit in the mind. The mind perceives a thought to have a defined form, which we call a "thing" or an "object." This thing is a limited form. It could even be called a fear thought since a fear thought is a thought that has a limit and appears to be solid. We are fearful when we think our fear thoughts are beyond our control (or taken away). The mind can never be satisfied when it focuses on a limit because the limit exists with the constant reminder that the limit (fear thought) will be, or could be, taken away. The nagging demands for "more" will also haunt our mind. How often does our lower mind choose to strive from the "getting" mode and forget to just be?

Greed will make a relationship unholy and it will make the partners feel unhappy. When the partners of a relationship focus on things as the source of love, then the relationship becomes unholy. In an unholy relationship, we have made the choice to settle for our limited things and beliefs instead of growing toward the awareness of abundance and demonstrating our creative potential. We fail to see the unlimited reality that exists within each other, and we choose to focus on behavior instead. Fear rules the minds that seek the attainment of things over the awareness of Spirit. Partners who do not work to correct these errors will never be able to reach union. By possessing a limiting belief in our mind, we are choosing to promote the concept of loss. The materially wealthy people are always concerned with what they could lose. The truly wealthy are those who experience no loss.

If your relationship has been built on materiality, then you and your partner must spend lots of time together in order to change that direction. Setting a holy purpose that is continually reinforced by you and your partner is the only method for successfully steering the relationship toward the creative level.

Material goals require an understanding of manifestation principles. Material goals are helpful, but they should not be valued more than the unifying goal. Money is useful, but there is no substitute for your Spiritual purpose. Part of your mind would prefer to focus on worldly goals and body goals rather than the unified goal. Choosing this preference is the same as putting the cart before the horse. When you notice that you and your partner spend a lot of time fighting and attacking each other, then you need to realize and admit that you are seeking Ego-oriented goals.

Unrealistic Goals

Your relationship must grow in the spiritual understanding of the definition of reality and the semantics of how the spiritual laws of abundance and increase work. Examining your goals is one of the best ways of discovering what you value. Are your values in alignment with spiritual prosperity?

A very important part of CO-creating is to be realistic. The right question to ask is, "What is real and what is not real?" What is unrealistic to one person can seem realistic to another, but the key to realism is in your consciousness. Super-consciousness can manifest anything but not for selfish gain.

Unrealistic goals are not attainable even though you may wish, fantasize, or pray for them. A person who makes $20,000 a year would be setting an unrealistic goal if he or she set a plan to make $500,000 next year doing similar job activities. Setting material goals or setting goals that expand our mental or emotional awareness must originate from an honest evaluation of where you currently reside in relation to those goals. Unrealistic goals are made by the Ego thought system because the Ego wants to keep you away from reality.

A degree of trust and respect can be lost when one partner fails to meet an unrealistic goal if the attainment of that goal was coupled with a promise to the other partner. The CO-creative process is devalued when unrealistic dreams replace the reality of Now. If the goal is a promise to be home in one hour to help clean the house, yet that promise was made from an unrealistic position, then a failure to reach that goal will cause a conflict. Don't make unrealistic agreements to appease a partner. These agreements will usually backfire, which will force you and your partner into a position of healing an issue.

How do you teach yourself how to set realistic goals when you are used to making unrealistic goals, dreams, and promises? First, ask the Holy Spirit for guidance. Second, affirm your unifying goals. Third, take an honest, small step. Finally, stay in communication with a willingness to change your behavior. Be open to the idea of sharing honest adjustments. For example, you thought it would take an hour to get home and you see the amount of traffic may force you to require two hours to get home. Pull off the road and make a phone call to your spouse. If you gave your word that you would be home in an hour, then communicate that the situation has changed and you need to reset the agreement.

When a person sets a large, unrealistic goal then he or she is feeling a need to prove something to someone by seeking that person's approval. In a No Loss Relationship, partners do not set goals based on a false need to prove something because love is never associated with performance or acquiring.

Financial Goals: Creating vs. Making Money

Money is not security, or happiness. It can't create nor produce health. We see money as the symbol of love, when it is just an illusion. We see money as a symbol or false idea of many things, and it ties us to our lower mind. The word "idol" comes from the concept of a false value placed upon an object or person. Undoing these false beliefs is a purpose for a Holy Relationship.

Couples who experience trouble with finances don't know how to create together, and they are living in a dream mind of "getting" money or fighting about money. Why do couples fight over money? The simple answer is that they are stuck in false beliefs and don't know how to change those beliefs.

All money problems are an indication that we are thinking too much from the lower mind. Money is not the answer, but at the same time it is not wrong or bad to use money. Like the body, money is a tool for communication and a means for teaching. Money is the by-product of creativity, like the waste material of food. Like fertilizer, money is necessary for growth and for the stimulation of future creativity.

Money is meant to follow creativity, not to be valued more than creativity. Many think they need money before they can be creative. They blame their blocks to creativity on not having money. If we find ourselves believing we want or need money to be creative or to finish a creative project, then realize that we have placed money in the wrong position within our project. There is never a lack of money because money is really printed-paper with a meaning that was assigned by our government

I remember as a child my grandfather had thousands of confederate dollars. I pretended I was rich, even though my grandfather knew the dollars were worthless. Money only has the meaning that we give to it. Everything will be provided to those who are clear about their purpose and are willing to "give" something valuable instead of trying to "get" something (like money).

If you are experiencing money problems in your relationship, then practice working on practical, realistic agreements and goals. Work on communication and your clarification of purpose. Carefully review your motivation and identify what you are chasing to feel good. Learn to exchange the pursuit of money for the desire to be more creative, and when the fear of lack comes to mind, use it as a reminder that you need to focus on a spiritual endeavor. Your money will always reflect your thoughts about how you are loved. An unloving relationship will always produce money problems, even if the couple has millions in the bank.

I have seen several couples with lots of money that fight over money regularly. "You paid how much for that dress?" shouted the millionaire husband to his wife. She screamed back, "Well, look what you paid for that boat!" True spiritual partners recognize the awareness of abundance and create from it.

Those who believe they want power because it will prove their wealth or provide them with a means to influence other people have forgotten the nature of life. Survival issues are meaningless to those who know they live eternally with Spirit. Earth becomes a vacation and a school for sharing, not a home to toil in or a place to fight for material needs. Those who are interested in making all of their relationships holy will be given instructions on how to do so and will be told of God's plan for their lives. There is no loss for those who follow God's plan because each moment is a joyous creative process. You are either following a spiritual purpose or attempting to be entertained in some meaningless pursuit. Nothing outside of you makes you happy or unhappy. You are solely responsible for happiness.

Goals Related to Behavior

In a Holy Relationship, each person has set the unified goal of being happy prior to any goals that involve any physical action. Each person has set a goal to release personal control over the outcome of any unified goals that are set by his or her partner. Each person has agreed to relinquish any conditions or judgments regarding his or her partner's goals. In addition, each person sees the escape from fear and the release from Ego thoughts as the way to healing. The unified goals of the relationship are reinforced, appreciated, and strengthened.

In stage two of an involvement, personalities may seem different and behaviors may seem to vary significantly from the behaviors that were enjoyed during the first stage of the involvement. Often, the Ego will point to what it "hates" in a partner's behavior. The "correction" of your partner's personality is not the means to becoming joined together. Personalities are formed by thoughts, beliefs, and patterns of expression. Personalities blend through acceptance, not from rigid criticism. For example, if you are in an unholy relationship with a woman, then you may express a desire for her to act a certain way so that her behavior will match your image of who you want her to be. In a Holy Relationship, you would want you both to behave in alignment with your unified and co-creative goals, beliefs, and agreements.

You can only improve your own character. My character goals are to tell the truth, to be more articulate, and not to procrastinate. I have enough to do without working on my partner's character. I can support her by setting agreements together (see Agreements in this chapter).

The Holy Spirit directs you in making choices that steer you away from "littleness" and away from pain. You become very little when you attempt to exert control over the behavior of your partners. It becomes a painful experience for you when you try to change someone else. It is easy to change your own thoughts when you have the guidance of Spirit. Your partner weighs something more than 100 pounds and your own thoughts weigh less than 1/1000 of a milligram. Which do you think are easier to move? Believe it or not, you think your partner's behavior is easier to move, but the only reason that you foster this belief is because you were not trained on how to release your own thoughts.

The number 1 goal of any relationship should be work on yourself, not on your partner. In other words, change your own mind, not your partner's mind.

Set a goal of not correcting your partner's behavior—or your own behavior, for that matter. Make a goal to only change inner thoughts. You are learning to transcend behavior, not to control it or require that it be a certain way. When you judge another person's behavior, you keep it current because you are replaying it in your mind. As a result, you inadvertently fail to notice the point at which the behavior has subsided or ended. It is the past. Stop trying to change the past. Instead change the thoughts that cause you to hold on to it. When you truly change a thought pattern (i.e. judgment), then you will discontinue the behavior that was associated with that thought pattern.

You will know that you and your partner are making mutual choices when you both feel happy and free of attachments to any specific outcomes. Actions taken from the Ego thought system do not change anything and do not make anything happen. Judgments from the Ego may change from liking to disliking, but the thoughts and beliefs stay the same. You do not lose when your partner is whomever they spontaneously choose to be. The partners of a No Loss Relationship understand that neither partner is hurt as a result of the behavior expressed by the other partner. If you think that someone else can hurt you, then the relationship has forgotten its holiness.

Let's say, you start to notice that you hate the way your partner leaves clothes all around the house. The behavior is sloppy, in your perception. You want to tell her to pick up after herself. If you make her behavior wrong and ask her to do what you want (even if she wants to be neater), then you are focusing on her form and behavior. Correction comes from looking at your unifying goal first. You must be joyous about the mess. You must practice the AAA mind healing method of Accepting, Appreciating, and Acknowledging the condition of the things in the house, even though you may still catch your mind calling it a mess.

Through this process, you are coming from a different space and a different view; you are addressing your own healing, not hers. In this example, you choose to examine your view of being neat and see it as an opportunity to change your programming regarding perfectionism with a new realization that there are many ways to see perfection. You can admit your process by sharing it with your partner, but you know that it is not a requirement on your part that she make a behavior correction for you to feel okay or satisfied. If she decides that she wants to change her behavior, then you can make an agreement that addresses this situation. If she does not indicate a desire to change her behavior, then you simply respond joyfully by picking up the clothes.

It is very difficult to learn not to correct your partner for his or her behavior. You do see differences, and you do start to dislike what your partner does. For this reason, it is important to understand your unifying goal and be willing to practice it regarding your partner's behavior. Think of it in this way: your partner's behavior is your way of becoming free of your Ego's control over you.

Goals

If the mind chooses to set goals that describe physical requirements for the body or set expectations regarding a person's physical appearance, then these goals and expectations are supporting a distorted perception of the real purpose of the body. Many people set goals for selfish reasons, such as losing weight to look good, wearing certain clothes to attract attention, or putting on makeup to impress people.

Remember that your ability to determine whether your behavior is coming from Spirit or from the Ego is not about the behavior itself, but understanding the reason that you do a particular behavior. Choosing to wear makeup is not the problem. Choosing to wear makeup because you perceive it as the only way that you can be attractive, and without makeup you feel you are lacking something is a distorted perception of the real purpose of the body. Are you dependent on makeup to feel okay about your appearance? Do you adorn your body with jewelry because you think you need to wear jewelry to feel okay about yourself? If yes, then this belief serves as proof that you consider the body to be your home, and you are forgetting that Spirit is your true home.

You have been behaving under these beliefs for most of your life, even though these beliefs are often the cause of sickness, feelings of "restlessness," and a sense of never being satisfied.

Every goal can be aligned with a spiritual value. Many spiritual people wear bright, elaborate clothing and fine jewelry because they see these items as actively reflecting spiritual rays or qualities. Clothing is meant to keep you warm, and the colors can reflect spiritual attributes. The fabric does not define you; it only has the meaning that you give to it. If clothing is used to improve your image as a body, then it serves the Ego. If it serves the purpose of the Holy Spirit, then it brings souls closer to the Light. If clothing is a symbol of our vanity, then the Ego mind is using the body to imprison the Spirit.

Goals that keep energy flowing through the body, like taking classes in yoga or Tai Chi, or running or hiking outdoors support the goal of staying healthy. These efforts for staying healthy can be combined with the goals of service and wholeness to the Spirit, mind, and emotions. Choosing to care for the body is never the problem. Making choices from the lower mind that use the body for the wrong reasons is a problem. Evil is a term that could be used to describe actions taken that represent wrong use of the body. In other words, an act referred to as evil is an indication that a person identifies him or herself mostly with the body and perceives him or herself as so separate from Spirit that he or she uses the body to do harm. To truly live, means, to do no harm. Choosing to set a goal that would harm your body, your partner's body, or any other person's body is a choice that originates from fear.

How to Set Spiritual Goals

If we are uncertain of what we want or what goal would be in alignment with our partner, then we can simply ask the Holy Spirit to clarify the goal so that it serves our greater goal to reach God. We ask these questions: "What is the motivation of this goal?" "What result do we want from this goal?" "In which direction will this goal lead us?" And "Is this goal in alignment with our unifying goals?" Asking these four very important questions will lead us toward our task of setting the goal with a spiritual focus. Who doesn't want a goal that will lead us to true happiness?

In the beginning, the power to discern the usefulness of anything lies in our ability to communicate with the Holy Spirit. It requires a willingness to ask, listen, and follow some specific guidelines. Guidelines will not only keep us in bounds, on the path, and on track, but they will also save time. Following these guidelines will prevent the Ego from using the object-thing (any physical thing) for self-glorification.

The Specific Guidelines for Object-Things

1. The object-thing is not cherished more than your relationship.
2. The object-thing is seen as temporal. It won't last, and must not be retained for selfish interests.
3. The object-thing is shared and given to all. It is not to be possessed or owned for oneself alone.
4. The object-thing has a useful purpose, which is to promote communication that will serve the good of all.
5. The object-thing is to be seen for it's now moment focus, not to be stored as a way to remember the past.
6. The Is-ness of the object-thing is to be observed first and before a decision is made regarding its usefulness.

The Specific Guidelines for People

1. The person is in your life to mirror your mind.
2. The person is in your life for healing and then creating together.
3. The relationship with the person is the means to teach you to communicate.
4. The person is a means to free you from limited perceptions.
5. The person is to be seen as a mind and not a body.
6. All the rules of object-things can be interpreted to apply to people.

Goal Setting for the Highest Good

Each day, if possible, set some goals with your partner. Call the goals: daily things to do. Many people are accustomed to following a "TO DO LIST," which is similar, but be sure to state the spiritual reason for doing each item on the list. This task doesn't need to take more than five minutes, and it places the mind in the service of the Spirit each day.

Each week, and at least once a month (perhaps on or just after the New Moon), has a longer planning session for the purpose of reviewing, revising, and clarifying your mutual goals. This is time well spent and can save years of uselessly pursuing unnecessary goals. If the television takes precedence to goal setting, then the Ego is winning and keeping you distracted. Most relationships stop working because partners don't take time to pray, plan, and prioritize their goals with a higher purpose.

When asking for a spiritual gift, make sure the request is in alignment with the highest good for you and for others. The gift will be given. No true request is ever denied. If the request is misguided or the purpose is not clearly aligned with the good of all, then clarification may be needed. Often, you look for outside confirmations for inner requests.

Looking for results in a specific form is an indication that you value the outer more than the inner, and that the Ego has pulled you away from the inner realization. For example, if you ask for a new car to make you look good and feel important, then this request serves your Ego. If you ask for a new car so that you can teach about relationships and do more healing work, then your request is to serve Spirit. The manifestation of the car can come in any form, type, style, or price.

When you are clear about the reason for each goal, then communicate the goal to your higher self, release any attachment to how it will manifest, and then listen quietly to what your next agreement or action step should be.

The Process for Setting Goals Created in Light with the Highest Good in Mind
1. Affirm the spiritual unification goal.
2. Ask for the material goal.
3. Clarify the idea. What is its spiritual equivalent?
4. Release any specific outcome.
5. Find the now moment agreement that best supports your part.
6. Reaffirm the spiritual unification goal.

Example:
1. Peace is my purpose.
2. I want a new car.
3. The car is an idea of being free and supports me to teach love in other parts of the city.
4. I release that I want a BMW or an Escalade.
5. I now agree to go to my banker and determine how much money I can borrow.
6. This goal of receiving a car is experienced in peace.

In our example, traveling is a way of becoming less restricted. It could represent several spiritual ideas, such as unlimited abundance, love, playfulness, adventure, etc.

All your desires for material objects are really just your inner desire for God. The temptations of the Ego are really your inner yearnings to know God, but they are twisted and misdirected. Partners who are in a Holy Relationship are able to untwist and correct these distortions that will then allow them to clearly understand the goal and the purpose. Partners use agreements as reminders for what they truly want.

Agreements

Your life works according to how well you keep your agreements.

Your truth is your purpose. Your goals are the means for reaching your purpose, and your agreements are the way to reach your goals. Setting agreements and learning how to keep them is a major part in being able to achieve a Holy Relationship.

Having agreements in place keeps you true to your word and able to create the reality of the love you desire. By setting and upholding agreements, you provide yourself with a way to overcome the influence of the Ego and to prevent yourself from lying to yourself and your partner. If an agreement becomes broken, then trust must be rebuilt and healing must occur in order to reestablish the agreement. I will discuss how to heal broken agreements later, but it is important to understand that anger projected at a partner is not the way to produce healing. Agreements made to yourself alone are really agreements made with your Ego. Sharing agreements with a partner supports the power of joining. Agreements made with your partner will support your unifying goals.

Agreements are the muscles of a Holy Relationship. You can make agreements to do the "baby steps" toward reaching your goals. Agreements teach you the process of taking realistic, practical steps toward what you truly desire. You will need to support each other in loving ways to make it easy to keep your agreements.

Agreements provide a way for you to practice keeping your word and overcoming the fears that lead to lower consciousness (animalistic behavior). By making an agreement with your partner, you do what you say you will do, and you provide a basic foundation for trust. As a result of upholding agreements, you will become more conscientious of your surroundings and more considerate towards other people. In addition, your efforts to uphold an agreement will help prevent you from acting selfishly. Agreements are very necessary for your stage of evolution.

Each agreement must be seen as a way of promoting the spiritual goals and fulfilling your purpose. If you and your partner have the same purpose and the same spiritual goals, then your efforts to maintain agreements will become easy. Partners in a Holy Relationship make agreements and learn how to keep them. You can only trust your partner when you both understand how to keep agreements. Many people think they reside within the relationship with certain agreements, yet they are actually living with implied assumptions and false expectations.

Healing Agreements Through Support

You and your partner need to agree that you will openly admit and discuss situations that occur when agreements are not fulfilled or completed. Agree to hold the discussion without criticism. Clarify the goal, be supportive, and be willing to openly discuss how the agreement can now be reached.

You must learn to receive support. You are not being receptive if you respond with an attitude that you "know it all." If you respond with a defensive attitude, then you are reacting against ideas that could be helpful. If you respond with a secretive attitude because you want to hide your thoughts, then you are not being receptive. If you feel angry towards your partner because he or she behaved irresponsibly, then recognize that your response is a reflection of how you can behave irresponsibly as well. Being supportive means that you choose a response that is gentle and tolerant. It also means being honest about your own process. An agreement is not meant to be used as a weapon to beat up your partner when the agreement is not met, regardless of the reason.

Compassion speaks for non-judgment and a gentle recommitment of focus. You and your partner are at the same level regarding the ability to uphold an agreement and to keep your word. You might say, "I hate this part/I like being superior." Or, "It's easy to see my partner not keeping his or her agreements." Your Ego is equally as destructive as your partner's Ego. Your partner's way of self-deception may not be in the same form, but his or her capacity to keep an agreement is the same as yours. Choosing to feel guilty or make your partner feel guilty about not keeping an agreement will not help to correct inner thoughts.

Search your mind to identify the thoughts that may be having an impact on your ability to keep an agreement instead of labeling your behavior as wrong.

As an example, suppose you and your partner made an agreement in the relationship to practice meditating each day for 30 minutes. Your partner admits at the end of the week that he or she missed three days. While examining the excuses and reasons (not from a place of guilt), he or she discovers that the reason for the missed days was due to a fear that if he or she completed the meditations as agreed, then he or she would not have enough time to complete the other agreements.

With honesty, you both share the fear of not enough time and the belief that there is too much to do. Even though you were able to keep the meditation agreement, you support your partner's concerns by correcting your own time issues as well. By addressing this agreement with compassion, you and your partner have joined with each other in the task of releasing that fear and recommitting to the agreement of meditation. When you and your partner choose to be supportive, then you share thoughts that not only strengthen the relationship, but also heal the blocks that could prevent you from CO-creating.

You are harmful to yourself and to your partners when you respond with anger. Feelings of guilt will arise in both people when one person reacts with anger. Don't teach your partner that he or she must live with guilt. Other people have already tried to teach through guilt, but this process will not successfully alter a person's behavior without negative consequences. The sense of shame and guilt prevents you from being able to accept support from other people. You are often hard on other people because you are so hard on yourself.

A supportive partner knows that it's okay to be the student as well as the teacher. Each holy partner is willing to be humble. If your defenses are stronger than your ability to admit the error, then the block is not removed. You will continue to sabotage yourself by not keeping your agreements.

Major problems occur in relationship when couples can't find ways to provide support, but also to receive support. Often, a person will say, "I care about you, so I want you to _____." This expression of caring is more of a demand because it is stated with a stipulation. Therefore the other person will respond with resistance toward the so-called "caring" feeling. People never like the feeling that they have to change something about themselves to be loved.

If you find yourself unable to accept support, then you are afraid of your creative powers. You and your partner need to make agreements regarding actions to take when communication becomes blocked. This blockage occurs when a partner refuses to accept support, and he or she needs something that will help him or her shift back to a space where he or she is comfortable accepting support.

It is also appropriate to have several plans that could be used to address support blockages. Plan A might be for you and your partner to sit and meditate for 10 minutes. Plan B might be to walk away from each other and take 8 hours apart with the trust that each partner will work on him or herself in his or her own way and then agree to meet after that period. Having several plans clearly defined will prevent drama and outbursts of emotional chaos.

When two people attack each other to the extent that abuse and deep resentment occur, then the task of repairing the mental split can require lots of effort. Wouldn't it be more valuable to have agreements that would help you avoid reaching this explosive state? Give your partner the right to resist help. Responding with gentleness is not about forcing an issue. Terrorizing a student makes you a poor teacher.

Daily Agreements

By making daily agreements with your partner, you will be able to practice watching your own thoughts. As you are following your agreements, you will also notice how easy and joyous your relationship can work. All spiritual practices must come from the task of keeping agreements. Agree to pray daily, meditate, or read some spiritual material. Partners who share a spiritually focused involvement let the Holy Spirit make all decisions for them, knowing that every choice will lead to love. The agreement is to never make a decision alone. The commitment to the relationship creates the willingness to join in all decisions. Nothing you say or do conflicts with your purpose. Each partner learns not to make private decisions without connecting with their unified goal and with his or her partner.
Because you are so used to making decisions alone, it will require a conscious effort in the beginning to implement the process of making joint decisions with a partner and
The Holy Spirit.

Questions You May Have

When it comes to making agreements, does that mean you need to decide even the little things together like what to wear or what to buy at the grocery store?
The surprising answer is yes. True communication goes beyond the body's language and beyond our five senses. If you ask couples what bothers them the most, they will often reply that it's "the little things that make me feel as though my partner wasn't being considerate of my thoughts or feelings." You think you can remain separate and still get love from a partner. The origin of most disagreements occurs when one partner makes decisions without first connecting with his or her partner. United couples can communicate beyond time and space. This means that they are not limited to being within physical proximity to discuss choices. This may seem like an advanced idea to people who are in the beginning stages of making a relationship Holy. Wouldn't you rather strive for Oneness than succumb to the idea that attaining Oneness is impossible?

When it comes to making decisions, you can consult the Holy Spirit first by setting your mind in joy. Next, you contact your partner mentally and use your intuition. You must learn that your minds are joined because you have spent so much time in your life learning that they are not. Learning how to listen by following what is heard is the final step. When you know your mind is joined, then correct decisions can be received.

The partners of a Holy Relationship practice the joined decision making process with a no-loss and no-guilt focus by being supportive. You self examine only to heal, not to criticize. Be happy in your learning. You can either join in mind or you can continue to live from the old pattern of doing it as you always have.

Does This Joining Process Take a Lot of Time?

At first, it may seem to require much thought and time to get still. I assure you, though, trying to make the "right" decision on your own will not only result in more wasted time, but it will often lead you further away from your purpose. How much time have you spent chasing or seeking after something that you believed would satisfy you only to find out that much of your invested efforts were useless?

How do you know you have connected with your partner, and how do you know that you are making the right choice?

At first, faith is required and your Ego will present you with lots of confusion and doubt. Many times you will forget to ask. Often, your Ego will tell you about your failures. Faith is a way of placing your mind in a state of listening and connecting with your higher mind. The Holy Spirit is on the other end of the telephone line. You have only forgotten the number. In every relationship, a spiritual energy cord runs between your mind and your partner's mind. You could dial your partner's number by remembering the essence (or even an image) of your partner. This essence could come to you as an image, a color, a feeling, or a sense of knowing, or of remembering that you are joined in purpose. You could do a self-created ritual, or you could just be certain. Finding out which procedure works for you and trusting in that procedure is part of the fun.

Learning how to trust your inner voice is a process that takes time, so be patient and gentle with yourself. Connecting with your partner is automatic, but it doesn't mean your partner needs to be literally thinking about you at that moment. Your partner's higher soul, the part that always loves you, is adding energy to your process through the faith that you have in your partner, and the answer to your question will arise through your being peaceful in the silence.

You will learn through practice that these decisions made through joining will not only strengthen your commitment to continue this process, but they will also enhance your awareness of the idea that you and your partner are really joined in mind. Feedback that supports this awareness is actualized when you and your partner share your experiences with each other. Be honest. You will know that a decision was made through this joining practice when you can acknowledge the fruits of the practice.

Never attack your partner when he or she attempts to practice joining and the results are not apparent. Also, you never want to attack your partner if he or she simply forgets to follow the joining process when he or she needs a decision. The results of truly joining are enormous because they will cause the mind to move into the creative level. Don't be too concerned with doing it right. Be open to noticing what it means to make decisions for the good of all.

A choice is never between two object-things but between a decision of separation and a decision that supports your unifying goal. If you arrive home after buying the groceries and you realize that your partner had said that he or she wanted yams, but you had mistakenly bought potatoes, then in this example, did you join? You know that you consciously practiced the joining process because communication had occurred prior to the decision. Perhaps you chose to forget your partner's statement about the yams because you really preferred to buy potatoes. Regardless, no attempt to practice the joining process is a failure.

When it comes to choosing between things, there is no right choice or wrong choice. The concepts of "right or wrong" and "good or bad" do not exist in the unified mind. The mutuality of your experience is the idea of nurturing your body to serve Spirit. Correction of the mind comes with the desire to seek the mutual benefit. Both partners must be willing to release the need to know the context of the mutual benefit, especially since each partner's perception may differ. In the example above, the choice of buying the yams or the potatoes is not the event that really matters. Understanding the manner in which the events play out at the level of form is not the goal. It is acknowledging that you and your partner joined in an effort to nurture the relationship.

This example may seem frivolous and insignificant, especially when you consider some of the larger problems that couples face, but the small issues will add up and can cause significant problems and resentments if they are not addressed. The ability to join for the sake of a decision requires the honest attempt of only one partner. The other partner may need to take an honest look inside and ask if an impulse was felt at the time of the joining attempt or if he or she were engaged in some activity that may have served as a distraction.

Can You Manipulate Agreements?

Agreements can be manipulated when you choose to listen to your Ego. I assure you, your inner teacher will not let you get away with it and your inner peace will not be complete. A day later, you could be reminded that you chose selfishly. With intuition, the lesson comes even faster. Believe me, you don't want to win against your partner. It is not real winning. It will only hurt you.

Let me repeat that illusions of special love and illusions of special hate are the same. Neither will really make you happy. If you find yourself "thinking" about something that happened in the past (whether it was an hour ago or several days ago), then these uneasy thoughts are an indication that your choice was out of accord with love, and your state of mind has moved into the Ego realm of resentment.

When approached at the level of form and behavior, resentment regarding a choice that was made will lead to guilt, and then to separation. When you feel anything other than peace, then this feeling is a sign that you attempted to act in a selfish manner, even though you may feel proud of the action that you chose. Pride is a form of self-centered Egotism. Pride and false righteousness serve as destroyers of any efforts in the process of joining. It isn't easy to catch yourself participating in your ways of manipulation.

Setting Goals for the 4 H's

It is very valuable to set goals in the 4 H's: Health, Happiness, Healing, and Holiness. They correspond to your four bodies.

Health is for the body level. It also includes material things. You and your partner can write down 10 goals that relate to your body and its maintenance and another 10 goals that pertain to material needs. Remember to clarify the goal spiritually.

For example:
I want to fix my teeth so that I can chew food properly and so my body will receive the nutrition it needs.
I want to exercise and do yoga so that I will learn how to circulate energy.
Material goals:
I want to buy a house and start a spiritual center.
Happiness is for your emotional body. Set goals for your emotional balance and set happy dreams that include adventure and exploration.

For example:
I plan to attend a spiritual class on inner peace and meditation to learn how to deal with my anger.
I plan to read a book about nonviolent communication with my partner.
Healing is the mental realm and can also apply to the emotional realm. Set some mental goals that work with your mind.

For example:
I want to increase my vocabulary and be more intelligible.
I want to heal my relationship with my sister.
I want to forgive myself for past mistakes with money.
Holiness is the realm of Spirit and relates to your unified goal and spiritual practices.

For example:
I want to increase my awareness of my spiritual guides.
I want to practice yoga every day.

When you and your partner review your goals in these 4 areas, then you will better understand your areas of interests. For example, if it is easy for you to list 10 goals or more in the area of health (body level) and only a few in the area of healing, then your priorities may be skewed towards a material focus. When goals in one level are listed with a purpose stated behind the form description, then they are integrated and useful in every other level as well. Most of you will consider one level to be at a higher priority than the other levels. Also, people tend to be stronger at accomplishing tasks within one level and weaker in another. That's fine; if you're highly mental, then set more healing goals and work on your emotional body. Everyone is striving for integration and wholeness in all areas.

Happy Dreams

Happy dreams are also reflections but the distortion is very minimal. You are in the process of learning. You must learn to move your state of being from specialness to wholeness. Even though it is only one step, you are learning how to take that step constantly. Most people take one step forward into wholeness and two steps backward into specialness until they realize that specialness doesn't work, and they become willing to give up all dreams about specialness. Some people are never willing to give up these dreams. They hold on very dearly as if they couldn't exist without them. Most people refuse to wake up from their false notions of what will make them happy. You must constantly learn to discern your dreams and find within them the hidden distortions that make you think happiness is in something or someone.

The experience of a happy dream becomes apparent when you look at your partner and come to the awareness that he or she shares your same dream, and you are not "getting" happiness from each other. You are extending happiness and joining in it. This type of dreaming is not a denial of participating in this world. You are participating in such a way that you don't get trapped into believing that your private mind is reality. All unhappiness is but the insistence that your private dreams are real.

Happiness doesn't happen in the future. If you think it does, then you are relying on a false dream. Happiness doesn't come from what you thought made you happy in your past, with the wish to repeat it. The process is in time and about time. Healing is not about waiting for time to correct errors in the mind, but the acceptance of what happiness is. Happiness happens now. Happy dreams are about creating in a now moment. Happy dreams are fun, and you never lose your purpose; it is a miraculous way of seeing this world.

When the partners of a Holy Relationship work toward healing dreams, then they examine them for aspects of "selfishness" and control. When you are supporting your partner through the healing process, you don't label their dreams as "bad"; you simply ask questions. The right, appropriate questions will lead to wisdom.

When exploring your wants, dreams, wishes, and fantasies, keep an open mind. Remembering that you need training in discernment. Expressions of anger and attack will not correct the mind. When practicing discernment, consider the following questions: What purpose does this dream support? Is this dream in alignment with your other goals? What will this goal teach you? What are you teaching others by acting on this dream? Review the principles to happiness and determine if the dream is against the principles.

Once I had a dream to take a trip to Hawaii, and I wanted to take a woman who I was see ing at the time. In the dream, the time we spent traveling and sharing together on the trip to Hawaii made our relationship stronger and happier. Who wouldn't want to take a trip to the beach with such a great guy like me? Upon further examination of the dream, I realized that it had elements of specialness, greed, and beliefs that the trip would make the relationship work better. I was attempting to prove that I was a great partner. The lure of the warm sun and romantic escapades danced through our heads until we realized that the purpose of completing this book and becoming friends first had more precedence. The happy dream became a ski trip and a weekend by a warm fire, typing away.

The illusions of happiness are caused by the misperception that happiness can be given or taken away by some objective other. You make someone special because your mind has projected that happiness comes from that person.
The ability to create fun in a relationship requires that each partner learn the principles of true happiness.

The Principles to True Happiness

1. Happiness is an internal awareness.
2. Happiness comes from the Now moment, not a past special perception.
3. Don't work for happiness and don't work to survive.
4. Objects and people are not responsible for your feelings.
5. Desires come from creating, not from getting.
6. Judgments cause pain, and a non-judgmental state of mind is happiness.
7. Freedom is an aspect of happiness. You must set something free before you can experience real happiness.

1. Happiness is an internal awareness.
Understand and teach that each person receives happiness first from within, and then you are able to extend it to another person. When a person understands that happiness comes from his or her inner self, then he or she is considered whole. Two whole beings extending to each other reaffirm the idea of wholeness; thus they create from it. If a person

doesn't see his or her happiness as originating from within, then he or she will think of him or herself as incomplete and empty, which will result in the mistaken belief that happiness can be fulfilled from an outside source. Two incomplete people think getting together will make them whole, but it never works. Two incomplete beings live as a reminder to each other of what they don't have. They never really "get" happiness or completeness from their mate.

2. Happiness comes from the Now moment, not a past, special perception.

Happiness is often associated with "getting", which is conveyed to you by the Ego-mind. The world promotes Ego-based ideas because the Ego makes alliances with other Egos. Romance that is sold to you because you think you "got" something in return is an exaggerated darkened emotion and not an expanded awareness. Each erotic excitement produces an adrenaline high, but like any drug, it has its side effects. Your emptiness would be filled by this person, only to find out the fire burned out sooner than you'd hoped, leaving you with a deeper sense of loss.

Again, you failed to find true love. The side effect of erotic love is emotional pain. This pain is so great that many people feel that they would rather give up on love and relationships and be alone than face the effects of that type of longing. The false concept of "getting," which is also known as the "I want" phrase, will lead to an obsession with romance.

When two people engage in sexual pleasures where the focus is directed on identification with the body, they are setting the groundwork for an excessive amount of emotional drama. No two people can join or find purpose within a relationship if the drama, which consists of switching between emotional love and emotional hate, becomes the predominate interaction. Like a small boat in a heavy storm, the rise and fall of the waves will sink the ship. Happiness will never be found until each person balances his or her own emotions first.

Few people know how to address and resolve this pattern. It is synonymous to a catch-22 because you rush into a romantic, sexual relationship hoping that the other person can fix that which feels "wrong" inside of you. Yet you need to fix that which is "wrong" inside of you before you can engage in a healthy relationship. Because you have lived with your Ego mind for several years, you carry with you a deep sense of unhappiness. Those of you who are chasing after a mate are simply saying, "Who can take away this unhappiness, can you?"

To create fun in your relationship, replace romance with the desire to join. Set your partner free from any fantasies that maintain that happiness comes from him or her. Replace specialness with wholeness and learn to see that you are giving first to yourself and then to a partner who is the same as you.

3. Don't work for happiness and don't work to survive.

Working for happiness, security, or spiritual favoritism is a mistake made by the mind that believes that you need to "pay" to know God. False teachings of God instill upon people that they have to pay back God or that God demands that you pay for what you have been given. "God needs your money to build greater churches, to have the best religion, and to help the poor." These ideas sound good, but God needs nothing from this material plane to work his or her plan effectively. You need these things only so you can remember to go within and listen. Offering money to spiritual institutions is not the problem; it's the belief that you "get" something for giving. What you always get is the now moment miracle; you never get something from the "give-get" mentality.

The lower mind falsely believes that exchanging as the means for "getting" insures "having." You'll work so that you "have." A false sense of being happy is established when you entertain such foolish concepts that you can pay for anything that God gives freely. Security comes from creating, not from possessing. The pure idea of happiness is blocked by the concept of possession and the need to own. The partners of a Holy Relationship have fun at everything and they remember the highest purposes of the relationship. When fun is lost, then working for it becomes a poor choice.

Examine your motives for working and what working means to you. Review the concepts regarding work that you were taught by other people. Meaning is the bus that takes you somewhere. To work for something that is already given is meaningless, unless you believe that you can no longer receive it. The nature of the statement "to work" is that it provides you with an opportunity to share your unique talents and your spiritual gifts. But to work for something material is to lose your spiritual identity. Knowledge cannot be replaced by working for physical security. Your values become upside down. Those who do work for material gain, believing their happiness comes from it, are sadly mistaken.

Complete the following sentence:
I have to _____ or else _____(what do you imagine will happen if   what you fear comes true).
I have to make money to pay the rent or else they will take away my home.
I have to work hard or else I won't have enough money.

Continue to repeat this sentence and fill in the blanks with every situation that you   can imagine. Fill up a page of "I have top's." Look at the fear motivation.
Next, complete the same sentence for a great relationship.
I have to _____in order to have a great relationship, or else _____.

Each "I have to" represents the concepts that you hold about work. It becomes your need to perform, which robs you of joy. Two couples can be doing the exact same task, one doing it from a place of "I have to," and the other doing it from the space of pure giving. The actions seem identical, but the inner attitudes of each couple differ, the latter experiencing Play, Joy, and Freedom.

4. Objects and people are not the cause of your feelings.

A person with an awakened mind has transcended the reactive mind and understands that he or she alone is responsible for his or her own feelings. When you are teaching yourself to awaken, you will need to practice constantly to align your behaviors and thought system with this understanding. You will fall asleep into the reactive mind if you choose to think that something outside of you is the cause of your emotions. Only in the support of a happy relationship can you teach yourself this truth regarding your own feelings. Don't expect the majority of people to understand this concept. Don't even expect yourself to believe it at times! Few people understand the power of being "centered in wholeness" and even fewer are able to maintain such a focus.

5. Desires come from creating, not from getting.

This idea teaches you how the universe remains in a constant state of Light, while the human animal's mind falls into fear. Desires are different from wishing, wanting, or begging. Desires come from the inner realms of the soul. By being a creator, you create from inner desires for the purpose of being whole. These desires are different than the Ego's yearning which can be described as wishing, wanting, and begging for the purpose of "getting something."

6. Judgments cause pain, and a non-judgmental state of mind is happiness.

Making judgments will cause you pain. All judgments of the mind cause a mental and an emotional interference of joy, which is a lowering of the vibration from the higher mind. The Ego believes it has the right to judge and is the cause of all our pain and sickness. The mind that learns not to judge or to control the material world is choosing to remember its pure Self. If you are in pain, remember that happiness teaches you that the universe runs just fine without your perception, your opinions, and your judgmental beliefs. You are so used to your patterns of thinking that you don't realize what it is costing you until you are ready to give up those patterns.

7. Freedom is an aspect of happiness. You must set something free before you can experience real happiness.

This idea is a contradiction to the ideas that you have learned in this world because most of the people in this world love to conquer and to make trophies. The world's ideas reinforce imprisonment by possession because the Ego will constantly remind you that you're drenched with limitation. All unhappiness originates from the belief in loss. You can't remain happy if you choose to contemplate what you don't have. The ultimate freedom that everyone is seeking is from limited perceptions. It is achieved through the practice of setting other people free. Forgiveness is the method that you need to learn to reach a state of freedom.

Loss in relationships is perceived when happiness is not recognized for what it is. If you feel rejected and abandoned, it is because you sought happiness in the wrong way. It takes a great amount of undoing to learn that happiness doesn't come from the illusions of love. It takes a lot of effort to learn how to discover these illusions of love. The sooner you learn to recognize that which is false, the more chances you will have to seek for that which is true. No relationship is a failure because every relationship provides an opportunity for you to learn more about that which is false. Once you realize that you experienced an illusion of love, you have learned something of great value, and you are ready to consider the relationship a success. True happiness and love come from the same source. The partners of a Holy Relationship examine and eliminate the ways in which they may be falsely seeking happiness.

The Unhappy Dream and Relationship Avoidance

Dreams happen in the day and in the night. Because we are dreaming most of the time, we must learn how to wake up. Dreams are images that we made in our mind. They are the reflections of reality that we distorted into our personal views of life. Moonlight is a reflection of the sun's light. Dreams are twisted reflections of life. Dreams happen when our minds are focused in the future or when we review a dream that we made and we call it our past.

The unhappy dream is our romantic special wish that we will get the happiness that we desire from another person. Secretly, we make up images of what love is, how it should act, how it should look, taste, smell, and feel. The more we value these images, the more we think we need them to exist. We then project them onto our target, that special someone who seems to match our dreams. This pattern is so unconscious to us; we are not aware of the mental processes of dreaming. We even call it "thinking." This thinking dream is supposed to bring us happiness, but as we discover, it fails. A major life lesson is to learn how dreaming fails to cause happiness. If we can understand this important point, then we are well on our way to discovering the way to true love. This view of the dream is the reason why we can't fail in relationships. If we really learn what doesn't work, then we are sure to find out what does work.

There are only two paths. When you choose to stay out of relationships, then this choice serves as proof that you haven't learned what doesn't work. You are not designed to avoid relationships but to enjoy the process of correcting your mind through the relationship experience. You will hear people make the following statements: "No, I am not in a relationship," or "No, I haven't found someone," and "The last relationship was so painful that I am not going to get into a relationship for a while," or "Men are @*&@#, who needs them," and "Women, who can understand them?" Such thoughts will only delay the healing process. Secretly, your Ego waits to repeat the pattern of special love. You are always in a relationship with some aspect of yourself.

The greatest joy partners can share is the process of healing the mind together. You can always find someone who wants a spiritual involvement because everyone is looking for a way to be truly happy. Learning the correct way to cause healing is really fun. Choose to create a Holy Relationship. Involvement in relationships is required to see your reflections, your expectations, and your dreams. Don't avoid relationships; just be more devoted to a higher purpose in a relationship. If you still feel that you were hurt by the last relationship, then do the emotional releasing exercise in this book, and take responsibility for your own interpretation of the involvement.

If you are unhappy, then stop blaming people for your unhappiness. Stop looking for the illusions of love, and start learning how to create happy dreams. Never let your Ego convince you that you aren't entitled to be in a relationship or that you shouldn't be in a relationship. Being able to notice the difference between miracles and erotic love will require a slight shift in perception. Once this difference is realized, you will never "see" yourself as alone again. The world needs miracle workers and teachers who are willing to have Holy Relationships. The world needs happy dreamers. You are here to demonstrate happiness through relationships, and there is no lack of students who want to learn of true happiness. If you teach yourself what happiness is, then you will never say, "I lack someone to be in a relationship with." A Holy Relationship by definition is the act of extending oneself to all selves.

This is the time for you to give birth to CO-creating in the nature of love. Have perfect faith that you and your partner can do all that is asked of you. Know with certainty that what you set out to accomplish will be supported by your higher mind because your higher mind is providing you with direction. Nothing will be denied and nothing will be lacking. Say to your partner, "In the name of our Holy Relationship I give all our dreams and goals to the Holy Spirit. I know they will be achieved as we are released from fear. I will not use these goals as a way to remain in limitation. I will use them for the purpose of healing relationships. In the name of love and our freedom, I choose to give as I receive, and see us healed together."

This year is the time to CO-create our happy dreams in peace and for the greater good of all. There is much to do, and now is the time to participate in the healing of our planet and the healing of our minds. Let all of our relationships be holy, and let us make this year a year to fulfill our purpose.

Let God's plan be done through us. Amen.

Making Decisions

You have already learned to ask for the support of the Holy Spirit and your partner when facing major decisions, then you can also be joined in love for the creation of your goals. This joining process will produce true happiness. Setting goals together and as one mind causes you to join in CO-creating and multiplies the power of creating.

When a major issue surfaces, pray together and ask for inner guidance. Teach each other the power of trusting and listening to the Holy Spirit. Remember, you are not accustomed to deciding this way. Most of the decision-making process for goal setting is done in selfishness based on separate interest. Rarely have you been taught to pray first and then listen for the answer regarding your need to make a spiritual goal. Happy dreams will sometimes require a plan, but when you catch yourself planning alone, then be aware that you are moving away from making your relationship create as one.

Communication leads to joint understanding. You are really learning that a Holy Relation ship is not about a "me against you, I get what I want" mentality. Using the Holy Spirit as the intermediary, a third power, between your separate goals will eliminate any power struggles. The Ego counsels, "Take your happiness at whatever cost; it's your right." The Holy Spirit counsels, "Happiness is dependent on your decision to join with your partner's mind." Most of the responses that we learned are the "do it your way" or "do it my way" pendulum of fear, or to listen to something which we likely heard from someone in authority or, "I'll do what I want," which is selfishness based on separate interest, or "Don't tell me what to do, I'll do what I want," which is a form of rebellion. When it comes to major issues, we were rarely trained to pray first and then listen and wait until we both get the same answer. This is the key to creating happy dreams.

Selfish planning for the future is one of the Ego's methods of getting what it wants. It is a process to learn to give plans to Holy Spirit; it is a process of trust and listening. What good are your private plans if they lead you to destroy your relationship?

You must learn that not getting what you want is not a sacrifice. The Ego loves to say, "I sacrificed my happiness/dreams for you." In a Holy Relationship, the goal is to join your minds and share your miracles; miracles are inspired when two minds give up selfish interests for love's expressions.

Learn to put all your ideas/dreams/ goals in a common journey, and learn they are not "Yours" nor are they your partners. Don't see them as belonging to either of you. See them as just ideas that can work for greater good or not while detaching from you vs. me. It's only an idea causing more listening to Holy Spirit and what can serve the All. True happy dreams cause no conflict to anyone. So always be willing to give up a personal plan, and trust that Spirit's plan for your life is greater than anything the ego can want.

Minor decisions like what to eat today, or what to wear, or should you stop off and have a drink before coming home, can also be made by joining your mind with your partner and asking the Holy Spirit for help. This doesn't require your partner to be physically present, nor does spoken communication need to happen. Joining in mind with your partner is an awareness of his or her spiritual presence. When the feeling of minds being joined becomes acute in your awareness, then a simple feeling that you receive can be an answer.

Practice is required, and it never hurts at the beginning of the relationship to ask as often as you can remember to join in mind and feel what it is like to know your partner is joined with you, regardless of physical locality. From this awareness comes the feeling of peace, joy, and certainty that whatever you decide supports both of you. It strengthens your commitment to your holy purpose.

Choosing to join before making a decision will require great honesty and open sharing. You will likely experience attempts that may appear to you to be mistakes or failures. Admit when you have behaved selfishly or in a controlling manner. Also, admit when you may forget the act of joining, make a private decision, and do what you want because you were following a habit. Be willing to correct your error without judgment. Practice forgiveness. You are in a relationship to be forgiven.

You will strengthen the joining process the more you practice and share the feeling you have. Watch how the ego makes you feel wrong either about practicing or doubting that a joining is happening.

When true intuition happens, and you know and it works for greater good, reinforce it with joy and double the knowing that it happened with an inner certainty. Then you can return to that successful feeling repeatedly. Once you got it, you always have it. Once Holy Spirit is working for you and your partner then you are CO-creating your life and have the mighty power of Spirit working for you.

CO-creating is the greatest experience we all can learn, and it applies to your work, family, friends, and the greater world as one. CO-creating changes so many lives and causes much happiness for all.

CO-creating is God in action because the whole is creating as one mind.
Learning to CO-create within a Holy Relationship will cause both of you to understand how creation works.

Complete the exercises for this chapter in Chapter 10.

CHAPTER 9

CHANGE IS CREATING

The Idea of Winning

The idea of winning comes from competition, judgment, and comparison. From the belief in separation you have made a world of judgment, where two people can be put against each other, where one wins and the other loses. This is the Ego's world where everything is seen from the state of duality. If you believe in winning at anything, then you think the competition has lost. You believe in the power of defeat.

When it comes to intimate relationships, the idea of winning is obscure. If the goal of a Holy Relationship is to be the same self, if they lose—don't you lose as well? How can you win a fight if you are only fighting with yourself?

In a Holy Relationship no separate self exists. The purpose is to experience a no-loss state of consciousness. In truth, nothing is ever lost. You can't win at someone's expense and call it success. Success in a Holy Relationship means there are no winners or losers, only the experience of creating in love and with love.

In perception, you make the idea of loss seem real. The correction of loss is a goal of a Holy Relationship. The only way the idea can be corrected is to look carefully at this point of view called winning.

In sports, we see how winning is everything. In this type of competition, the game is played so that one team wins and the other must lose. Everything is measured by the success of winning. Watch the Super Bowl or the World Cup. See the emotion, the drive— there can be only one winner. Each losing team walks away wondering what went wrong. An entire city can go into a sta te of depression, frustration, and anger about how their team placed second, thus labeled the "loser." O.J. Simpson is our most famous example of the Competitor. Most saw him as a winner, the most successful type of person you can be in America—until the wheel turned and the dark side surfaced. Winning at any price destroyed him and his relationship. The need to be the best drove his marriage to disaster. Could anyone say he had a winning marriage?

I remember being very upset because my favorite team lost in the playoffs after following them throughout the regular season. They won so many games. How could they lose? My mind was outraged. The entire team and all the fans were in states of disbelief and disappointment. The next day, I watched another playoff game seeing two different teams compete. I wasn't very involved in either team. I watched one win and the other lose with little to no emotion. I saw how my specialness attitude toward my team that caused my disappointment, and how in reality, my mind made the winning so important. I saw winning and losing for what it really was, just a made-up game in my mind. I had bought into the system of competing.

Winning is taught in so many ways in our society that it seems quite natural and carries over into our intimate involvement. Winning means there is something to gain or to get. It is more about being better than it is a sport, a game.

"Winning is everything" is a self-deception, an Ego lie, a way to promote the separation. Love is everything. If you buy or invest into this type of thinking in any area of your life, it must carry over into other areas of your life. First sports, then business, then the effects creep into your family. You push your children to win at any cost, and you find yourself unwilling to forgive or be wrong.

For men it comes very early, as most are encouraged to enter into sports, be strong, and be a winner, don't show emotions or be weak, and you must succeed in business. Get the best job and compete to be with the best-looking woman.

For women, it comes first in school, some in sports, and then against each other. Who looks the best gets the most successful man. Women can also feel as though they were competing for better jobs and higher pay.

When competing enters the dating process, the man wants to win the woman, or the woman wants to be won over. This game is very dangerous, and the outcome is always that someone is seen as a loser and is rejected. If you see yourself as a loser in any relationship, admit you were playing the competition and trying to win. Any feeling of losing has to be matched with the idea of winning.

With each disappointment, a fixed expectation exists, claiming you lost. If you can teach yourself that this was only a dream in your mind and you had nothing to gain through competing, the idea of loss vanishes. The same holds true for success and failure, right and wrong, true or false. Duality means one idea is split in two. Becoming aware of your duality-driven way of thinking and repairing the split is a process of healing. Forgiveness brings the split together in your mind and shows you that once joined, you see a bigger picture of Oneness.

Chasing after another man or woman when you have a current relationship is an adulterous form of competition. The mind becomes more split. When the purpose of relationships is to end separation, you must stop doing or thinking ideas that promote further splits. Competing only splits your mind.

Can we play sports or be great in business if we don't complete? Isn't there a healthy type of competition? Evolution is our most natural form of competition. Creatures evolve and change, and it seems each creature improves to survive. To exist, some creature feeds off another while others feed off them. We have animal-humans that do the same thing. Evolution is a system whereby growth happens, but the whole is kept in balance. Human animals seem to dominate the planet, but we still need plants and animals to survive. So we can't really say that we win at their expense. It serves us not to misuse our resources from the mineral-plant-animal kingdoms. Nature doesn't see loss either, it only sees transformation and the whole. Our competitive mind only sees part of the whole and tries to discard the rest. In a natural way of competing we include all and don't judgments. We eliminate the concept of less than. Each moment our performance is perfect in itself, provided we don't compare.

In life, there exists a state of consciousness whereby you play not to win against the other, but to express the maximum performance for the good of all. Competition is an Ego perception. You can reach maximum performance and be happy with that performance and not compare. You don't have to judge yourself nor another self. If this happens out of habit, recognize that you can release this perception by choosing contentment. The "I've got to win" attitude is never at peace. Always having to be better and reaching for the highest means you never get there.

Be satisfied with yourself and all that happens around you. Another's achievement is really yours. It's all of humanity's. Your achievements can be shared and not kept for self-glorification. Don't make sport of your relationships.

This is not a popular concept. Most of the population will have a hard time understanding this, for the way of learning through separation is deeply rooted into our thinking. Winning, success, and competing are rooted into the ideas of prosperity as well.

In these games, a score is always kept, for the Ego is great at remembering who wins and who loses. Winning will always eventually remind you of your shortcomings (losses). Yes, that critical voice inside your head is the scorekeeper, keeping an eye on the competition. When your relationship has tallied up enough losses, you think, "I guess it's time to end it." You forget about how you have fabricated what winning really means.

Every relationship in which you have been rejected or abandoned, or one that you believe failed or in which you got cheated, is evidence that you believe love is based on competition. The more your mind proves you have to compete, the more you will lose. Prove instead that you have never lost in any relationship that you never have been rejected, nor have you won. This means the Ego must be silenced. The only way to be rejected is to "want your way more then their way." Rejecting is not possible if you want what is mutually real and good for all. Let go and give to your partner whatever they ask for, and their receiving is yours as well.

Those who witness loss keep repeating patterns until they back track and teach themselves that even in their earliest memories, they didn't lose. In each moment there is just the moment, the best you did. The perfect thing happened no matter what you called it or how you judged it. Some feel that giving up a competitive spirit is a sacrifice. They could even point to others who appear less successful and say, "I don't want to end up like them, so I must compete to get somewhere." The fear of being less than or not having something comes from a self-created concept of being incomplete. If all memories of incompletion are erased from the mind that thought them, what are you left with?

The fear of losing can even be projected as lack of enthusiasm. The fear of losing passion or excitement is an old trick the Ego loves to play. Those who learn not to judge easily find within themselves all the passion and enthusiasm they need. They know it comes from Spirit, and doesn't need to be manufactured through competition.

You say, "I like the feeling of winning, and it's worth the risk of losing. Even if I do lose I can quickly bounce back to trying to be a winner again." Couples do this quite often in arguing, fighting, and making up, believing they are winning when they fight, and that making up is a way of trying to be a winner again. What is never admitted is how the mind becomes stuck in this lower game, and the more it is reinforced, the harder it is to transcend it.

We mostly compete with our partner in our communication and our need to be right about our points of view. Competition creeps into arguing. Two people have different points of view about an experience. They discuss that perception with the added demand to be right about their point at the expense of proving their partner wrong.

If you prove you are right you think you win, but just because your partner seems to be defeated doesn't mean he or she has changed his or her perception. Your partner has suppressed his or her point of view and pretended to take yours. So what do you win? He or she has not changed and you have gotten nothing. Maybe a false sense of power—that later proves you are powerless.

Your powerlessness shows up when you are not aware of the separation, or the distance you have created, by needing to win or be right. People who are very intellectual can be the loneliest people on the planet if they think they gain power from being correct using information. You can't join with intellectual information alone. It requires love, which comes from the heart, the center. It requires a feeling of both parties being joyous together.

Think carefully: do you feel you have to be the winner in your relationship when it comes to discussing points of view, and in what way does your partner show resentment or play the victim? What is your strategy for winning a disagreement? Do you just keep talking, repeating your points of view until you wear down your partner, until they become your opponent? Do you back down but hold hidden grievances? Do you start to express lots of emotion to prove your point, or silently walk away knowing you are right?

Whatever strategy you use underneath the Ego's voice is saying, "You must be a winner because I know you are really a loser." In every fight, a winner must emerge, and a loser must accept being less than. Can you really be happy with a partner being a reflection of your lesser self?

What many fail to see is that the game leads to divorce and smothers real love. One day they wake up and realize they both feel like losers because it seems impossible to regain the awareness of no competition. So many couples after 15, 20, or even 35 years of marriage are getting divorced. Ask them; they never got past the level of competing with each other. To have a Holy Relationship and achieve Oneness you must outgrow the idea of competition.

You have to work within yourself to experience the state of no loss. It requires effort to choose forgiveness over competition. Being right at the expense of making your partner wrong costs much more than you think you are gaining. This false sense of pride is the downfall of every relationship. It destroys unity. To reverse the demand to be a winner you must see what it costs you and how the payoff is meaningless.

The payoff for being a winner is attention, but attention without true joining is really aloneness. Many a person has become a winner to the world's standards of what a winner is, only to find the feeling very fleeting and the emptiness so great they have to go fill it with something. If you compete in a relationship and don't correct it, you will never feel love. Love has no winners or losers. Love's only purpose is to be itself. Love never competes nor compares itself; it simply is.

Stop all forms of loss, by ending the dream that you can win at the expense of another. As you do to other it will be done unto you. The higher mind sees how you have constructed these false concepts of winning and will always be working to balance it. It waits in readiness to teach you how you have been harmful to yourself by buying into this dream of being "better than." It requires your willingness to listen for as long as you wish to play the game of competition. No one will stop you, and you can keep striving until you wake up and find yourself alone, older, and suddenly spinning into the loser realm. No one has ever escaped this experience. Even the most "successful" must look at the entire process of wholeness.

These are some of the ways our Ego convinces us we are "winning":

Making more money than other people.

Being better at sports.
Acting superior by knowing certain information.
Not willing to see another point of view.
Not sharing, keeping certain possessions to ourselves.
Holding grievances against what happened in the past.
Fighting or arguing instead of saying, "Forgive me."
Avoiding conversations.
Demanding sex or any other gratification through selfishness.
Being the "best" child in the family and repeating it with our partner.
Overworking or overachievers.
Being overconfident and aggressive.
Being judgmental or critical.
Using verbal tones that would push someone away.
Thinking we know what the future should bring.
Bargaining for a lower, unfair price at the expense of others.
Negotiating or compromising for what we want.
Acting independent of what our partner thinks.
Not discussing or communicating—giving someone the silent treatment.
Hiding information or not telling the truth.
Avoiding dealing with important issues.
Holding onto bigotry or prejudices.
Demanding that we get our way.
Trying to be right about religious beliefs.
Using our physical strength in harmful ways.
Any form of attack.
Any perception of lack, rejection, or loss.
Any way we make our partner feel guilty or pointing out others faults.

Can you add anything to this list?

Do you see ways that your Ego tries to persuade you to win? Do you see how winning is a value you have placed over joining? Isn't it clear that by playing the winner, someone who you could love now must play the loser? The Ego counsels that you love losers by pitying them; you feel sorry for victims, you provide charity for the less fortunate who aren't winners like you. The do-gooders always want to be known. They hardly ever give anonymously. Advertisers promote top name athletes because everyone wants to be associated with a winner. A winner wants to be promoted, but the underlining motive of the Ego is glory. Glory to the person, to its performance and to false image—all indicating you have forgotten your spiritual nature.

If a thief steals my wallet and I think of him as the winner and I play the victim, it is easy to see what I think I lost. What do I gain by seeing I am not a victim? The answer is, I see my soul. Victims can't transcend the physical behavior of the act in which they were victimized. The vision is upon what happened with their added story, their interpretation of the facts. Victims have an interpretation of what the event means in their evolution. It becomes their prediction of the future and, most of the time, includes a view of lack.

All victims believe in lack, loss, and death. They have to perceive a winner and a loser and something taken away. Never attempt to tell people they aren't a victim if they believe they are. They will try even harder to convince themselves and you. Only the mind of the perceiver can change a perception of lack.

Only by realizing that you can't lose—which must be taught from within—can the inner mind transcend a victim mentality. No outside source is convincing in comparison to the miracles of Spirit. Raising the consciousness of the victim-loser focus requires grace. You can become ready and willing to shift out of limitation by asking to be shown a higher perception. Each time you teach yourself, you become a miracle worker for others to learn, and they too can change their focus from loss to creation.

Living in victim hood only proves you want this world of separate bodies, where one overpowers the other, one wins, and another loses. Your Holy Relationship would have you undo all beliefs in duality and heal every split thought. Real ideas are forever in the mind that thinks them. A healing relationship spends time looking at false notions of the Ego, laughing, correcting them, and witnessing the reality of Spirit—the no-loss state of consciousness.

A No Loss Relationship avoids the personal hate cycle by taking the special love out of the relationship and directing that energy toward the greater good for humanity. It doesn't mean that the couple doesn't spend quality time with each other. It simply means their focuses include a wider scope of interest. That broader view prevents them from attacking each other with lower views of what the other is or isn't doing.

In a Holy Relationship, you're cute, fun and funny. Your intelligence is worldly. You're humble and authentic, you take responsibility for yourself, and have the willingness and ability to observe and be honest with yourself. Your energy is light and playful, and you can let go and allow yourself to be vulnerable. Most importantly, you know the value of self-love and understand that how you see yourself is how you will see the world, and how you see the world is how you will experience the world.

No Problem Relationships

Let me realize my problems have already been solved

Wouldn't it be considered a miracle to have a relationship where you had no problems, no fears, no guilt or shame placed upon you? What would it be like to be involved with your mate with a clear understanding of how to solve every problem using the same method for correcting errors? What would it be like to know you and your partner agreed on this method and practiced it regularly and enjoyed sharing in the process of correcting problems? Did I hear Heavenly? Isn't this what everyone is looking for?

Most couples approach problem solving in different ways. They try to solve the problem in their relationship using the way they were taught. All problems are fabricated by the lower mind of fear, so why fight about problems that aren't even real? Couples argue about what is the best way to solve their differences, making the fight a problem in the problem. Even if they are in agreement about having a problem and attempt to brainstorm ways out of the problem, they usually end up disagreeing on which solution is really the best. One may give in and allow the other to win but will still hold on to a solution to use it at a different time or remind the other how it could have been solved had the other solution been used. Notice the guilt if the solution didn't work.

The first mistake most couples make is they don't both get to the place of admitting they have a problem. Denial, avoidance, pride, or fear prevents them from acknowledging they are in a limited point of view. False pride will project a positive view or project the problem onto someone else, thus preventing the couple from jointly taking responsibility. If you say it's your partner's problem and not yours, you are denying the power of joining. If you attempt to fix the problem for your partner before joining, the problem may get temporarily fixed (a patch) but never resolved. Substitution becomes a method used to solve a problem—get rid of the old for something new. It can be the same as changing a job, a religion, moving to a different city, or looking for that new toy to entertain you.

Problems never get totally solved unless both join in mind and agree on the method of correction. Problems that seem to be solved by you have only temporary remedies. Problems that make other problems, never correct the original error. If you solve your individual problems but make a bigger problem for your partnership or others, you seldom find peace. Joint decisions lead to strength in unity.

Whenever you make a problem in your mind, you have also made an answer to that problem somewhere in your mind. The answer is at the same level as the problem, if provided by the Ego. The answer is not the way to solve the problem, but the mind that made the problem believes it is. For example, if in doing the family budget you discover that you are $200.00 short of the money needed, the answer may seem to go out and get another job and make the extra money. The problem is still lack of money.

The Ego will give you a remedy that treats the symptom in every case of sickness. Western medicine rarely treats the cause. The mind that creates problems is sick indeed. To go out and work another job to earn extra money becomes another problem. The next problem may be, "I'm tired of working so much." Those who solve problems by using their lower mind are constantly going from one problem to another. Life then becomes one big problem. Yet this is not life.

Problems, no matter what the form, all have one thing in common. Problems occur because we see in a limited way. We see only a limited part of reality by judging. It matters not how many problems we think we have. For each problem at its core, has the same mistake.

The cause of all problems is they each have the same idea of loss woven into the perception. I have repeatedly said that there is no loss and that any concept of lack is a made up belief, a perception of the lower mind. All problems are some form of a belief in loss. If we sift through the mental garbage of each issue that presents itself as a problem, the core root (cause) is a fixed limitation you have imposed on Is-ness. If you retain any belief of loss in your lower mind and come up with an answer, that answer becomes your next problem. It will keep recurring over and over and over again until the inner core causes are changed.

The Ego doesn't want you to recognize this or admit it to your partner. This is why it offers you another answer. Its solution, which by the way is another limitation, is the denial of admitting its weakness. The Ego can only think in limited forms anyway. When a Holy Relationship learns how to look deeper to the cause of the loss and find how it was perceived, you then start to watch problems vanish. Without a cause, no problem can remain.

Each problem has at its core, which is the concept that you are separate from the whole. If the whole offers you everything, what is lacking is your belief that you are not connected to the whole. This is simply a perceptional error, as all loss is a misperception. Your false

185

pride will not want you to look at this while it produces fear. The more afraid you become, the more real the problem, the lack, seem to be. Fear attempts to get you to turn away from looking at causes in your mind. Fear attempts to get you to solve your problems by yourself, because it can offer you its own solution.

With the help of your partner and the Holy Spirit you can release a perception, a mistake in looking at life. In a healing session you can look to the inner thoughts at the core of your self esteem and find experiences where you thought of yourself as "less than." Each belief of lack, when properly corrected, teaches that loss is impossible. When loss is corrected you realize what you have, and that is enough.

The key to healing your beliefs in lack is looking at what you have done by not remaining joined to the whole. Apply the AAA (Acknowledge, Acceptance, Appreciation) method to your problems and watch them dissolve. Don't fix it, dissolve it. Don't correct a problem with a problem. You have problems on the level of the material, which comes from the belief 'you don't have = lack. You have emotional problems, which means you have lost the awareness of happiness. You have intellectual problems, which means you think you lack intelligence, or you never had it, or your opinion is right against another that is wrong.

Any spiritual problem is an evaluation that you feel separate from Spirit. It is important to identify the level of where you perceive your problem to be. Work up the levels, going from the physical to the spiritual, until all levels are problem free and aligned to truth. Suppose you believe you lack money, and the core of lack comes from the belief that in childhood a parent told you repeatedly you were stupid and wouldn't amount to much. The correction is to remove all loss on every level of Self. You are worthwhile, you are smart enough, and as you adopt this new awareness of Self, your finances will reflect it. When you look at the whole, there is certainly no lack of dollars out there. The government never stops printing them. Money is simply a belief in how loved you feel.

Money is always a reflection of how you create or play with others in the good of all. It is a mirror of your abilities to connect with the whole and CO-create. The poor are simply those who believe in separation and remain disconnected from the CO-creative process of joining.

Your problem demands a win/lose scenario. Loss is perceived, so all you can gain is the game of all errors the lower mind makes. Each problem that exists has a belief that someone must lose, and someone will gain at the expense of the one who loses. If the problem is someone stole your favorite stereo, the problem is that you lost and they gained. The car dealer loves to present you with the problem that they lose and you gain the better deal. You often believe you can get a deal from the one you love causing them the problem. As a child, you expect your parents to sacrifice and give to you, to buy you the best toy and finest clothes; "All the other children have them." As an adult, you carry these ideas into your intimate relationships. Most couples make problems by sacrificing and by stealing from each other not even being aware they are acting out old patterns of taking.

All stealing comes from the idea that one loses and another wins, which is the core of selfishness and lower mind thinking. Believe it or not, it is always taught to children in several unconscious ways.

Children learn to win at another's expense, and it's a game they pick up very quickly in school. When these beliefs carry over to adulthood and into a Holy Relationship, they must be seen as a problem and corrected accordingly. You need to look at the concept of sacrifice within yourself. It is the core of your belief in scarcity.

Judging that others have more creates the idea of less, which leads to a sense of lack and takes the mind into a conclusion of loss. You also can do advance work with your partner by going back and reviewing experiences in childhood where you learned to steal, feel less than, take advantage of another, and fight believing you won. Call it the problem.

The Steps to Correcting Problems: The No Loss Point of View

1. Join with your partner (mentally) in a moment of silence. Ask for help in looking at this problem, from both your partner and the Holy Spirit.

2. Admit the problem according to your Ego version of it without coming up with an answer. Write or verbalize the problem as specific. "I don't have enough money to pay the bills." "I am $110.00 short of paying my rent that is due in the next 4 days." "I feel stuck and unable to find the right job."

3. Edit the script, and remove any ideas of lack, loss, or limitation. Cross out "don't have," "short of," "due in the next 4 days."

4. Ask for help in seeing other lack issues that are similar in your past. Edit those past errors as well. Keep asking for help from Spirit to show you any missed beliefs in lack.

5. Apply the AAA mind healing method of Acceptance, Appreciation, and Acknowledgement of what happened to the situation. Look for the Is-ness of the situation. Share this with your partner to see that you are both in agreement.

6. Allow time and space for your partner to also remove any similar belief in lost that the problem triggered for him or her. Repeat steps 2 through 5.

7. Together, spend a few moments in silence and meditation again. Listen to your deeper intuition of what is the next step in CO-creating. You both will get very similar answers. A practical action step will be given that serves both your partnership and the whole. It follows your purpose and continues your spiritual goals.
The still small voice of your intuition gives you a "now" moment part to play in joyous celebration of life. It requires no sacrifice or loss to anyone.

8. Write clearly the new directive, and make any agreements with your partner that seems appropriate. The key to CO-creating is the joy you feel. There is only creation in reality, and that is done out of joy.

There are no problems in CO-creating with the creator of life unless you make yourself separate from it. Problems are steps out of limitations. Every form has a limitation and is a limit. Limits will never satisfy you.
Whenever we configure that someone else won at another's expense we claim an injustice occurred, and the crime calls for answers, or punishment, or justice. If someone loses, we figure someone must have won. A problem is made when a mind thinks of injustice, and only the Higher Mind can solve that problem by showing us the whole mind.

What really happens is we forget to recognize who our partner is to us. We block our minds from seeing the Spirit within. The issue in relationships is we always fail to see what our true essence is and recognize that our partner is the same. The other issue of relationships is we think the other is different from us. The only problem any relationship has is its fears of joining and making separation seem like the better answer.

No problem can exist to couples that learn to form a triangle with the Holy Spirit. All problems dissolve in its Light. It is better to dissolve a problem than to believe that you fixed it. Be aware of avoiding problems or pretending that you "fixed" it with some physical action. If you don't heal the mind the so-called "solution" will reoccur, which is the proof that the problem was never corrected. Real answers are permanent and never change. Wouldn't you prefer the answer rather to making up a false solution?

Giving and Receiving

The aspects of giving and receiving are major issues in any relationship. They are a source of confusion and deception about being loved. We like to think of ourselves as people who give graciously and selflessly. We believe that we give out of a desire to express love and appreciation for another person. We may even feel that we would sacrifice everything to show how much we love a person. However, in truth, most of our giving is based on a thought system that supports acts of exchanging and bargaining. We often know that we should give without retaining any hidden agendas, expectations, or demands; yet, often, unbeknownst to us, the thought system of our lower mind still governs our needs.

In the beginning of a relationship, we are seldom concerned with what the partner gives to us in return because we are so excited what we think we are getting. We do not realize that we will soon be playing out an old pattern of our sense of loss that is based on a false idea of unbalanced exchanges. These patterns in regard to the acts of giving and receiving that were originally developed through childhood experiences are so entwined in our experiences with our present partners that we need to make a conscious effort to see them.

While we may believe that we are giving unconditionally, our shadow subconscious mind is looking for what is being returned. Within this secret bargain, we are determining if this partner can fulfill the role of maintaining our specialness in the manner in which we identify ourselves. In other words, we have set an expectation that our partner behave a certain way to uphold our identity, even though this perceived identity is based on specialness that was established during experiences of loss or disappointment throughout our childhood.

You can recognize these expectations when you notice feelings of being ripped off, cheated, or used. Have you heard yourself say, "He or she used me?" It can be very difficult to listen to your hidden wants. You often don't link what you are giving with what you are expecting.

While this idea of giving and receiving may be a bigger problem than you realize, at the center of the Ego thought system are the ideas of sacrifice and the fear of being controlled, which may be even more difficult to admit and recognize. Be willing to explore these beliefs in your relationships because looking at them is how you heal them.

Within the secret bargain you try to give away the role of maintaining your specialness, and you try to take on the role of maintaining your partner's specialness. You bargain, plead, demand, beg, attack, need, want, and pray with the expectation that your special love/hate partner will give you that which you perceive you do not have.

Love is the experience that is felt when you become aware that giving and receiving are the same because you can but give to yourself. Anything that you perceive as not yourself becomes an illusion about reality.

The Ego mind is always looking "to get" that which it can take as a "good deal." The "me" that is based on the Ego thought system is only interested in itself, and it looks for what it doesn't have and tries to fill the void through a false method of receiving called "getting, taking, or stealing." When partners are looking to each other to fill this void, then the situation can be seen as "Negative + negative = a double negative experience" or a "fight to win" mentality. Two insane minds cannot establish the Oneness until one partner becomes sane enough to stop and ask for help. Take a few moments and try to recall any memories where you and your love partner were both trying to "get." You should be able to recall a lot of examples, but if your mind doesn't allow you to recall them, then ask for help. You tend to want to stay unconscious about this issue because an imbalanced mind values its specialness.

You have learned to bargain for a little bit, your part, and a tiny scrap of something to claim as security against a world that wants to take it all away. You think that your love partner may be like other people you have experienced who are ungrateful for what you give them. Many types of twisted scenarios have evolved from an unfair, unbalanced mind regarding the ideas around giving and receiving. The "I am" which is only interested in the "I am" looks for what it has and sees that as receiving. You extend what you have or you project what you don't have. In creation, there is never lack so the Spirit is always giving to itself. The receiving is the same as giving because the mind sees itself as the everything.

In the Ego world, the idea of payment for services is core to the idea of exchange. Think of all the ways you get paid or are not paid for the ways you give. It's a good thing that, at the age of one, you didn't have to go out and earn your milk. It requires two to make an exchange, and if two different selves are negotiating on who wins (at the expense of the other), then you make an unfair arrangement. Consider how quickly your love relationships can slide into this false programming of bargaining. The gesture of falling back into these old habits occurs either because you grew up learning about unfair exchanges, or because you decided in your Ego mind that you were mistreated or abused in some way. You surmised that you must look out for your own separate interest. Through the healing process, you realize that the truth has no concept of unfair or unjust.

The healing process may provide opportunities to take a different perspective of past experiences. If you experienced a situation where you felt that you were not appreciated for your contributions, then you may have started to believe that you don't have anything to give. If your identity became based on a self-concept that you have to give to get noticed, then you may have followed a path that allows you to be a workaholic or a caretaker. If your self-concept is based on a sense of lack, then you may have followed a path where you can feel that there is nothing to give or where you feel that you need to be a hoarder. Through past experiences, you learned to become a taker. If other people urge you to give because of the belief that it's more blessed to give than to receive, then you may give begrudgingly, or you give but believe that you are sacrificing something that you don't want to give up. When the idea of sacrifice starts to convince you that life is not giving your fair share, then you look to your love partner to somehow make up the slack. This added responsibility laid on to your partner, who has similar feelings of lack, makes for two very un-giving people.

When two people are trying to get something from each other, they are engaging in the most dysfunctional expression of love that is possible. The Ego never gives out of a sense of abundance because the Ego thought system was made as a substitute for abundance. This substitution is why the concept of "getting" arose in the Ego's thought system. Appetites and yearnings are "getting" mechanisms, and they represent the Ego's need to confirm itself.

The imbalance of giving and receiving began when you started making "deals" with God. It's no wonder that so many people emphasize that type of God. God's "lets make a deal" show is now playing on planet number three. Can you pick the lucky number and win? You even make a God who has the power to withhold or grant you your special lacks, depending on how "good" you behave and whether you act "right" or not. "God, give me _____, and I will _____ (be good in exchange)." You still perceive that you are separate from Spirit.

Love can't be seen as an exchange where loss can be perceived. Love is not about one person winning at another person's expense. These ideas of giving and receiving are only a game of "getting."

Love energy is never lost, limited, taken away, or withheld. Any appearance of these ideas is an indication that you have done something to yourself to block your ability to perceive the love-Light energies. That block is some form of imbalance in the idea of receiving. Learning how to recognize it and how to correct it is the higher purpose of a Holy Relationship.

The partners of a No Loss Relationship are always willing to give and receive as one. They share with no concept of sacrifice, and neither believes in the idea that one gains by the other one losing. When you are in a No Loss Relationship, you see that your partner is you, the truth, and the same Self. When you are so deeply in love, why do you forget this? Then, go out and prove that it is not the other person that is giving you what you want. Why would you want to act out old patterns with your new partner? Letting go of old patterns is the only way. It's the greatest way to understand the healing purpose of all relationships.

The No Sacrifice Relationship

You can tell if you believe in sacrifice by how you feel. All tiredness and forms of guilt, grief, and unfairness come from perceived lack. All demands, expectations, future wants, and wishes to control reality and make it turn out a certain way come from the idea of sacrifice.

A Course in Miracles states, *"Guilt is the condition of sacrifice, as peace is the condition for the awareness of your relationship with God. Through guilt you exclude your Father and your brothers from yourself."*

Sacrifice is the belief that something can be taken away from someone and given to someone else, and that the exchange will bring benefit to the giver who made the sacrifice. The person who made the sacrifice feels the need to atone for some wrongdoing by offering something good. It is a payment made to an idol god.

To sacrifice is the choice to give up, to be without, and to suffer loss. When you associate giving with sacrifice, then you are choosing to give only because you believe that you are somehow getting something better, and can therefore do without the thing that you give. Your confusion of sacrifice and love is so profound that you either begin to define love as sacrifice, or the act of making a sacrifice becomes a requirement to believe that a person is expressing love. However, sacrifice is actually an attack on love.

Sacrifice is a notion that is totally unknown to God. It arises solely from fear and establishes a view of love that is fearful and requires an effort. When sacrifice is part of a relationship, it promotes the belief in loss, which in turn, makes payment and punishment real. You must learn to make payment unreal and unnecessary in your Holy Relationships. You need to pay nothing for what is already yours. Everything God gives is given freely and with no need to be paid back and no need for anything to be done for it. Love demands no sacrifice.

Overworked and Underpaid

Relationships that have been built with no established agreements and unclear communications will eventually lead to feelings that can be expressed through the old axiom "overworked and underpaid." It is not possible for you to give to a different Self and not be aware through your Ego mind of what is being given back to you. The "what's in it for me" attitude will preside by keeping an eye open for your own separate interests. Without clear communications in the relationship, it is easy for you to perceive your efforts as a sacrifice. When you feel as though you have sacrificed your time, energy, or something physical, then you are experiencing feelings of hate for your partner. You are not expressing love for your partner if your acts of giving feel like a sacrifice. Since sacrifice is derived from the Ego thought system, forgiveness becomes impossible. The Ego believes that forgiving a person is to lose any hold that you perceive that you have over that person.

It is not possible for the partners of a Holy Relationship to have separate interests. This idea only occurs within special relationships. Couples who are interested in making their relationship holy need to learn how to recognize when they are making bargains like those that may include negotiations of who gets what, who does what, who gives what, who pays the cost, and who gets the pay off. One may ask the question, "Is our relationship just a business?" The imbalance of giving and receiving is not corrected by practicing ideas of tracking measurements, keeping scores, setting obligations, and getting even. These thoughts only work to further you from the awareness of one Self.

Overpaid and Overworked

In the eye of Is-ness, the idea of "unfairness" is based on a mistake made in perception. You cannot be unfairly treated. If you perceive that you are being unfairly treated, then you must feel that you are being attacked. This belief is but another form of the idea that you are being deprived by someone else, not yourself. Your projection of the cause of sacrifice is at the root of everything that you perceive as unfair. This projection can be recognized in a situation where you compare yourself to another person and you believe that you were not justly acknowledged or compensated for your contribution. This projection may also occur from an opposing idea where you perceive that you are overpaid, overcompensated, and lucky to be acknowledged at all. You may have doubts that your recognition is justified.

A person who sees himself as a victim feels compelled to overwork to be a pleaser and this effort can turn into an expression of passive aggressive anger. Caretakers who overwork often suffer in their minds. They are so focused on being a pleaser that they are unable to recognize and appreciate the real rewards of being a giving person.

Underworked and Overpaid

In one way or another, every relationship the Ego makes is based in the idea that by sacrificing itself, it becomes bigger. The "sacrifice," which it regards as purification, is the root of its bitter resentment. When a person considers himself as "better than" other people because of a shared view that he is paid a lot a money for performing a small amount of work, then this idea allows him to create a false sense of his own importance and entitlement. A person who is "underworked and overpaid" tends to use his rewards to maintain an image of "high status" and "above other people." When the Ego crashes, the person may wonder why he feels no love and may try to "buy it." "Better than" is an unbalanced view of life, and how life will always seek balance.

The Four Levels of Giving and Receiving

Level A: Level of Oneness
Partners involved in a level A relationship seek to understand the nature of Oneness. By agreeing to join for a Holy Relationship, partners are choosing to understand the truth of Oneness through its practices. Oneness, or Spirit-God-Self, can only be experienced through a Holy Relationship. Holy means Oneness. This experience is one of enlightenment, which is a characteristic of all spiritual teachers.

It is also called truth. When you master the nature of giving and receiving as the same and you know you are giving and receiving as one, then this great truth becomes who you are. Choosing to practice giving and receiving within every relationship is a very fast path of attaining realization as truth. All pain will disappear in your relationship, which is as innocent as your relationship with Spirit. Without pain there is no need for sacrifice; and without sacrifice, there must be love. You seek to give to the one Self. You receive for that Self simultaneously.

Level B: Level of Equal Exchange - the Win-Win Agreement
When you are involved in a level B relationship, you give to win, and you make agreements so that both partners win. When loss is experienced, you feel the loss together, even though one of you may have stronger feelings about the loss. Any exchange that occurs within the relationship is orchestrated to uphold the giving and receiving agreement. You agree to support the mutual cause, and you share in the gain. You uphold the agreement in the interest of fairness and righteousness.

Life is good because you can share and care for people; you love in a way that is mutually beneficial. Then, the tests begin and the challenges of maintaining these balances cause the relationship either to advance toward being holy or to slip into levels C or D. The idea of "getting" is not the same concept as "receiving." The idea of "taking" is not the same concept as "someone giving to you." Neither a belief in giving with a motivation to take and get something in return, nor any belief in winning can occur without leaving some negative energy with the agreement.

If you can see the true win in every situation for everyone with no concept of loss whatsoever, then you would easily advance to level A. The Ego energies must be transformed or they will remain to undermine the giving, and they can lower you toward level C. No one loses; nothing is taken away from anyone; and everyone gains through your holy vision. It signifies the end of sacrifice because it offers everyone his or her full due. There is no other way that the idea of sacrifice can be removed from the world's thinking process.

Level C: Level of Sacrifice Giving to Get - No Agreements

There is one mistake within the level C relationship. The mistake rests in the whole idea that loss is possible and that loss could result in a gain for anyone. Your hidden plan is to win at all cost and make certain that you get something from someone. Desperate and alone, you resort to acts of grabbing, bargaining, and stealing. Your thought process convinces you that, by "getting" you are doing someone a favor and sometimes that favor is for yourself. Any other way of seeing it would inevitably result in a demand for payment.

The more the idea of giving is tainted or imbalanced, the more a person is led to ideas of demands and sacrifice. At this level, the Ego is always voicing its view towards the idea of sacrifice. Choice is the leeway that you have between the higher and the lower levels of giving. Choosing to feel the needs of sacrifice can only cause you to feel tired and fatigued. Pain is the effect of the belief in sacrifice.
Continuing Sacrifice Only Leads to Level D

Level D: Darkness; Taker or Stealing = Fear

Level D can also be described as "darkness taking from darkness." Originating from this level are the feelings of being lost, the feeling that you are completely alone, and the feeling that you are fighting to survive against other people, God, nature, and life itself. The only option is to take as needed to survive. The idea of taking whatever you can to attain power, pleasure, or special attention is the Ego's grip. Thinking only of your lower self, you pretend to care about the other person, and you give just enough to make sure you get what you want. In other words, your focus is, "Me first. You lose."

You read about the four Ds (The Dent, The Damaged, The Destroyed, and Death-The Void) and how they affect your life in a negative way. It is the imbalance of giving and receiving that lead to the experiences of the four D's. This imbalance continues from one life into the next life, and it is often reinforced through childhood experiences and relationships with parents. This imbalance continues to be a way of life until you ask for help. When you practice the ideas of the No Loss Relationship, you learn how to give and receive as one and how to lift yourself and your partner to a higher level.

The Changing of an Involvement is Not the End

In a No Loss Relationship, there is no ending because what remains as real is always continued. A Holy Relationship is committed to purpose, healing, and CO-creating, and if it turns into a "B" relationship, a change is required in form but not in content.

Changing an involvement from the view of the lower mind is an ending, a loss, and a death of the partnership or friendship. Most Ego-based relationships provide each person involved with an opportunity to use the ending to validate an unloved aspect of one's self. The partners involved in a dark-hearted involvement often feel that possession is the way to keep love. Therefore, when a partner senses that he or she is losing control of that possession, it is interpreted as a threat that can produce anger, fear, and jealousy. These fear-based emotions can instigate harmful behaviors that are often witnessed in domestic violence court cases. Dramatic relationships often end poorly since Ego-based behaviors are motivated by an interest in generating pain and discomfort. However, there is another way of changing an involvement besides breaking up.

The partners involved in a Holy Relationship choose to experience only unconditional love. Each partner realizes that all relationship changes are based on a non-judgmental agreement. Realizing that the agreement supports a higher cause and a greater experience of joy and peace, partners agree to freely move into different spaces or activities without any sense of possessiveness. Freedom is love.

The Holy Spirit welcomes a change in the partnership when that change is necessary for spiritual growth. Even though the partners of a Holy Relationship may experience emotional pain and a sense of loss of attachment, they choose to use those feelings to seek greater healing and to deepen love. They choose not to project that pain in a way that might harm another person or oneself. Grief is as natural as the rain, and feelings of grief lead to grace when given to the Holy Spirit. Few people can escape the emotional pain that occurs when the lower mind's attachment to specialness perceives it is being threatened. However through the thought process of the Holy Relationship, a person can learn to transcend that pain and dismiss the urge to resist it.

Resistance to change can generate great pain and an unnatural grief. Unnatural grief and a sense of loss are based on selfishness that is controlled by your Ego, which wants you to suffer and feel unlovable. When you accept the change in your involvement by consciously giving all of your feelings of grief to the Holy Spirit, and you choose not to pass blame onto your partner, a greater purpose can be received. It takes great mastery of unconditional love to realize that all change is for a higher purpose. Once you have given all of your relationships over to the Holy Spirit, your acceptance of all change becomes an expression of freedom for all. Grief will turn into lightheartedness and a quiet inner joy. Fighting against a change, even though you and your partner are not mutually creating a shared purpose, only serves to prove your loyalty to the Ego and not to the true love of the Holy Relationship.

The qualities of a Holy Relationship are sustained in regards to content, understanding, and purpose. Partners never resist change that is for greater good. Greater good is that which is mutually agreed upon with Spiritual guidance. If your partner is requesting a change in the involvement, then the Holy Spirit is asking you to release your partner, to trust Spirit and to let go of the form of the partnership. Spirit is not asking you to stop loving your partner. Spirit is asking you to set your partner free.

A commitment to "loving" is a different idea than the commitment to retain a connection as fixed in form. Many people are confused about commitment because their definition rests on expectations that couples should stay together for reasons established in lower agreements, such as false security or pleasure.

True commitment is based in higher agreements of purpose and mutual creating, and the commitment will last as long as the creations have meaning or serve your enlightenment. The partners of a No Loss Relationship have no attachment to bodies or keeping the form fixed in a special way.

The "end" is always a beginning of the continuum of life and love. Look forward to new creations always, and make everything new. Bringing in the newness of creation is an expression of God. Seek that newness more than the past. Make a decision to release your attachments to the past. Exchange something old for something new every day. With or without your partner, you are whole and complete.

Place your trust in the Holy Spirit and your need for spiritual growth. Releasing another person is a process for which you may request help from the Holy Spirit. If you continue to harbor feelings of betrayal, abandonment, and disappointment, then you are choosing to reinforce the lower mind's concepts of false love.

When you focus on a past love, then your current moment retains a false attachment to the old. When you choose to invite in the new, then you will open yourself to see the greater, higher purpose. Full acceptance of a change is an indication that you value that which the new brings. New purpose is not a loss but a gain toward a higher purpose. Whatever your brother or sister needs for his or her spiritual growth is honored, even if that change does not seem to align with your needs. This perspective is your choice to live the new or higher love.

You will be asked to demonstrate this choice in your lifetime to prove that you understand that love, by its defined existence, is released and free. No one can avoid these lessons because all form must change to bring in the new. When you pass, move on, and release correctly and without bitterness, then you connect truly to Spirit. This true connection to Spirit is the real purpose of any Holy Relationship.

The end of this book is the beginning of the teaching. The end of reading is the beginning of living what you understand. You must put down your learning and practice your knowledge. Let go and let God. Let God change everything for you. Accepting all change is what causes you to be closer to Spirit because you value formlessne ss.

Complete the exercises for this chapter in Chapter 10

CHAPTER 10

WORKBOOK

Chapter 1: The New Paradigm

List 5 past partners you have had: names and dates of the involvement (list more if you like).

1.
2.
3.
4.
5.

What is the longest relationship you have kept in a loving condition? Do you consider yourself having a 'successful' fulfilling relationship now?

List common interests you have with them, hobbies, or activities, such as hiking, music, and arts, church:

1.
2.
3.
4.
5.

Are you more likely to be rejected or do the rejecting in partnership?

Do you get out of a relationship quickly, or tend to hang on even knowing that it does not serve of you?

Have you been in a violent partnership? Verbal or physically.

Are you prone to arguing with your partner?

What 'dark' issues have you seen show up with a partner?

Do you see any recurring patterns of repeating behavior with new partners that happened from past involvements?

Are you more independent or codependent?

Do you have an issue of being honest?

Have you ever changed a relationship to follow a certain spiritual practice?

Are you the silent type or one who will process an issue until it is resolved?

What do you dislike most about your physical appearance?

What are your predominate feelings during any given day?

List 3 of the biggest mistakes you feel you have made in relationship:
1.
2.
3.

List 3 of your most negative personality traits that you recognize that have harmed your involvements:
1.
2.
3.

List 3 of your most positive personality traits where you have received lots of attention from others:
1.
2.
3.

List what makes you feel the 'best' when you are with your partner:

What are the 'worst' treatments you have experienced from another love partner?

What are you most valuable lessons learned about Specialness?

Chapter 2: Attraction to Specialness

Write spontaneously without much thinking or judging. Do not be critical or analytical about your answers. Watch how you feel when writing down answers. Make a note of any dark feelings that might surface. Exposing specialness is meant to be freeing and revealing, not steeped in judgment.

List 5 relationships that you viewed as not joining or achieving your dreams:
1.
2.
3.
4.
5.
    What caused the ending of the relationship?

List 5 physical attributes they have in common, such as tall, all blonde, all dark-skinned:
1.
2.
3.
4.
5.

What attracted you the most about your past partners?

List 5 physical features you are mostly to look for in a person:
1.
2.
3.
4.
5.

List what you believe have been your greatest problems in relationship:
1.
2.
3.
4.
5.

List what you like best about your partners' emotions, happy, outgoing, peaceful, intense, etc.:

1.
2.
3.
4.
5.

Briefly describe the best times you have had with a lover and why/what you experienced:

1.
2.
3.
4.
5.

What do you like best about sex, sensuality, and affection?

1.
2.
3.
4.
5.

Give your partners a grade (A, B, C, and D) on their ability to please you physically then emotionally, mentally, and spiritually:
Name: physical grade _ emotional grade_ mental grade_ intelligence grade_ spiritual grade _

1.
2.
3.
4.
5.

List the problems you had in these involvements: anger, lack of commitment, poor communication:

1.
2.
3.
4.
5.

List what dreams you had about them: getting married, living together, buying a home, and having kids:

1.
2.
3.
4.
5.

Write a short bucket list of unfulfilled dreams (things you want to do before you die):

Imagine you could have the perfect partner show up with the following qualities and attributes, exactly as you would want them to be. Below, list 20 aspects or things you are looking for in your perfect partner
1.
2.
3.
4.
5.
6.
7.
8.
9.
10.
11.
12.
13.
14.
15.
16.
17.
18.
19.
20.

Personal Growth
List what you have done in the way of personal growth, such as couple counseling, reading a book, and taking a workshop. Be specific:
1.
2.
3.
4.
5.

What would you do differently in any relationship you felt dissatisfied with?

What do you like most about your dad?

Your mom?

What do you dislike most about your brothers or sisters?

What negative aspect of your mother do you feel you are still living with (then, of your father)?

What negative traits did dad display in dealing with mom?

What resentment do you still have toward your parents? Explain the experiences that created this:

What was the best quality of character you received from dad, then your mom?

Do you see any similar behaviors showing up with partners that match similar issues with parents?

Dream Work Sheet

Write down your "sleeping" dreams for a month.

What are your predominant waking dreams about? Money, sex, play...

List your greatest fears:

What dreams of change do you have about your partnership?

What dreams are you learning to correct (dreams of forgiveness, etc.)?

Chapter 3: The Components of a Holy Relationship

Many times you know which path you are on by its effects and other times you are not sure or in between paths or wishing you could switch path. It never works to switch paths unless you are fully content with the path you are on, so be sure you have fully embraced the path you are on and learned its benefits as well as its challenges.

1. Do you think of yourself as a natural leader?
2. Are you in a committed partnership?
3. Do you feel lonely often?
4. Do you think of yourself as an independent person?
5. Does your life work serve many people?
6. Do you run a large company or work for a non-profit?
7. Are most of your intimate relationships long term?
8. Do you think of yourself as a monogamous person?
9. Do you have casual relationships?
10. Have you had more than 15 lovers or are promiscuous?
11. Have you been single for more than 9 months?
12. Do you like Internet dating?
13. Do you consider yourself successful at dating?
14. Are you a free spirit and change places often?
15. Have you mostly lived alone?
16. Do you like living with roommates or in a community?
17. Do you have more than 18 friends?
18. Are you close to your parents?
19. Are you happily married?
20. Do you believe in open marriage or a swinger lifestyle?
21. Do you like being alone at night?
22. Do you sleep alone (separate bed) with or without a partner?
23. Do you like to work on projects by yourself without help?
24. Are you an active leader/minister in a church or spiritual center?
25. Have you had more than 3 marriages?
26. Are you bothered by crowds or big cities?
27. Do you like drinking alcoholic or doing recreational drugs?
28. Do you like group sports?
29. Do you work out by yourself mostly?
30. Do you watch lots of TV or go to movies alone?
31. Are you popular with the opposite sex?
32. Do your artist pursuits require you to be alone a lot?
33. Do you meditate regularly?
34. Was your childhood spent alone?
35. Where you a introverted in childhood and then became extroverted?
36. Did your parents have a good marriage?
37. Did you fight lots in childhood?
38. Do you think you had a violent past?
39. Do you have a deep desire to be political or change the world?
40. What path (see below — 1, 2, or 3) do you feel you're currently on?

Path 1= The Many   Path 2 = Holy Relationship   Path 3 = No-one
Answers

1. Yes = 1. No =2	2. Yes = 2. No= 3	3. Yes =2. No =3	4. Yes =3 No =2
5. Yes =1 No= 2	6. Yes=1 No =2	7. Yes=2 No=1	8. Yes=2 No =1
9. Yes=1 No =2	10. Yes=1 No=3	11. Yes=3 No=2	12. Yes=1 No=3
13. Yes=1 No=3	14. Yes=1 No=2	15. Yes=3 No=2	16. Yes=1 No=3
17. Yes=1 No =2	18. Yes=2 No=1	19. Yes=2 No =3	20. Yes=1 No=2
21. Yes=3 No =2	22. Yes=3 No=2	23 Yes=3 No=1	24. Yes=1 No=2
25. Yes=2 No =3	26. Yes=3 No=1	27. Yes=3 No=1	28. Yes=1 No=3
29. Yes=3 No=2	30. Yes=3 No=2	31 Yes=2 No=3	32. Yes=3 No=2
33. Yes=3 No=1	34. Yes=3 No=2	35. Yes=1 No=2	36. Yes=2 No=3
37. Yes=1No=3	38. Yes=3 No=2	39. Yes=1 No=2	

40. Path 1 = 3; path 2 = 6; path 3 = 9.

Count the number of 1's you get =_____
Count the number of 2's you get =_____
Count the number of 3's you get =_____
If you get mostly one number you are definitely on that path.
If you get a mixture of 1's and 2's you are on path 2.
If you get a mixture of 2's and 3's you are on path 2.
If you get a mixture of mostly 1 and 3's you are path 1.
If you get lots of 3's and a few 1's and 2's you are on path 2.
Only if you get mostly 3 are you on purpose to be on path 3.

Write about your path and what you are learning on it.

The Meaning of Words

Take the word "communicate" and write 5 ideas that you associate with it, and 5 experiences or events that you associate with those meanings.

Communicate

Write down 5 beliefs you have about how you communicate with a partner

Ideas	Events, situations
1.	1.
2.	2.
3.	3.
4.	4.
5.	5.

Try out different words, such as "family," "sex," "happiness," "home" or "desire." If you do this with your partner notice how different your ideas are and how different the experiences are. If 100 people were put in a room and did this same exercise you would find no one would have your same list.

Chapter 4: Guidelines for Creating and Maintaining a Holy Relationship

Agree to the guidelines by signing them below. Tear out the page and hang it on the bathroom mirror, on the refrigerator, or any place that will serve as a reminder. Spend several sessions memorizing them and refer to them often until they are built into your inner programming. The largest problem most relationships have is that they have no agreements about the relationship. Therefore, each partner tends to resort back to the behavioral programming and mental images that he or she grew up with.

We often expect our partner to know if we feel that a particular behavior is unacceptable to us! This assumption is wrong. Assumptions are like ships without rudders or boats without captains. Most couples fail to set agreements before they choose to become sexually and emotionally entangled. As a result, no friendly method to heal can occur when the lower personalities try to destroy the involvement. Be certain they will try!

Guideline 1: The New Paradigm
Talk about the effects of specialness from your past relationships.
From questions in Chapter 1 keep the discussion open as to what specialness is.
Write about the ideas of being "better or less than" and keep asking how they where created in your childhood.

Guideline 2: Open the Heart
What does open the heart mean to you and what does it mean to your partner?
What practices do you do that open your heart?
What do you notice when your heart is closed or you're not connected to the ones you love?
What are the ways you spend time focused in your heart?
        Discuss the heart darkening awareness you have felt. (Greed, envy, jealousy, fear of not being loved or alone.)
How have you changed your mind about greed?
How do you see envy differently?
Who have you been jealous of? _____ Why?
What fears have been showing up around being alone or not loved that you can trace from the heart?

Guideline 3: Act as Mirrors (Equals) and Heal One Another
List 5 ways you see your partner mirroring similar behaviors or beliefs, such as poverty, anger, fears, interests, hobbies, or talents. How are you alike?
        1.
        2.
        3.
        4.
        5.

What ways do you think you are different and are not mirroring similar ideas?

Guideline 4: Create a Safe Space for Sharing and Healing

Where do you do healing together?

What space is devoted to healing?

What time commitments have you made for your healing?

What causes you to feel unsafe in sharing beliefs and fears with your partner?

What are the tone ranges you are comfortable with?

Do you or your partner fail to keep tone agreements and or turn arguments into shouting?

 List ways that you feel unsafe with your partner?

Do you withhold healing because of unsafe agreements or feeling with your partner?

What does your partner do to make you feel unsafe?

What do you do to yourself to magnify the unsafe feelings within?

What are you both agreeing upon to increase the healing experiences?

Guideline 5: See the Is-ness In Each Other

What is the Is-ness in your current perceptions or understandings?

How have you used the awareness of the Holy Spirit to help in your healing?

Describe other words or ideas for Is-ness.

Create a 5 to 10 minute meditation for seeing Is-ness of each other. Schedule when to practice it.

Describe the effects of being in Is-ness with your partner?

How have you witnessed healing from learning to align to Is-ness.

What feeling do you associate with Is-ness?

Guideline 6: Love Your Partner as Yourself

List your agreements about non-violent communication.

How are you practicing the golden rule with each other?

How do projections contribute to seeing differences?

Where do you think you have the same issues but you make them different?

What is the Spiritual Consciousness of love that causes you to see the other as
 yourself?

What differences do you keep about your partner?

Guideline 7: Have No Separate Interests or Ways to End The Relationship
We all feel separate and alone and want out of fear.

How often do you feel alone? _____% of the time.
What are the withholdings or lack of sharing you keep thinking you have with
   your partner?

How do you leave the relationship when a fight happens? Withdraw or become
   increasingly argumentative?

Who ends the relationship usually, you or your partners?

How many little ways do you end or feel a death of connection through the week?

Guideline 8: Choose To Be Happy
What is happiness to you?

What are your happy dreams with your partner?

List some happy agreements you and your partner have made.

List some controlling demands you have made on another.
Do you set aside time to experience pure happiness, without attachment to what
   form it takes?

Guideline 9: Enjoy Spiritual Disciplines with One Another
List 5 practices you want to do with your partner.
   1.
   2.
   3.
   4.
   5.

List 3 practices you do differently than your partner.

     1.

     2.

     3.

List ways you feel you can receive more support in doing certain practices.

What support does your partner give you?

What growth are you charting together?

Guideline 10:   Not My Will But Thy Will Be Done

     What is your partner's greater purpose?

What is yours?

What is your joint or mutual higher purpose?

List action steps you both want to do together toward your higher purposes.

What added agreements or guidelines have you come up with together?

Write in your Holy Relationship Journal how you see the Guidelines helping the relationship and where they can be improved.

     Read the guidelines to each other ___ times per week.

Chapter 5: We Are One

The A B C's of Involvements: How to Spiritually End, Change, or Transform an Involvement

How many B level relationships can you identify?

How may "A" involvements do you recognize? (Mother, father)

List the purposes of the Ego and the spirit for all A and B relationships.

What is your special purpose for all C related relationships given from your spirit?

List all your close friends and then your semi-close friends.

Do you see a common nature or purpose or interest?

List the relationship that you resisted change with.
1.
2.
3.
4.
5.

What are the common feelings you have when changing an involvement?

What was the specialness you had trouble letting go of?

What other fear emotions surfaced when attempting to let go?

What feeling of control and possession did you feel?

What messages lived with those emotions? (Such as, I will never love again, I am alone, I never am good enough for love, etc.)

Discover Your Perceptions

Perform this exercise to demonstrate how you perceive your past and current relationships.
1. Draw a small circle and put yourself in the middle.
2. Draw a larger circle around the small circle.
3. List your "A" relationships in the space between the inner circle and the outer circle.
4. Draw a larger circle outside the second circle.

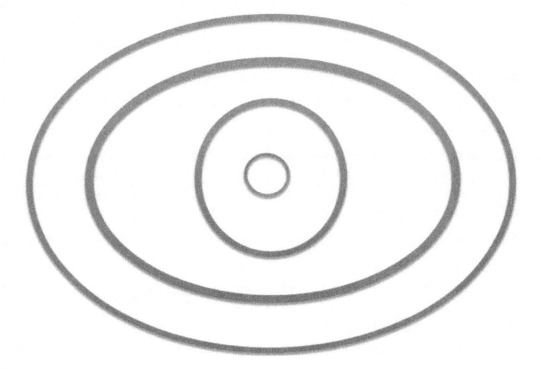

5. List your "B" relationships in the space between the two outer circles.

6. With an even larger circle, do the same for your "C" relationships.

7. Then, finally, draw a really, really large outer circle for everyone and everything else. When you are determining where to place the relationships among the circles, notice how a person may have moved from an outer circle to an inner circle or vice versa. When you are determining where to place the relationships among the circles, notice how a person may have moved from an outer circle to an inner circle or vice versa.

8. Identify and write down the purpose for each relationship.

9. Write down the lessons that you feel the relationship was designed by Spirit to teach you.

10. Write down any agreements that you feel was made regarding each involvement. Are you keeping those agreements even though a person may have moved from one circle to another?

For clarity, you may choose to create a separate set of circles for different areas of your life. For example, one set of circles could show your past and present intimate relationships, one for your past and present friendships, and one for your past and present business relationships.

TRUST

Write about three relationships where trust or communication was broken.

   Your partner's name _____ Your age at the time _____ What happened that caused you to be fearful of them

   What changed in your perception of them?

   How Does Mistrust Feel?

   Describe the feeling and where it is in your body

   What self-concepts did you make up about yourself

   Placing trust in another and not in Spirit can mean you are listening to false dreams Or expectations or their ego lies.

   List any awareness of them

Issues: Liar

How do you lie?

How often do you catch yourself in a lie?

   Admit some dark Ego lies

   What are the core feelings you have before a lie or right after

Lie vs. Truth

The lie is _____ the truth is_____ the feeling is_____

The lie is _____ the truth is_____ the feeling is_____

The lie is _____ the truth is_____ the feeling is_____

The lie is _____ the truth is_____ the feeling is_____

Let go of any judgments or deceptions of who you are as a liar.

I let go of

Give any shame or disappointment to Spirit.

Same vs. Different

Here are the steps to unraveling a difference:

1. Recognize that you are not at peace or experiencing love with your partner. Notice that you don't like the way you feel when sharing a point of view or story.

2. Ask for help from your partner and Holy Spirit.

3. Admit that you are locked into a perception of being right about a difference and that you have a judgment. See both sides of the judgment and the circumstances that surround that judgment.

4. Make a clear choice to join with your partner and put your love first. Be still.

5. Inwardly release the need to hold on to the difference. Feel the surrender and the joy of releasing.

6. Share the thought that you are releasing and admit any false concepts you perceive.

7. Affirm the truth of your sameness and source with your partner.

8. Make an agreement of CO-creation with each other.

Chapter 6: Body or Energy

The Range of Feelings:

> 0 = stillness, death
> 1 = indifference, numbness, avoidance, fear
> 2 = depression
> 3 = uncertainty, doubt, indecisiveness
> 4 = sadness, deep to mild
> 5a = defenses: guilt, shame, blame
> 5b = attacks, anger, small upsets to rage
> 6 = pleasure and/or pain, self-gratifying sensations
> 7 = acceptance and gratitude
> 8 = happiness, humor to pure joy
> 9 = love, bliss
> 10 = divine awareness, cosmic consciousness

Tolerances Chart

Chart your emotions for a month with your partner and determine your state of emotional constitution.

Set some goals with you partner to uplift your state of emotional being. Set a monthly meeting to review emotional goals and what it requires to shift feelings to higher states of bliss. Set a healing session day and time and practice sharing feelings and where they are in relationship to body and chakras by following the steps in Sharing Feelings in chapter 6.

List emotional expressions that exceed your comfort zone.

Notice tolerance levels for certain situations by using the following chart.

Date	Event	Emotions felt	Emotions expressed	Tolerance	Experienced
6/14	Fight	anger	fear	Low 4	pain in heart
8/14	Party		excited joy	High 8	playfulness

Emotional Release Exercise

Make a special time to work with your partner for Emotional clearing.

Remember that emotional feelings are not good or bad, or not acceptable. They are just thoughts in motion. It's how you release them that matters and learning how to target them, not at someone or yourself.

When you are feeling any emotion other than Love, teach yourself to release the feeling to the wholeness of Spirit.

1. Sit in a comfortable chair. Sit up straight. Feet on the ground, neck straight too.

2. Have no distractions for 20 minutes. Ask your partner to provide support and nurturing and ask them not to judge or analyze your feelings. Learn together to tell the difference between feeling and thinking. Just feel into your body and open to whatever feelings are there.

3. Breathe several big breaths deeply, and keep doing this for 3 to 5 minutes. Each big breath is designed to help you feel more and relax into your feelings. Your partner can be your coach to remind you to feel and relax and keep breathing.

4. Remember the event or person or thoughts that triggered a fear emotion, but don't talk about the story of it, just keep feeling into it.

5. Feel the places in your body associated to the feeling (tightness in stomach, hurt in the heart or another body part). Connect that to a chakra or center. Breathe more and be more aware of that area and any memories associated with that area.

6. Now, as you release your breath, let go of the feelings and imagine them going into the whole sky (or ocean) or released into outer space. Like a volcano, blow it up and out. Like a mushroom, or nuclear explosion sense it goes up and away and out in every direction, released and dispersed away from the center.

7. Make sounds or allow sounds to be made. Express the emotion fully and keep doing it until you feel lightness or clearing. Do it a little longer to be sure you expressed it all. If it's sadness and it's genuine to cry, cry with full expression. Same with anger, get really angry but let it go to the entire Universe.

8. Shake or quiver, and swirl it up and away. Forgiveness is giving the feeling to Holy Spirit. Like throwing up poison, or spitting, give it away completely.

9. Let whatever feeling you have turn into sounds and expressions until your empty.

10. Feel empty, feel free of them. Observe the sounds you make and see without effort, if they are changing naturally on their own. Often more harmonious sounds start to vibrate as you clear. Don't control it or force. Allow them to change without conscious thinking, but if you feel joy or laughter or inner lightheartedness, bring it fully through and listen to it. Listening to joy is following the Voice of Spirit within.

11. When you released waste produced from your body, you could see what it was. Similarly, fear and other emotions have waste and after it's been eliminated you can identify it. Remember, it's all error thinking known as Fear, and no matter what its story is, you are removing the beliefs in lack and loss.

12. Practice together and take turns supporting and helping the other release emotional fear. Clearing errors is like cleaning the body of toxins, it should be done often.

Enjoy the practice. Learning to breath together is very rewarding. Admitting errors and clearing them bring much happiness to each other.

Chapter 7: Body and Energy

List 5 past energy bonds you recognize that are light and freeing.
1.
2.
3.
4.
5.

List 5 past energy bonding's that are dark and where are they connected to you.
1.
2.
3.
4.
5.

Whenever you continually think of someone where is the cord connected in your body?

What heart energy bonding are you aware of?

What energy cords are still in your sexual chakra?

What cords do your parents still have with you?

Create a cord cutting ritual with your partner to unbind you to old attachments.

Understanding the 4 D's

List 5 ways you feel your emotions swing and how they cause damage to yourself or others.
1.
2.
3.
4.
5.
List 3 relationships that became destroyed by darkness.
1.
2.
3.

List causes within your inner mind that caused the destruction to occur.

List 5 relationships that died in form, either from natural change or destructive patterns.
1.
2.
3.
4.
5.
List 5 ways you see darkness showing up in your life.
1.
2.
3.
4.
5.

Talk about the thickness of energy in your life.

How do you use luminous energy daily?

Manifestation of Ego Defects
It is always important to catch the Ego and expose light upon it with your partner without guilt, or shame, or fear of recognizing the Ego nature.
List 3 examples of each defect you notice, feeling them in your body awareness

1. Trust

Lack of taking responsibility for situations:

Extreme planning

Indecisiveness

Anger toward someone or Higher Spirit

2. Honesty

Dishonesty—cover-ups

Shutting out others

218

Failure to admit faults

Aware of lying

3. Tolerance

Perfectionism

People pleasing

Tolerating sexual abuse or loss of personal morality

4. Gentleness

Expressing feelings explosively

Incorrect expression of anger

Wanting the other to change

5. Joy

Lack of passion or commitment

Physical or mental illness

Depression or broken heartedness

6. Defenselessness

Embarrassment

Inappropriate social behavior

Irresponsibility

7. Generosity

Helplessness

Envy

Financial problems

8. Patience

Controlling the reality of others

Score keeping

Arguing about facts

9. Faithfulness

Self-centeredness

Making others special or more equipped to make decisions for you

Doubting yourself

10. Open-mindedness

Jealousy

Wanting someone to have your values

Closed of fixed way life has to be

What are some core beliefs that you find about your Ego (lower mind)
    My Beliefs are Awareness in Body Centers
1.
2.
3.
4.
5.
Shift: Lift and Gift Exercise
Write three beliefs you want shifted into love.
1.
2.
3.
Write a positive affirmation or love statement to yourself and ask Spirit to show you what a   lifted state feels like.
What are the descriptive words to describe the lifted awareness? (Joy, bliss, excitement)
    1.
    2.
    3.

The gift. Each challenge can offers some growth or benefit for yourself or others or as a purpose for healing the lower mind and the world.

What are your spiritual gifts, what has Spirit gifted you with?

Example: addiction lifted to pure pleasure is then gifted with self-control, then teaching others to overcome addition or lower self-esteem issues.

Gratitude Practice

Start cultivating gratitude by having sessions with your partner and praise ceremonies.

Make lists of what you are grateful for:

God is...

Write a letter to Spirit thanking and praising your gift that you recognized.

I understand the presence of God shown to me as

Power Struggles

List 5 ways you identity a power struggle with your partner.

1.

2.

3.

4.

5.

In what ways do you get out of control with your communication and increase or magnify the arguing?

Chapter 8: Unified Goals and Agreements for the Body, Mind, and Spirit

What is your purpose ?

What is your partner's purpose?

What agreements are you failing to keep?

What is your special function?

What is happiness to you?

What are your happy dreams with your partner?

Choose a date to practice setting higher purpose and affirm your purpose as one.

Write some agreements of Support and how you support your partner in keeping his/her word?

List how you are demanding (which issues) and how you are not supporting change?

List some happy agreements you and your partner have made.

List some controlling demands you have made on another.

Do you set-aside time to experience pure happiness, without attachment to what form it takes?

Joining

How do you keep from joining your partner?

What objects have you made into an idol or made special?

What is your fear about becoming ONE with your partner?

What clubs or organizations do you join?

How do you remain Independent and not join or stay an "outsider"?

Making Decisions

What major decisions are you making together?

List your ideas   List their ideas
1.
2.
3.
4.
5.

Blend the ideas and Give them to Spirit

1.

2.

3.

4.

5.

What does your inner Guidance tell you that are mutual and real?

Minor Decisions

What minor decisions have you been making without your partners physically present but know you are calling upon them?

1.

2.

3.

What feedback are you getting from your partner about making decisions as One heart?

List 3 daily agreements per day and journey how you are keeping them.

1.

2.

3.

What 4H Focus (goals) Does Your Relationship Have?

Write down 20 goals, 5 goals for each body. List 5 goals that relate to your physical self, 5 that relate to the mental, 5 that focus on your feelings, and 5 ideas that would increase your spiritual awareness. Compare your list to that of your partner's and talk openly about how you can support each other in reaching these goals. In our section on happy dreams, we will teach you how to evaluate these goals, spiritualize them and make agreements with your partner to manifest them. We will be showing you how to direct your will or aim toward these ideas. Each idea when manifested, and each goal when achieved, brings you closer to a complete realization of what makes a Holy Relationship.

Physical Goals

1.

2.

3.

4.

5.

Mental Goals
1.
2.
3.
4.
5.

Emotional Goals
1.
2.
3.
4.
5.

Spiritual Goals
1.
2.
3.
4.
5.

List How the 4 S's Have Effected Your Past Relationships

Describe how the lower mind seeks this way of thinking.

Specialness:
Example: my attraction to Jane's legs made me focus on her body more than her Spirit.

Security:
Example: my insecurities got the best of me with Jane. I became controlling.

Survival:
Example: our money problems became the source of our fighting.

Sexuality:
Example: one of us was obsessed with affection and sex.

Describe Some of the Feelings and Situations You Notice in Each of These Areas

Specialness: excitement, disappointment, anger, the need to feel good

Security: frightened, unsure, doubt myself

Survival: fear, anger, doubt, questioning

Sexuality: romantic, exotic feeling, sexual high, passion, upset, disappointed

Chapter 9:

The No Problem Solution

1. List the problem

2. Edit the ideas and admit the lack concepts.

3. Look for past events or situation of similar nature

4. Ask together for Holy Spirit to bring the light of truth into both of your awareness. Meditate on completion and fullness.

5. Write an action plan for creativity and now-moment giving.
What traits do you like about you close friends?

Guidelines for Creating and Maintaining a Holy Relationship

1.**Admit that you do not know how to transform your relationship from specialness to holiness. What is this relationship for? Create a purpose and a vision for the relationship**. Pray together in a peaceful state of mind asking that the Holy Spirit to be in charge of making the relationship holy. Be willing to learn.

2. **Open your heart.** You're with the perfect partner because he or she is able to teach you how to know your higher mind. Don't substitute another person for your partner in Holy Relationship; include everyone. Have no secrets and hide nothing from each other. Strive to put an end to jealousy, envy, and greed, and all the lower emotions of the mind.

3. **Act as mirrors (equals) and heal each other**. God's children are equal and the same. Neither of you is less or more advanced than the other. Refrain from being "better than" or "less than." Be open to being both a student and a teacher to each other. Nothing happens that is not affecting both of you. You're both equally dealing with the same issues. Make choices that promote joining.

4. **Create a safe space for sharing and healing**. Start by sharing feelings first and be willing to use your feelings as a vehicle for healing. Communication is for growth and healing. Tell the truth about your experiences. Choose to work past the Ego illusions of communication. Don't hold grievances against your partner. Practice forgiveness by not attacking each other when faults are discussed. Admit your own errors, but don't seek out your partner's errors. 5. **See the Is-ness in each other**. Admit judgments for the purpose of correcting them. Don't make them real. Ask the Holy Mind to judge for you and show you the true perception, which is called the Is-ness. Agree to disagree by allowing each other to have a different perception of the situation.

6. **Love your partner as yourself**. Agree not to be verbally or physically abusive. Do nothing to each other physically without his or her full consent. While it is appropriate to release emotions in verbal form, it is not appropriate to focus the anger or sadness toward your partner. Proper expression of feeling is to be targeted into the Holy Spirit, not your partner. You have the right to leave the space if the verbal expressions of your partner would trigger an emotional reaction in you that surpasses your comfort level. Pray while your partner is releasing.

Make peace within yourselves and make your home a priority. Practice the Golden Rule.

7. **Have no separate interests or ways to end the relationship.** Turn all decisions about the relationship over to the Holy Spirit, and make no major decisions without each other and the guidance of the Holy Spirit. Share the miracles and inspire them to happen. Create fun and happy dreams.

8. **Choose to be happy.** Admit expectations and addictive needs with the willingness to see them as healed. Make no demands, rules, or conditions of how the relationship should be in form. Understand pure happiness as a way of being.

9. **Enjoy spiritual disciplines with each other**. Pray and meditate daily, both morning and evening. Commit to spiritual principles that apply in your daily practices. Affirm spiritual truths daily.

10. **Not my will but Thy will be done.** Find a purpose for the relationship that is greater than your personal interests are. Holiness works for causes greater than sensational pleasures, power, or survival. Let the Holy Spirit show the way of serving God's Plan for humanity. Build trust in God's plan for your mutual freedom.

ADD your Guidelines here.

cut here

cut here

Manifestation of Ego Defects:

1. Trust
Lack of taking responsibility for situations.
Extreme planning.
Indecisiveness.
Anger toward someone or higher Spirit.

2. Honesty
Dishonesty, cover-ups.
Shutting out others.
Failure to admit faults.

3. Tolerance
Perfectionism.
People pleasing.
Tolerating sexual abuse or loss of personal morality.

4. Gentleness
Expressing feelings explosively.
Incorrect expression of anger.
Wanting the other to change.

5. Joy
Lack of passion or commitment.
Physical or mental illness.

6. Defenselessness
Embarrassment.
Inappropriate social behavior.

7. Generosity
Helplessness.
Envy.
Inadequate or unfulfilled sex life.
Financial problems.
Irresponsibility.

8. Patience
Controlling the reality of others.
Score keeping.
Arguing about facts.

9. Faithfulness
Self-centeredness.
Making others special or more equipped to make decisions for you.

10. Open-mindedness
Jealousy.
Wanting someone who has your value system.

cut here

cut here

Temperament

1 = Indifference, numbness, avoidance and fear

High = unaware of the fear, the numbness seems normal, spends lots of time feeling alone and distant from others, always separate.

Coping = aware of the fear, hiding but doing little about problems or causes, avoiding communicating or sharing, denial of effects of problems.

Low = trouble admitting feelings but still taking minor actions, others can tell that he or she is avoiding dealing with issues at hand.

2 = Depression

High = staying depressed for months, not dealing with daily issues.

Coping = aware of being depressed but not seeking help and little is changing.

Low = getting medication and advice but not practicing much of what they are being told to do.

3 = Uncertainty, doubt, indecisiveness

High = no goals, no purpose, no spiritual practices.

Coping = doubting sometimes, hoping but procrastinating, stalling, indecisive.

Low = asking for advice but often from the wrong sources, making choices but not following through. Little to no risk taking.

4 = Sadness: deep to mild

High = holds sadness in and doesn't let others see it, cries often, deeply saddened by many perceived losses.

Coping = expressing sadness to loved ones but not resolving the cause of it, not finding forgiveness.

Low = mildly sad, frowning, pouting, or denying the feeling of sadness.

5a = Defenses: guilt, shame, blame

High = very protective of self and others, feels lots of shame or guilt.

Coping = argumentative or stays in small groups that share beliefs and opinions.

Low = blames partner to make him or her "wrong," holds onto defenses but keeps them more to him or herself.

5b = Attacks: anger, small upsets to rage

High = expresses opinions easily and often, keeps an appearance of being mildly upset or holds anger, can be self-critical.

Coping = expresses anger with self-justification.

Low = unhappy with feelings, ashamed but seeking help while looking for correct methods to deal with the emotions.

6 = Pleasure/pain, self-gratifying sensations

High = addictive behavior to wanting to be punished.

Coping = finding balance in both pleasure and pain.

Low = looking for new ways to find pleasure (spiritual methods) and learning to source the true causes of pain.

7 = Acceptance and gratitude

Low = practicing more and more.

Coping = finding more reasons to be grateful and forgiving.

High = singing, praising, practicing being in the Is-ness often.

8 = Happiness/humor to pure joy

Low = humor, laughter, joking.

Coping = enjoying both inner and outer joy.

High = constantly happy, unperturbed by things or people.

9 = Love, bliss

Low = glimpses of bliss, deep meditations, brief moments of revelation.

Coping = glimpses of bliss happen more and more, longer periods of uninterrupted peace.

High = awareness of always being One with God; enlightenment.

cut here

cut here

The Range of Feelings

0 = stillness, death.
   Absolute 0 represents an awareness of infinity in the direction of fear and
   could be described as a snake biting its own tail.

1 = indifference, numbness, avoidance, and fear.
A denial of emotions or stuck in darkness.

2 = depression.
Sluggish to no movement.

3 = uncertainty, doubt, indecisiveness.
Slight mental activity with no action.

4 = sadness, deep to mild.
Movement in the emotional body, crying pains.

5a = defenses: guilt, shame, blame.
Physical avoiding to hiding or self-protection.

5b = attacks, anger.
Small upsets to rage, physical activity begins to express itself.

6 = pleasure and/or pain, self-gratifying sensations.
Felt in the emotional and physical body.

7 = acceptance and gratitude.

8 = happiness.
Humor to pure joy.

9 = love, bliss.

10 = divine awareness, cosmic consciousness.

cut here

cut here

Contact Robert Wood at www.spiritaura.com or 303-570-0840 for future classes, work-shops, and special counseling sessions related to developing your Holy Relationships.

Feel free to contact Robert to establish a Holy Relationship workshop in your area.

The No Loss Relationship audio CD version of this book will be available at www.spiritaura.com.

Other teachings and workshops are also available at www.spiritaura.com.

CPSIA information can be obtained
at www.ICGtesting.com
Printed in the USA
FSOW04n0123051115
12938FS